AF255039

WANT TO TAKE YOUR **ABLETON PUSH SKILLS** TO THE NEXT LEVEL?

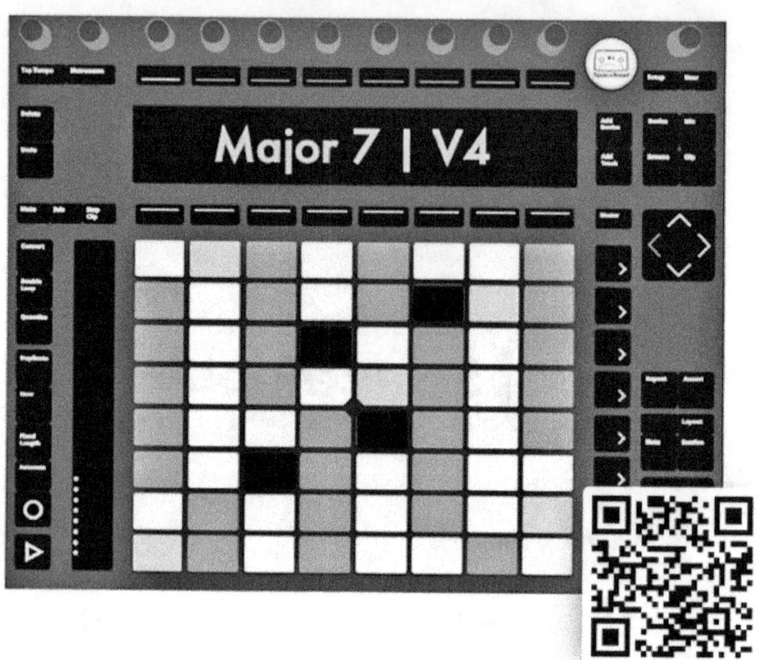

TRY THE PUSH CHORD GUIDE
Available as PDF

This is a ready-to-print, PDF chord shape guide for use on the Push 1,2 & 3 Controller, and **features 42 chord types and finger positions**. Each image is given its own page, with some space underneath to write personal notes on how that chord makes you feel which makes it a perfect guide for new composers wanting to hone their ear training.

LOOKING FOR SOME INSPIRATION?

AVAILABLE IN PRINT AND E-BOOK

The Ultimate Producer Handbook features 100 song blueprints for 10 different genres including, Synthwave, Techno, Trance, Drum & Bass and more.

200+ FINGER DRUM TABS

IN 14 MODERN GENRES

Available on Amazon

Spacefood.ca

MAKE MUSIC, EAT PIZZA.

THE FINGER DRUM GENESIS

BY AARON SPACEFOOD

TO MY STUDENTS

It has been an incredible honor to be part of my students' musical journeys. Every new student brings a unique perspective on music, fresh challenges, and most importantly, a new friendship. The journey of discovering and mentoring aspiring producers has been like a magnet, drawing in amazing people who share my passions and interests. Teaching music production has connected me with talented individuals from all corners of the globe, each with their own distinctive goals and styles. I am profoundly grateful for the opportunity to know all of you personally and to contribute, even in a small way, to your musical paths. Thank you all so much!

SPECIAL THANKS!

The *Finger Drum Bible* series would not have come to life without the expertise and encouragement of my good friend Brandon. "Thank you" can hardly capture the depth of my gratitude. Who would have thought that a seemingly random interaction on Reddit could blossom into such a dedicated and rewarding friendship? It's these serendipitous moments that make me believe in destiny or some higher plan. Never doubt your incredible skills, impeccable taste, and boundless passion – you have it all! Knowing you has been a true joy, and I eagerly look forward to our weekly hangs. Thank you for being a part of my life, Brandon!

I owe endless thanks to my partner, Carmen. Through the intense, challenging days and countless adventures, you offer unwavering support, encouragement, and an environment that fosters creativity, positivity, and a healthy work/life balance. Your perspective and priorities keep me centered and motivated to pursue my dreams, no matter how out of reach they may seem. You're always open to taking the leap, and regardless of where we land, you're joyfully there for the journey. You truly are my partner in life, navigating the unknown together. You make even the most mundane activities exciting! I am completely twitterpated by you! <3

CONTENTS

THE BEGINNING

HOW TO USE THIS BOOK

STRENGTH BUILDING EXERCISES

THE BASICS

CORE PERCUSSION SOUNDS

RUDIMENTS

ONE FINGER DRUMMING (EASY)

THREE FINGER DRUMMING (MODERATE)

FIVE FINGER DRUMMING (HARDER)

FOUNDATIONAL RHYTHMS

CONTENTS

SAMPLE MUSIC

HISTORY OF SAMPLE MUSIC

MUSIC CHOPS

FAVORITES

CONTENTS

MIRRORED

DRUM FILLS

GLOSSARY OF TERMS

GLOSSARY OF LINKS

CONCLUDING MESSAGE

ABOUT THE AUTHOR

BONUS

THE BEGINNING
THE BEGINNING
THE BEGINNING
THE BEGINNING
THE BEGINNING
THE BEGINNING
THE BEGINNING
THE BEGINNING
THE BEGINNING
THE BEGINNING
THE BEGINNING

WHAT IS THIS BOOK?

Thank you from the bottom of my heart for choosing *The Finger Drum Genesis.* This book represents countless hours of practice and meticulous preparation. My hope is that it equips you with the foundational knowledge to kickstart and sustain your journey in finger drumming, empowering you with strength and confidence.

So, what exactly is this book? In essence, it's designed to be your go-to guide for learning how to finger drum. I've compiled the most essential information and exercises to help you become a well-rounded rhythmist. Inside, you'll discover everything from key terminology to detailed descriptions and diagrams of vital musical concepts. Additionally, there are strategies for optimizing your practice time, essential rhythms to enhance your repertoire, strength-building and safety tips, and audio examples accessible via QR code. You also get links to downloadable drum kits.

From the outset, I wanted to create a tangible resource—one that you can annotate, decorate with stickers, and carry with you anywhere, without the hassle of another monthly subscription. As music hardware becomes increasingly portable, you can take your kit outdoors and enjoy making music in the fresh air and in the company of friends—just as music is meant to be experienced. This book allows you to study and practice without needing a constant internet connection.

After a year of refining my methods with the original *Finger Drum Bible*, I'm confident that *The Finger Drum Genesis* surpasses its predecessor in ease of use and diversity. While both books complement each other well, the tablature in *The Finger Drum Genesis* is refined and more user-friendly for all skill levels.

In summary, this book is a treasure trove of information and visuals designed to help you fulfill your potential as a finger drummer!

WHO IS THIS BOOK FOR?

This book is designed to benefit finger drummers of all skill levels and contains fundamental knowledge that will benefit both beginner and intermediate levels.

The book builds a strong foundational knowledge of common rhythmic instruments, and sounds, strength building exercises, safety tips, encouragement, and finally transitions to a set of essential patterns all drummers should know.

No music theory? No Problem! The unique grid-style tablature is easy to understand, even if you have no prior musical experience. Concepts about counting time and reading the grids are thoroughly described and illustrated in the beginning chapters of the book.

You'll be drumming in no time at all!

WHY IS THIS BOOK NEEDED?

Although finger drumming has been an art form since the '80s, there remains a lack of sufficient resources to educate aspiring finger drummers. Beyond hardware manuals, there is little available that fosters real intrinsic musical skill for finger drummers. This book aims to develop a wide range of essential skills required for fluid rhythmic performances using an 8 or 16 pad drum machine. The book takes a holistic approach to teaching finger drumming, starting at the very basics, such as common sounds, finger strengthening exercises, pad layouts, and progresses through a series of chapters on Rudiments, Foundational rhythms, and ideas on integrating melodic sample chops into a pattern.

This is by no means an exhaustive resource but provides a strong foundation of rhythm styles, rudiments, and techniques to assist beginners in becoming versatile and flexible electronic percussionists. This book solves the problem of not knowing what or how to practice by providing easy-to-read tablature and clear diagrams. Finger Drummers can consider themselves well-rounded pros by mastering everything contained within these pages.

The unique tablature created for this series of books helps to expedite the learning process by bypassing the learning curve inherent in traditional notation. There are aspects of this tablature that integrate some traditional concepts, but overall, a learner can open the book and easily understand what to do.

This book contains a variety of foundational rhythms in both electronic and acoustic genres. However, the content caters to the modern electronic musician by offering tablature of popular electronic genres that are commonly forgotten within acoustic drumming literature.

Often I hear of aspiring finger drummers getting stuck trying to decide on the most ideal pad layout. This book has included a meticulously considered layout, called the Standard Pad Layout, that is both ergonomic and flexible. You'll find clear diagrams of this layout along with links to download example sounds, Expansions, and Ableton Racks to get you started quickly. As an added feature, there is a chapter that explores two additional layouts for speed playing and sample chopping.

With consistent practice of the concepts in this book, you will strengthen the essential skills needed for finger drum mastery. Those skills include:

1 Developing a sense of timing and consistency. Every rhythmist requires a keen sense of timing, which is something that can be practiced and improved. Following the recommendations in this book will help increase your feel for consistent timing.

2 Utilizing all fingers and thumbs independently. A capable finger drummer can unlock complex patterns by utilizing all 10 fingers independently. The rhythms in this book aim to develop your finger and hand independence so that you may also perform complex rhythms with perfect accuracy.

3 Building adjacent and non-adjacent finger combo strength. Some patterns require awkward combinations and positioning of fingers on the pads. The patterns and exercises in the book will assist you in building the muscle and mental strength to handle strange combos.

4 Naturally introducing fills and flourishes. Nothing lifts the energy of a rhythm quite like a good drum fill. The culmination of varied patterns coupled with increased strength and control will build your ability to quickly switch between patterns and feels to create intriguing rhythmic transitions, naturally.

My personal hope is to see a torrent of new finger drummers who have realized their aspirations with a little boost from this book!

HOW TO USE THIS BOOK

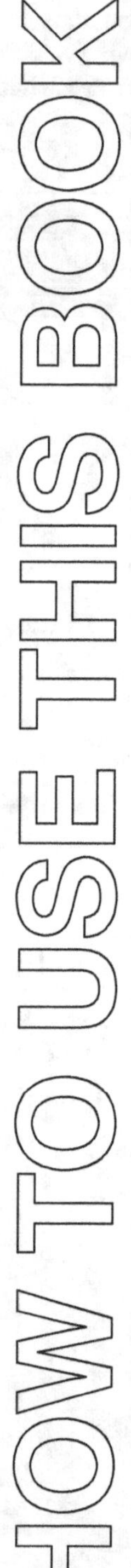

POSITIONING

The angle and posture you'll be using to engage with your finger drumming setup is a crucial factor in the ease of use and safety while practicing and performing. It may seem unusual to consider safety when practicing a musical instrument, but repetitive motion injuries are no joke. Proper posture will save you from the long-term discomfort of *Carpal Tunnel* and *Cubital Tunnel* syndrome. These are both results of repetitive strain injuries that impact the nerves passing through channels within the wrist and elbow causing tingling, numbness, and pain.

ARM POSITION: Your arms should be relaxed and hang comfortably by your sides, not extended too far forward or pulled too far back. Bend your elbows at approximately right angles (90 degrees), positioning them in such a way that they feel natural and not forced.

It's crucial to adjust the height of your chair or the position of the controller so that your forearms are approximately level with the controller's surface or slightly above it. This positioning helps keep your wrists in a neutral, flat position, rather than angled up or down, which can contribute to strain over time. By ensuring that your elbows are not splayed out to the sides and your wrists remain straight, you reduce the risk of developing repetitive strain injuries that can occur from prolonged improper positioning during play.

WRIST ALIGNMENT: Keep your wrists as straight as possible to avoid strain. There is no need to excessively twist your wrists to conform to orientation of the controller. Adjust the height of your seat or the position of the controller to help maintain a strain-free and ergonomic wrist posture.

CONTROLLER ORIENTATION: Selecting the right controller orientation is crucial for comfortable access to all pads and to prevent the need to stretch or strain during play. Here are some common orientations and their advantages:

Traditional Horizontal Orientation: In this conventional setup, the controller is placed directly in front of you with the bottom of the controller aligned parallel to your shoulder span. This arrangement provides a straightforward, direct approach to the pads, making it easy to navigate and familiar for beginners or those used to traditional keyboard or desk setups.

Diamond Orientation (45-Degree Angle): My personal preference for orientation is setting the controller at a 45-degree angle, also known as the diamond position. This orientation positions the controller's corners so two face directly towards and away from you, with the other two corners to your left and right. This setup allows for equal access to all of the pads using both hands, facilitating a more ergonomic reach and potentially reducing the risk of wrist strain. It provides a balanced approach, especially beneficial when using complex finger drumming techniques that require quick, simultaneous access to multiple pads.

Your Choice Based on Comfort and Ease: Ultimately, the choice of orientation should be determined by what feels most comfortable and natural to you. It's important to consider how each setup affects your ability to reach all pads without unnecessary stretching or straining. Experiment with different positions during your practice sessions to determine which orientation provides the best combination of comfort, ease of access, and efficiency in your playing style.

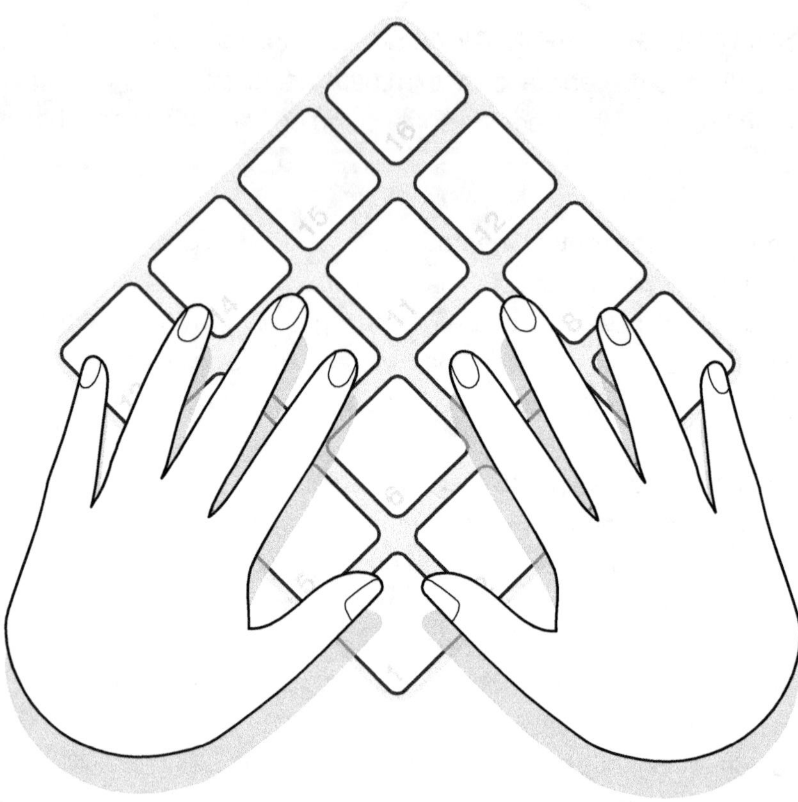

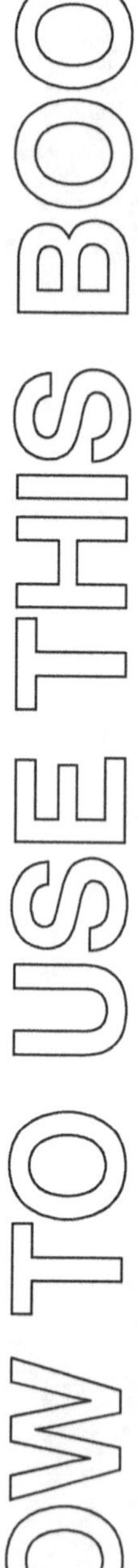

FINGER USAGE: This diamond-shaped controller layout, shown above, optimizes the accessibility of all drum pads for more intuitive and efficient tapping. It aligns the pads with your fingers to minimize the need for reaching or straining. Specifically, the thumbs (1) are used for the lower pads, typically set for bass and kick sounds. The index fingers (2) are positioned to trigger the central pads, ideal for snares and other mid-range tones. Meanwhile, the middle (3), ring (4), and pinky fingers (5) can easily strike the upper pads, suited for hats, percs, and other peripheral sounds.

STANDARD PAD LAYOUT (SPL)

The Standard Pad Layout (below) is thoughtfully designed for ergonomic use and supports both single and double-handed play. It is structured to align with all the rhythms featured in the *Finger Drum Genesis* and *Finger Drum Bible*, ensuring a cohesive learning and practice experience. Additionally, the layout includes options for customization, allowing you to modify the pad assignments according to your personal preferences and playing style. This adaptability lets you optimize the setup to best suit your individual drumming needs while also offering a concrete configuration to support building muscle memory and ultimately allowing you to play the pads without looking down at your fingers.

DOWNLOAD SPL KITS:

TOM 3 (MID) `13`	TOM 2 (HIGH/MID) `14`	TOM 1 (HIGH) `15`	CRASH SPLASH CHINA `16`
TOM 4 (MID/LOW) `9`	PERC FILLS CLAVES `10`	OPEN HAT `11`	PERC FILLS TAMBO `12`
TOM 5 (808) KICK 2 `5`	SNARE 1 `6`	CLOSED HAT `7`	PERC FILLS SHAKER `8`
TOM 6 KICK 1 `1`	CLAP ALT SNARE `2`	SNARE 2 (ACOUSTIC) `3`	RIDE `4`

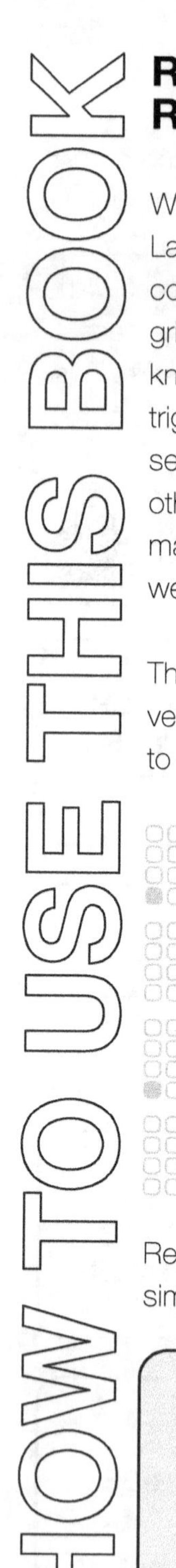

READING RHYTHMS

With the Standard Pad Layout configured on your controller, reading the grid-style tablature involves knowing which pads to trigger at each step in the sequence. Unless otherwise indicated, for the majority of the rhythms and exercises in this book, each step (which we call 'Grids') is equal to a 1/16th note count.

The diagram above visually guides you on how to count each step verbally as you progress through an example of a 1 bar beat (equal to 4 quarter notes).

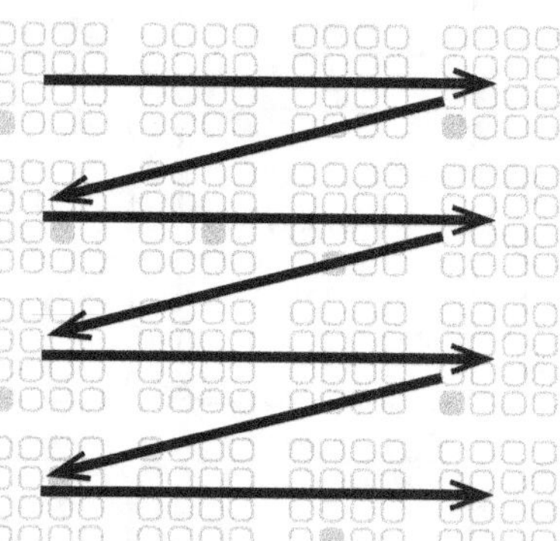

To read the Grids, begin at the top left corner. Follow the row from left to right, just like reading a sentence in an English book.

When you reach the the end of the first row, drop down to the first grid on the next row.

Repeat this until you get to the bottom. If the rhythm continues, simply start at the top left corner of the next page

GRID STEP VALUE
The value of a grid will be indicated by the following icon, or simply a fraction at the corner of the grid set.

16   1/16

ALTERNATIVE READING #1
JUST QUARTER NOTES

To comfortably ease into a new rhythm, consider starting with just the first column of an pattern in this book. This column exclusively features quarter notes, making it an excellent starting point for beginners or for warming up. Practice at your own pace until you are confident with the quarter note pattern before exploring additional methods.

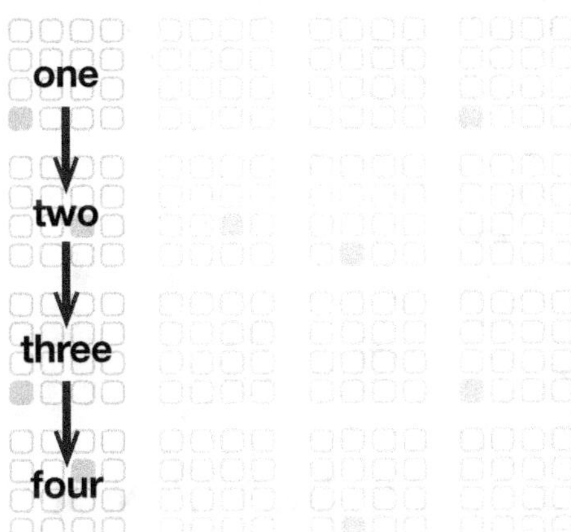

ALTERNATIVE READING #2
JUST EIGHTH NOTES

If you've mastered the quarter notes and want to challenge yourself further, try incorporating eighth notes by focusing on the first and third columns of the rhythms. Temporarily skip over the second and fourth columns. Move smoothly from left to right across the first and third columns, and as you do, count out loud: "One, And, Two, And, Three, And…"

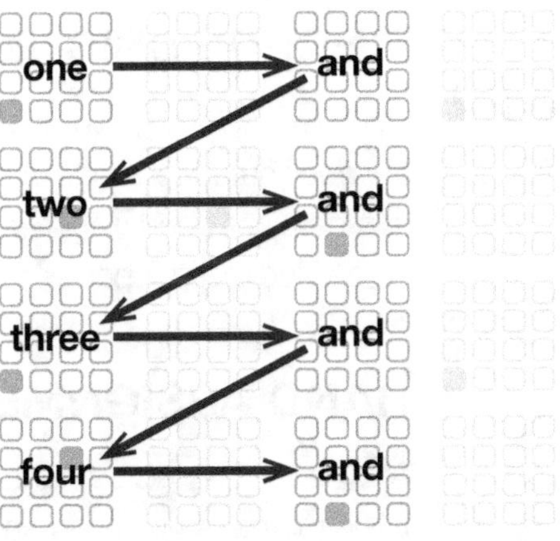

Personally, I prefer to practice row by row. I'll repeat just the first and second rows until I have them memorized, then add the next two rows. Rinse and repeat until I've memorized the full grid-set!

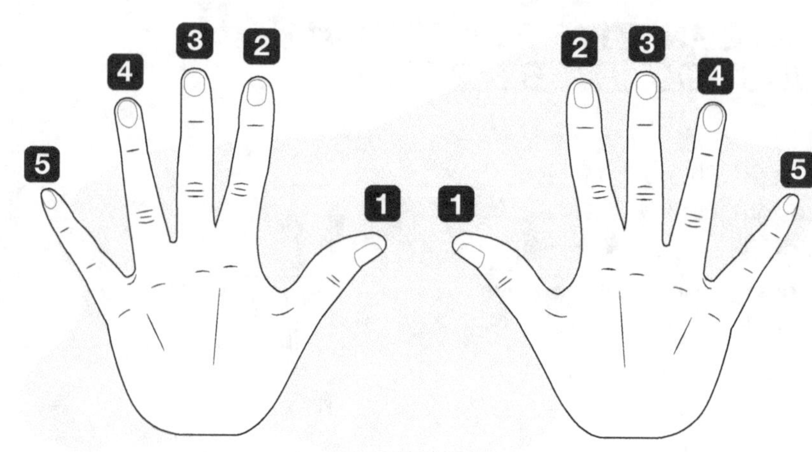

FINGER NUMBERING

To differentiate each finger, this book assigns each finger (and thumb) a number from 1-5, respectively starting from the thumbs (1), pointer fingers (2), middle fingers (3), ring fingers (4), and pinky fingers (5).

FINGER ASSIGNMENT

In the examples shown on the right, you'll notice that specific fingers are designated for triggering the pads. This is indicated by the finger numbers assigned within each pad. These instructions are unique to the Rudiments chapter to guide your practice efficiently.

HAND ASSIGNMENT

At times, a suggested hand will be recommended using one of three methods illustrated and described on the page to the right. The hand assignment will vary by step, across an entire grouping of steps, or both hands may be used during the same step with individual pads highlighted.

You can easily identify the corresponding hand by referring to the legend located above the pattern.

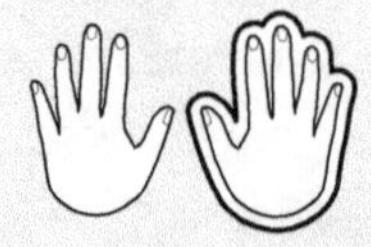

#1 SINGLE PAD ASSIGNMENTS

At times, both hands will be used simultaneously to trigger different pads on the same step and are differentiated using an outline (as shown above). Unless otherwise indicated, your right hand will be used to trigger pads highlighted with an outline (▣). Filled in black squares without an outline (■) are usually assigned to your left hand.

#2 SINGLE STEP ASSIGNMENTS

If only one hand is required for a step, the entire grid will be outlined. In the above example, the right hand (outlined) is suggested to trigger the pads on the first and third steps, while the left hand handles the pads on steps two and four.

#3 MULTI-STEP ASSIGNMENTS

When multiple adjacent steps use the same hand, more than one grid will be outlined, as shown above. For this reason, you might also see entire rows and full sequences outlined.

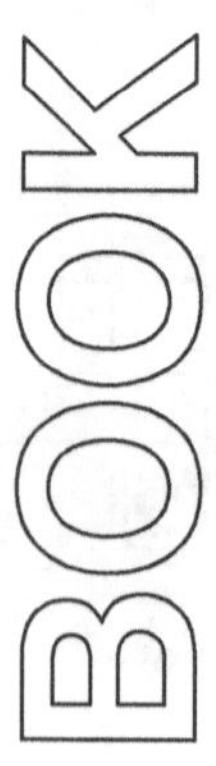
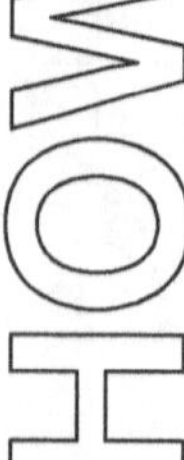

QR CODES

In as many places possible, I've included QR codes you can scan with your phone camera. Depending on their placement, the code will automatically link you to a supporting resource such as audio examples of sounds and rhythms, free downloads of drum sample packs, MPC Expansions, Ableton Drum Racks, and other useful resources.

If you're unable to scan the QR codes, I've included a complete link glossary at the back of the book!

TEMPO

The suggested tempo is included along with most of the rhythms and exercises. You'll always find it listed as **#BPM.**
Set your metronome or metronome app to the suggested BPM and practice, practice, practice! It's okay to start slow at first and work your way up to the full tempo.

DOWNLOADS

Use this QR code to access all of the downloadable resources included with the *Finger Drum Genesis* and *Finger Drum Bible* series.

ENJOY!

ALTERNATIVE LAYOUTS

This book introduces several alternative pad layouts that cater to different styles and techniques of drumming. Notable among these are the Mirrored layout, which is excellent for rapid drumming sequences, and the Sample Chops layout, ideal for blending drum one-shots with snippets of recorded music into a single 16-pad arrangement.

When practicing with an alternative layout, look for a Layout Marker in the corner of the pattern's tablature. This marker is your guide to understanding the specific layout being used, as it corresponds to the Layout Diagram found at the beginning of the chapter. Additionally, pre-configured kits for these layouts can be downloaded via the QR code provided or accessed directly from the Downloads Page.

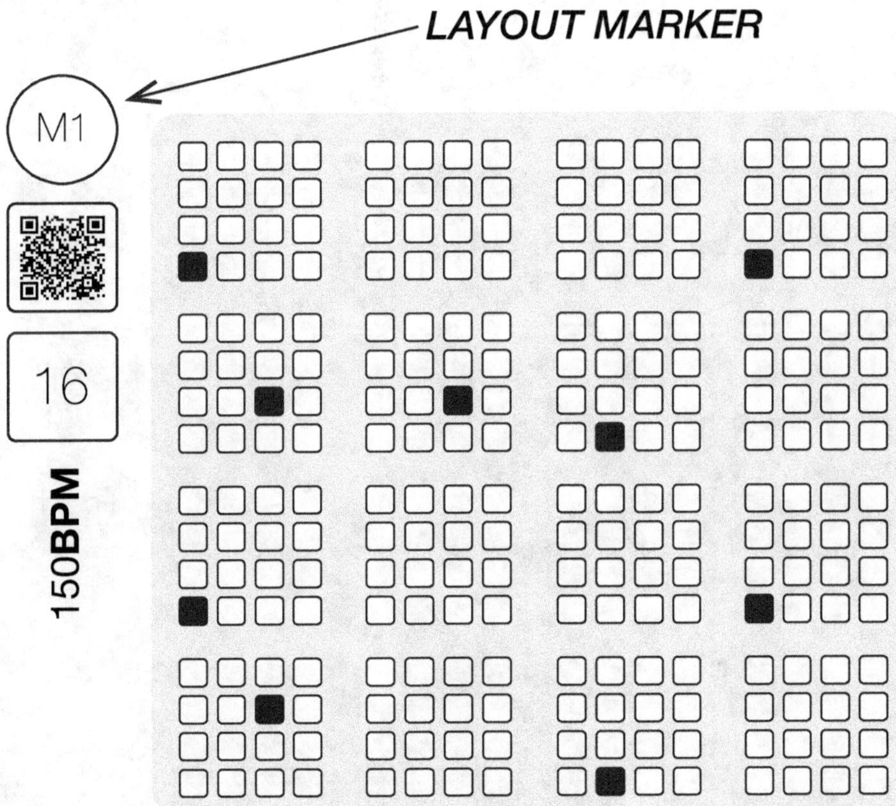

"We are what we repeatedly do.
Excellence, then, is not an act,
but a habit."

~ Aristotle

(Summarized by Will Durant)

STRENGTH BUILDING EXERCISES

PALMS DOWN

1.Begin by placing your dominant hand flat on a surface, ensuring that your fingers are spread comfortably apart. Press your palm gently against the surface to stabilize your hand.

2.Start the exercise by lifting your thumb off the surface while keeping all other fingers pressed down. Ensure that only the thumb moves, and the rest of the fingers remain in contact with the surface.

3.Hold your thumb in the lifted position for a duration of 5 seconds. Focus on maintaining a steady hold without any shaking or other finger movements.

4.After the 5 seconds, lower your thumb back to the surface. Next, lift your pointer finger and hold it in the air for 5 seconds. Make sure that while you're lifting the pointer finger, your thumb and other fingers remain flat against the surface, ensuring you are not straining any part of your hand.

5.Continue this sequence with each finger on your hand: first the middle finger, then the ring finger, and finally the pinky, lifting each for 5 seconds.

After completing the sequence with all fingers, lift all five digits simultaneously for 5 seconds before returning them to the surface. Once completed, switch hands and repeat the entire sequence with your non-dominant hand to ensure balanced strength and dexterity in both hands.

It's important to perform the exercises gently and without straining to avoid injury. If you experience any pain or discomfort, stop the exercise and consult a healthcare professional if the pain continues.

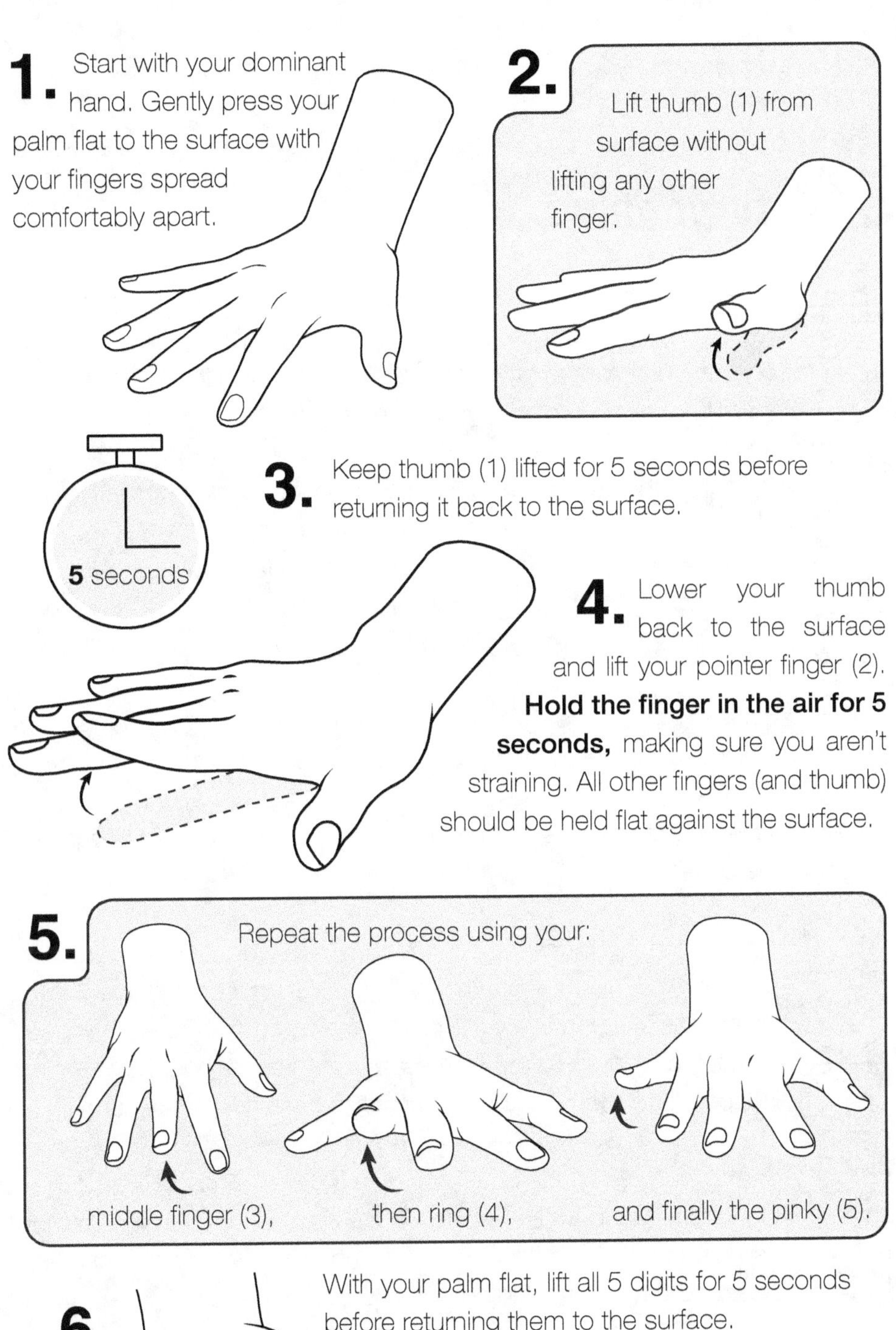

1. Start with your dominant hand. Gently press your palm flat to the surface with your fingers spread comfortably apart.

2. Lift thumb (1) from surface without lifting any other finger.

5 seconds

3. Keep thumb (1) lifted for 5 seconds before returning it back to the surface.

4. Lower your thumb back to the surface and lift your pointer finger (2). Hold the finger in the air for 5 seconds, making sure you aren't straining. All other fingers (and thumb) should be held flat against the surface.

5. Repeat the process using your:
middle finger (3),
then ring (4),
and finally the pinky (5).

6. With your palm flat, lift all 5 digits for 5 seconds before returning them to the surface.

Switch hands and repeat!

TIP TAPPING

1. Start by positioning your hand with the fingers curled slightly, placing only your thumb and finger tips firmly against a flat surface. Ensure that the palm of your hand does not touch the surface to maintain proper form throughout the exercise.

2.Begin with your thumb (labeled as '1' in the diagram). Firmly tap your thumb against the surface 10 to 15 times. Ensure that each tap is deliberate and lifts as high as is comfortable without causing strain. During this tapping, keep all other finger tips pressed against the surface to stabilize your hand.

3. Next, move on to your pointer finger (labeled as '2'). Tap this finger against the surface 10 to 15 times, similar to the thumb. Make sure to lift the finger as high as comfortable for each tap, while keeping all other fingers, including the thumb, in place against the surface.

4. Continue this process sequentially with the remaining fingers: start with the middle finger (labeled as '3'), then the ring finger (labeled as '4'), and finally the pinky (labeled as '5'). For each finger, repeat the tapping 10 to 15 times, ensuring each finger lifts independently while the others remain in contact with the surface.

5. After completing the taps with each finger on one hand, switch to the other hand and repeat the entire sequence. This exercise not only helps in building finger strength and dexterity but also ensures balanced development in both hands.

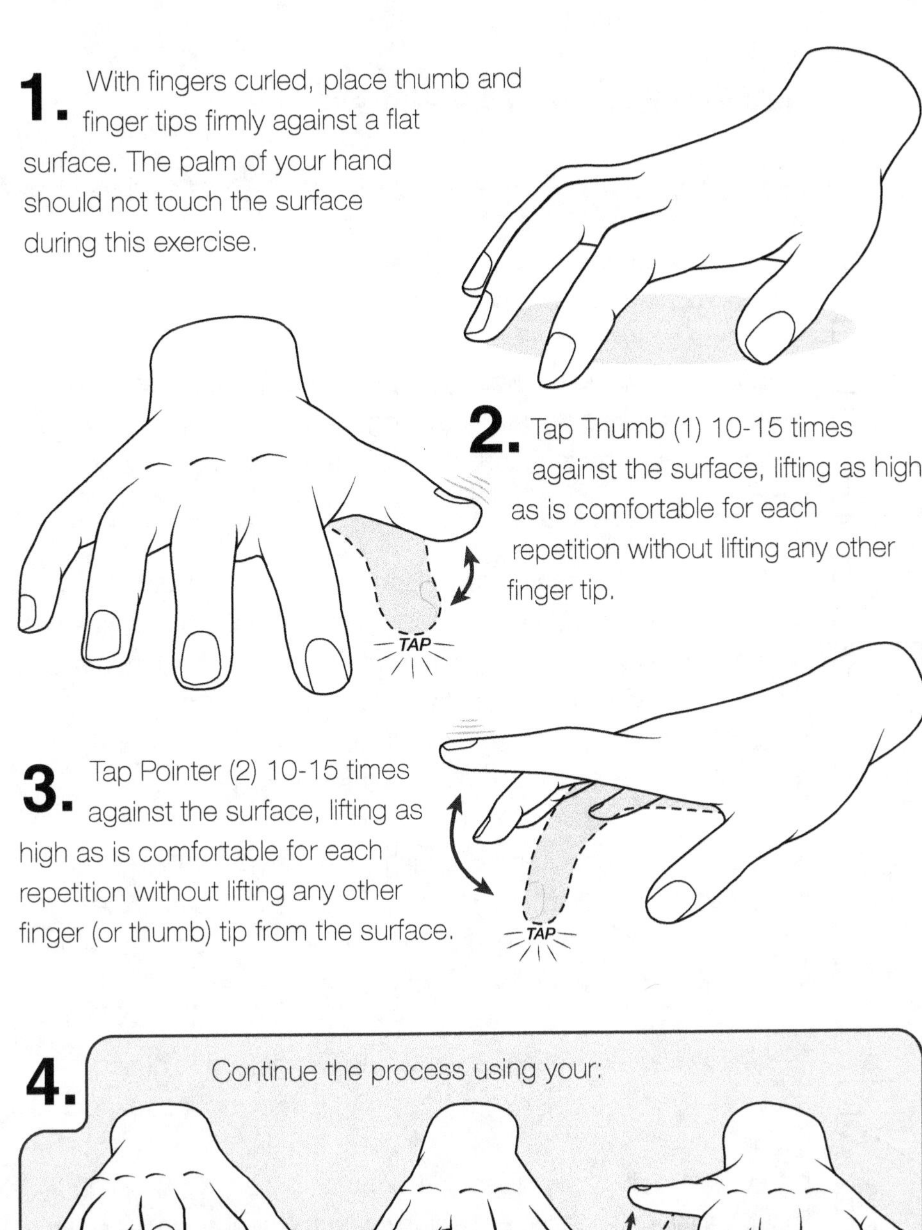

Switch hands and repeat!

INVERTED TIP TAPPING

1.Begin the exercise by positioning your hand above a flat surface with your palm parallel to it, ensuring it does not touch the surface. This initial posture is critical for the exercise as it ensures your hand is prepared for the movement without any support from the surface.

2.Anchor your hand by placing only your thumb on the edge of the surface. Make sure your thumb's edge is comfortably pressed against the surface to stabilize your hand while the other fingers remain free to move.

3.Start the tapping sequence by using your fingertips only, beginning with the pointer finger (2), followed by the middle (3), ring (4), and pinky (5) fingers. Tap each finger against the surface one at a time in this order. Ensure that your thumb remains stationary and pressed against the surface throughout this sequence. Repeat this cycle 10 times before proceeding to the next step.

4.Change your anchor finger to the pointer finger (2). With the pointer finger now anchoring your hand, all other fingers except the pointer should be hovering above the surface. This change will test the dexterity and independence of your other fingers.

5.With the new anchoring setup, initiate the tapping sequence again, starting this time with the thumb (1), then moving to the middle (3), ring (4), and pinky (5) fingers. Tap each finger against the surface in this new order, ensuring that the anchor (pointer) finger remains stationary. Repeat this tapping sequence 10 times.

6.Continue this exercise by rotating the anchor finger through each finger on your hand. After completing the sequence with one anchor, switch to the next finger as the anchor and repeat the tapping cycle. Once every finger has been used as an anchor, switch hands and repeat the entire exercise with the other hand to ensure balanced training.

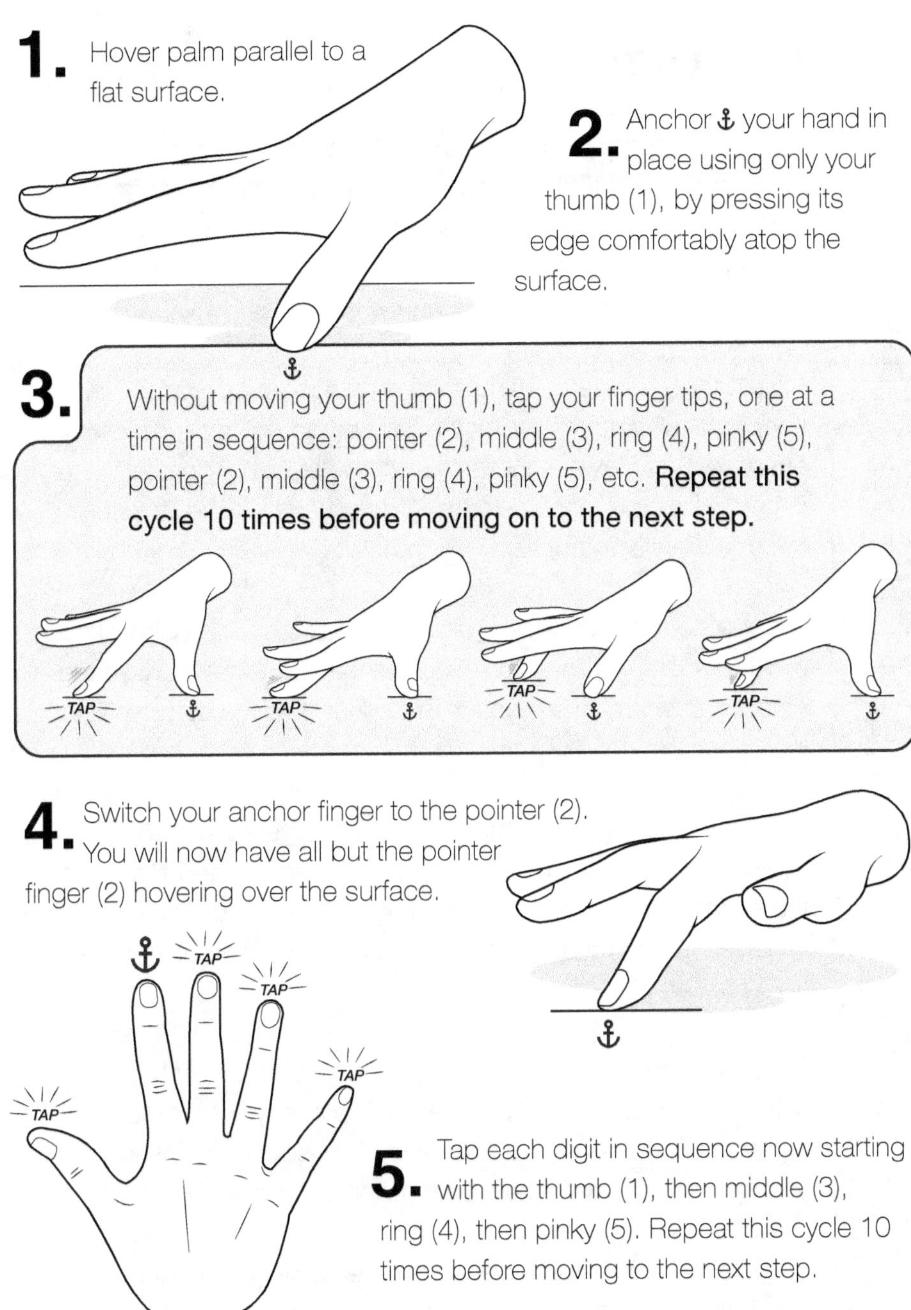

1. Hover palm parallel to a flat surface.

2. Anchor ⚓ your hand in place using only your thumb (1), by pressing its edge comfortably atop the surface.

3. Without moving your thumb (1), tap your finger tips, one at a time in sequence: pointer (2), middle (3), ring (4), pinky (5), pointer (2), middle (3), ring (4), pinky (5), etc. **Repeat this cycle 10 times before moving on to the next step.**

4. Switch your anchor finger to the pointer (2). You will now have all but the pointer finger (2) hovering over the surface.

5. Tap each digit in sequence now starting with the thumb (1), then middle (3), ring (4), then pinky (5). Repeat this cycle 10 times before moving to the next step.

6. Continue until each finger has been the anchor ⚓ once.

Switch hands and repeat!

PAIR LIFTS

1.Begin by positioning your hand with fingers curled, placing only the tips of your thumb and fingers firmly against a flat surface. Ensure that the palm of your hand does not touch but remains parallel to the surface. This starting position is crucial for effectively isolating finger movements during the exercise.

2.Start the exercise by lifting pairs of fingers off the surface in a specified sequence. First, lift the thumb and pointer finger together, ensuring they move simultaneously while keeping the rest of the fingers anchored to the surface. After completing the lift, return them to the starting position.

3.Continue the sequence by lifting the next pair: the pointer and middle fingers. Again, ensure these fingers lift together while the other fingers remain stationary. Return them to the surface after the lift.

4.Proceed with lifting the middle and ring fingers as a pair, followed by the ring finger and pinky. Each pair should be lifted cleanly off the surface while maintaining the anchor with the uninvolved fingers. This step requires careful control to prevent other fingers from moving.

5.After completing the lifts with all pairs, ensure that only the selected pairs are lifting from the surface at any given time; all other digits should remain firmly anchored. This isolation helps to strengthen individual finger coordination and dexterity.

6.Cycle through all the finger pairs repeatedly until you feel comfortable with their movement. Aim for smooth, controlled lifts, focusing on each hand separately before trying both simultaneously. Once you have mastered the sequence with one hand, switch to the other hand and repeat the entire exercise to ensure balanced strength and agility in both hands.

STRENGTH BUILDING

1. With fingers curled, place thumb and finger tips firmly against a flat surface. The palm of your hand should not touch but should be parallel to the surface.

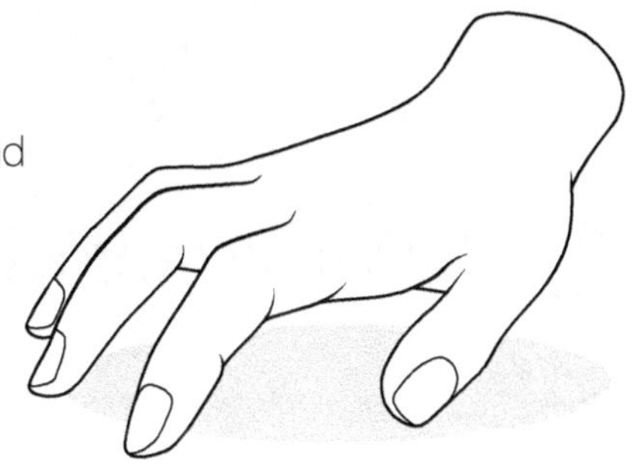

2. Repeatedly lift pairs of fingers from the surface starting with your:

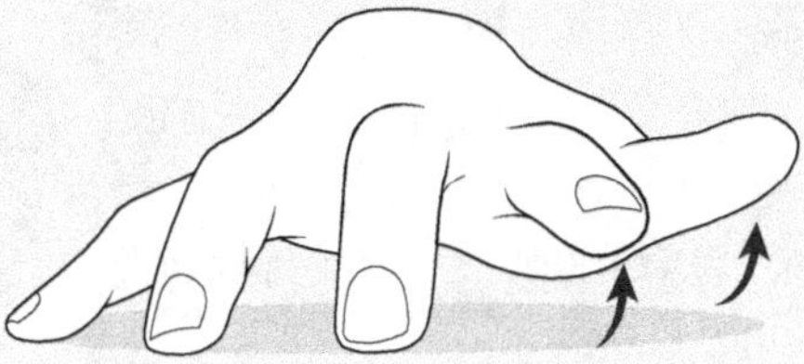

thumb (1), and pointer (2),

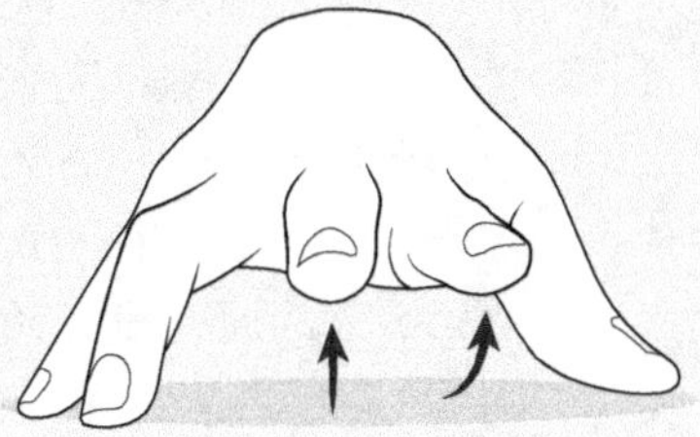

then pointer (2), and middle-finger (3),

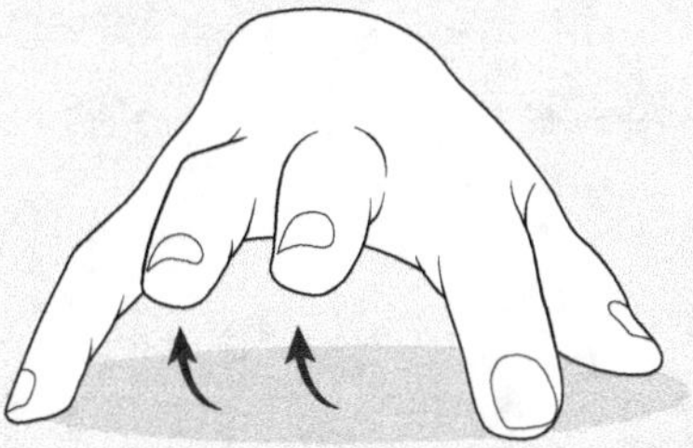

middle-finger (3), and ring (4),

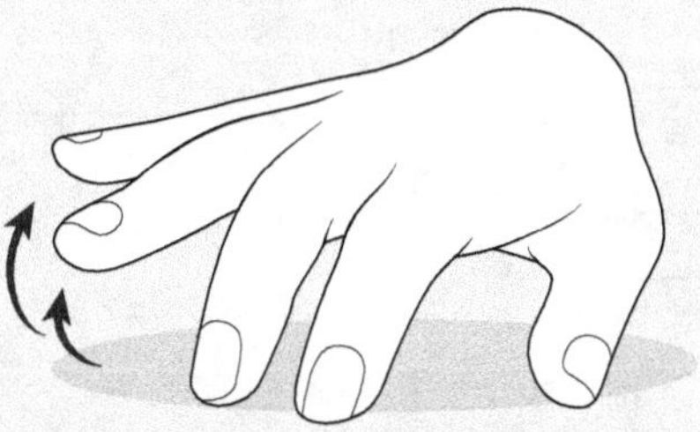

and finally ring-finger (4), and pinky (5).

Be sure that only the selected pairs are lifting from the surface; all other digits should remain anchored.

3. Cycle through the finger pairs until you feel relatively comfortable controlling their movement using each hand separately, and simultaneously.

Switch hands and repeat!

NONADJACENT PAIR LIFTS

1.Begin by positioning your hand with your fingers slightly curled and the tips of your thumb and fingers pressing firmly against a flat surface. Ensure that the palm of your hand does not make contact with the surface, but remains parallel to it. This will help isolate the finger movements for the exercise.

2.Start the exercise by lifting specific pairs of fingers off the surface while keeping the other fingers anchored. Begin with your thumb and middle finger, lifting them simultaneously away from the surface. Ensure that during this movement, the rest of your fingers stay in place, touching the surface.

3.Proceed to the next pair by lifting the pointer finger and the ring finger together. As with the previous step, make sure to lift only the designated fingers while the others remain firmly pressed against the surface.

4.Continue with the last pair by lifting the middle finger and the pinky simultaneously. This should be done with the same care as the previous steps, ensuring that only the selected fingers are raised while the others stay anchored.

5.Repeat the sequence of lifting each pair of fingers multiple times. This cycle should be continued until you feel comfortable controlling their movements. It's important to practice using each hand separately and then together, to develop equal skill and strength in both hands.

1.

With fingers curled, place thumb and finger tips firmly against a flat surface. The palm of your hand should not touch but should be parallel to the surface.

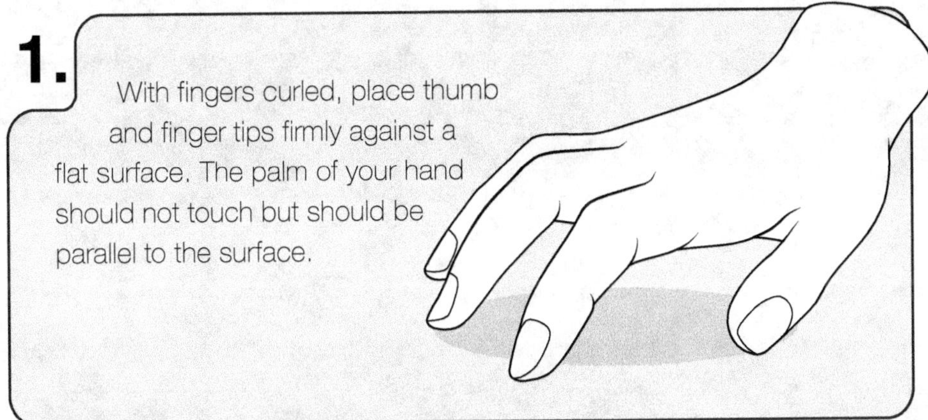

2. Repeatedly lift pairs of fingers from the surface starting with your:

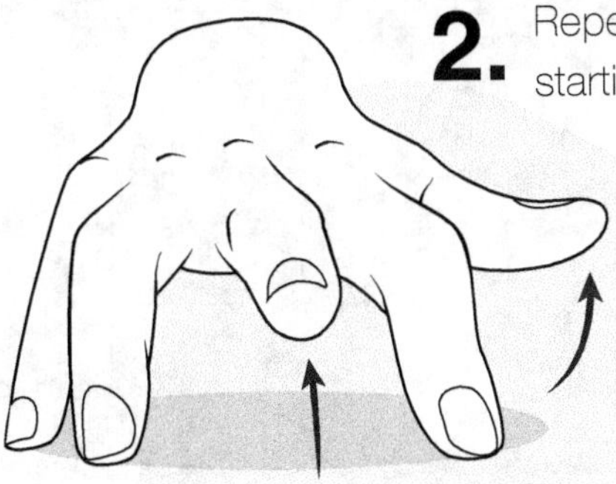

thumb (1), and middle (3),

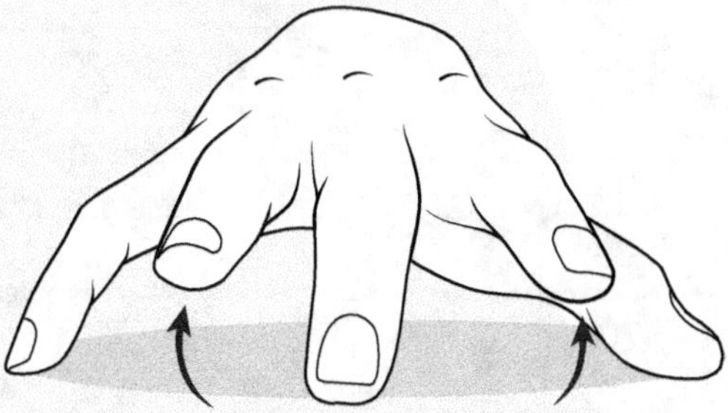

then pointer (2), and ring-finger (4),

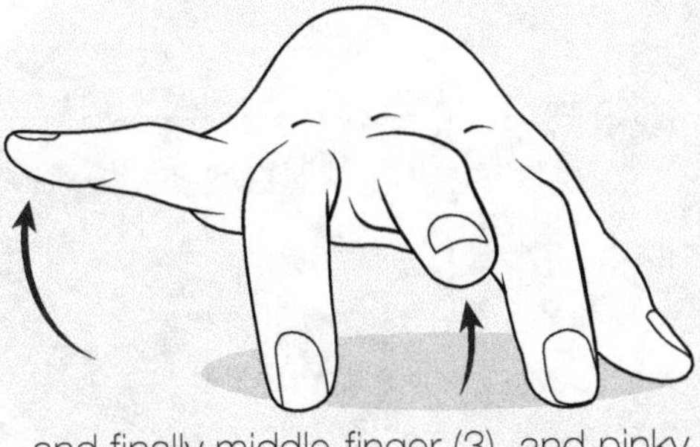

and finally middle-finger (3), and pinky (5).

Be sure that only the selected pairs are lifting from the surface. All other digits should remain anchored.

3. Cycle through the finger pairs until you feel relatively comfortable controlling their movement using each hand separately, and together.

"The journey of a thousand miles
begins with one step."

~*LAO TZU*

THE BASICS

BEATS, RHYTHM, AND TIMING

Rhythm is a fundamental element of music, shaping its flow and giving it life. It determines the pattern of sounds and silences, guiding how a piece moves through time. Understanding rhythm involves grasping several key concepts, including Beats Per Minute (BPM), note values, and time signatures.

WHAT IS RHYTHM?

Rhythm is a sequence of musical notes and rests in time, defining when a note should be played and for how long. It drives the pace and feel of the music, making it lively, mellow, or somewhere in between.

BEATS PER MINUTE (BPM)

BPM measures the tempo of a piece, indicating how many beats occur in one minute. Different musical genres have typical BPM ranges, such as 115-130 BPM for House music and 160-180 BPM for Drum & Bass. In this document, we provide rhythm patterns with corresponding BPMs.

COUNTING BPM WITH A METRONOME

A metronome is a valuable tool for counting BPM and maintaining a steady tempo. It ticks at a consistent pace, which you can set to the desired BPM. Practicing with a metronome strengthens your sense of timing, helping you become a more proficient musician. If you don't have a physical metronome, consider using a smartphone app.

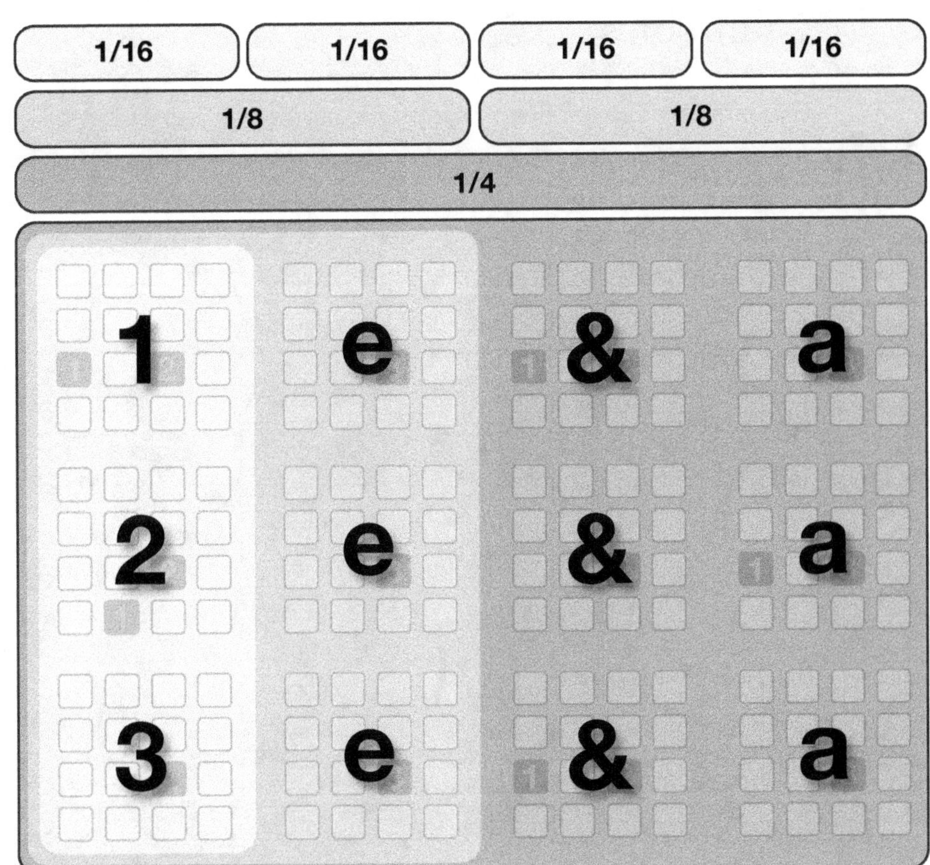

Note value diagram

QUARTER NOTES 1/4

Explanation: Quarter notes are a fundamental rhythmic notation, representing a single beat in 4/4 time, the most common time signature. One quarter note per beat forms the foundation of rhythm.

Visual Representation: In the Finger Drum Bible Series, a quarter note is visually represented as the first grid of each row, unless indicated otherwise. This shows its consistent presence at the start of each measure.

Counting Quarter Notes: To count quarter notes, each beat corresponds to a single quarter note. In a measure of 4/4 time, count "1, 2, 3, 4," with each number marking a quarter note.

EIGHTH NOTES   1/8

Explanation: Eighth notes are rhythmic units worth half a beat in 4/4 time, making them twice as fast as quarter notes.

Visual Representation: In the Finger Drum Bible Series, eighth notes are represented by the first and third grids of each row, unless indicated otherwise, showing their quicker, alternating nature.

Counting Eighth Notes: Counting eighth notes divides each beat into two parts. In 4/4 time, this is expressed as "1 and 2 and 3 and 4 and," with the numbers marking the main beats and the "and"s representing the eighth notes between them.

SIXTEENTH NOTES   1/16

Explanation: Sixteenth notes are rhythmic units worth a quarter of a beat in 4/4 time, making them twice as fast as eighth notes.

Visual Representation: In the Finger Drum Bible Series, each grid represents a sixteenth note, unless specified otherwise, showing their rapid succession.

Counting 16th Notes: Counting 16th notes involves dividing each beat into four parts. In 4/4 time, this is counted as "1 e & a, 2 e & a, 3 e & a, 4 e & a," with each syllable representing a 16th note.

In traditional musical notation, time values for notes are represented using symbols consisting of different shapes and stems. These symbols are placed on a five-line system called a staff.

QUARTER NOTE

EIGHTH NOTE

SIXTEENTH NOTE

PRACTICING RHYTHM

Find a quiet space where you can concentrate. You'll need a metronome or a metronome app on your phone. This will help you maintain a steady tempo while practicing.

START SLOW

Set your metronome to a slow tempo, around 60-80 BPM, to begin. This tempo will allow you to focus on keeping time without feeling rushed.

CLAPPING OR TAPPING TO THE BEAT

Quarter Notes: Start by clapping or tapping your hand on a table to each beat of the metronome. This means one clap or tap per beat, creating a steady rhythm: "1, 2, 3, 4." Repeat this for several measures to get comfortable with the basic timing.

Eighth Notes: Once comfortable with quarter notes, practice dividing each beat into two. This means you'll clap or tap twice per beat. This creates a rhythm of "1 and 2 and 3 and 4 and," with the numbers representing the main beats and the "and"s marking the eighth notes.

16th Notes: Once comfortable with eighth notes, progress to 16th notes by dividing each beat into four. This involves a quick "1 e & a, 2 e & a, 3 e & a, 4 e & a," where each syllable represents a clap or tap.

PRACTICE ALONGSIDE MUSIC

Choose a Song: Select a song with a clear, steady beat that matches your comfort level.

Clap or Tap to the Beat: Begin clapping or tapping to the beat of the song. For an extra challenge, identify and clap or tap along with specific rhythmic patterns, such as the bassline or melody.

Count Aloud: To solidify your sense of timing, count aloud while clapping or tapping, '1, 2, 3, 4' for quarter notes or '1 and 2 and 3 and 4 and' for eighth notes.

GRADUALLY INCREASE TEMPO

Increase Metronome Speed: Once you're comfortable with slower tempos, gradually increase the BPM by 10-20 increments. This will help you adapt to different musical speeds.

Practice at Various Tempos: Work at different tempos, from slow to fast, until you feel comfortable with each.

RHYTHM EXERCISES

Alternating Rhythms: Alternate between quarter notes, eighth notes, and 16th notes within the same measure. This strengthens your rhythmic versatility.

Syncopation: For an advanced challenge, try clapping or tapping on the "off-beat," or between the main beats. This creates syncopation, giving your rhythm a more dynamic feel.

STAY CONSISTENT

Practice daily, even if for just a few minutes. Consistent practice helps reinforce your sense of rhythm and timing over time.

RECORD AND EVALUATE

Record Your Practice: Use a voice recorder or phone app to record your clapping or tapping.

Self-Evaluation: Listen to the recording and assess if your rhythm is steady and accurate. Make adjustments as needed and try again.

SWING

Swing is a rhythmic concept commonly associated with jazz
music and its derivatives. Here's what it means:

SWING IN RHYTHM

Uneven Eighth Notes: In practice, swing often means playing eighth notes
in an uneven pattern. For example, in a 4/4 time signature, straight eighth
notes are evenly spaced at 1/2 of a beat each. In swing, the first eighth note
(on the beat) is longer, taking up 2/3 of the beat, while the second eighth
note (off-beat) is shorter, occupying 1/3 of the beat.

Groove: The combination of this uneven, laid-back feel gives swing music its
characteristic "groove." This rhythm makes swing feel more fluid, relaxed, and
bouncy compared to straight time.

SWING IN STYLE

Versatility: Swing isn't limited to jazz; it can be incorporated into many
musical genres, such as rock, pop, and electronic music, to give them a
different feel.

SWING IN PRACTICE

Interpretation: Musicians often interpret swing differently, ranging from subtle
to pronounced. The degree of swing can vary greatly depending on the style
and artist.

Grid Tablature: In *the Finger Drum Bible series*, including this book, swing
isn't always explicitly notated. Instead, tablature might include a note
indicating "swing feel," or it might be expected that you intuitively apply it
based on genre conventions.

CORE PERCUSSION SOUNDS

This chapter delves into the essential percussion sounds integral to modern music production. Each section focuses on a specific drum or percussion element, such as the kick, snare, hi-hats, and more. I've included valuable information for all technical levels, detailing unique sound characteristics, frequency ranges, and typical uses in various genres. By examining these elements, you'll learn to recognize common percussive sounds in a production and understand the role each element plays in evoking emotion and energy changes. To enrich your experience, I've included QR codes next to each illustration. Scanning these codes will allow you to hear examples of each sound, providing a practical understanding of their applications.

KICK/BASS DRUM

The kick drum, or bass drum, is a large, cylindrical drum with a diameter typically ranging from 18 to 26 inches (45 to 66 cm). It produces a deep, low-frequency thud essential in almost all contemporary music genres.

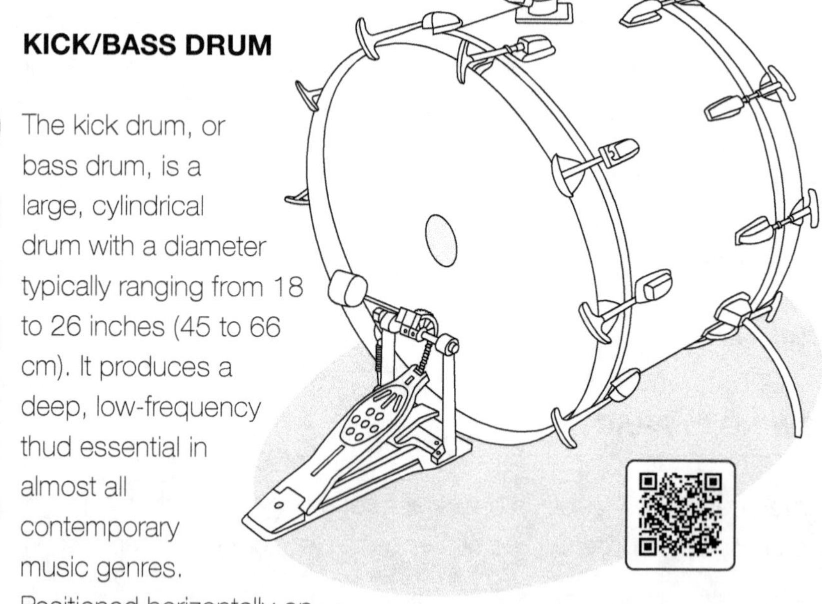

Positioned horizontally on the floor and played with a foot pedal, it serves as the fundamental pulse of a track, providing a steady, anchoring rhythm that drives the tempo and establishes the beat's foundation. The fundamental frequency range of the kick drum generally falls between 50 Hz and 100 Hz, with harmonics extending higher.

SNARE

The snare drum is a cylindrical drum with a depth ranging from 5 to 8 inches (13 to 20 cm) and a diameter of about 14 inches (35 cm). It has metal wires, known as snares, stretched across the bottom head, producing a sharp, crisp sound that contrasts with the low thud of the kick drum. Typically placed on the second and fourth beats in common time, the snare's snapping character adds dynamic variation and rhythmic definition to the beat. The fundamental frequency range of the snare drum is usually between 100 Hz and 250 Hz, with the crisp "snap" sound occurring around 2 kHz to 4 kHz, and harmonics extending higher.

TAMBOURINE

The tambourine consists of a circular frame, usually made of wood or plastic, with metal discs, called jingles, embedded in the frame. It produces a bright, jingly sound through the shaking or striking of these metal discs. Although it may be surprising, the tambourine can be heard in many electronic genres, including House, Drum & Bass, Garage, and many more. It is an excellent substitute for closed hat or ride patterns, adding variation or extra energy to a track. The fundamental frequency range of the tambourine typically falls between 2 kHz and 8 kHz, with harmonics extending higher.

OPEN HIGH HAT

When the hi-hats are struck while apart, they produce a longer, more sustained, and resonant sound. This variation introduces dynamic accents and enhances the rhythmic texture, providing a breathy contrast to the sharper closed hat sound.

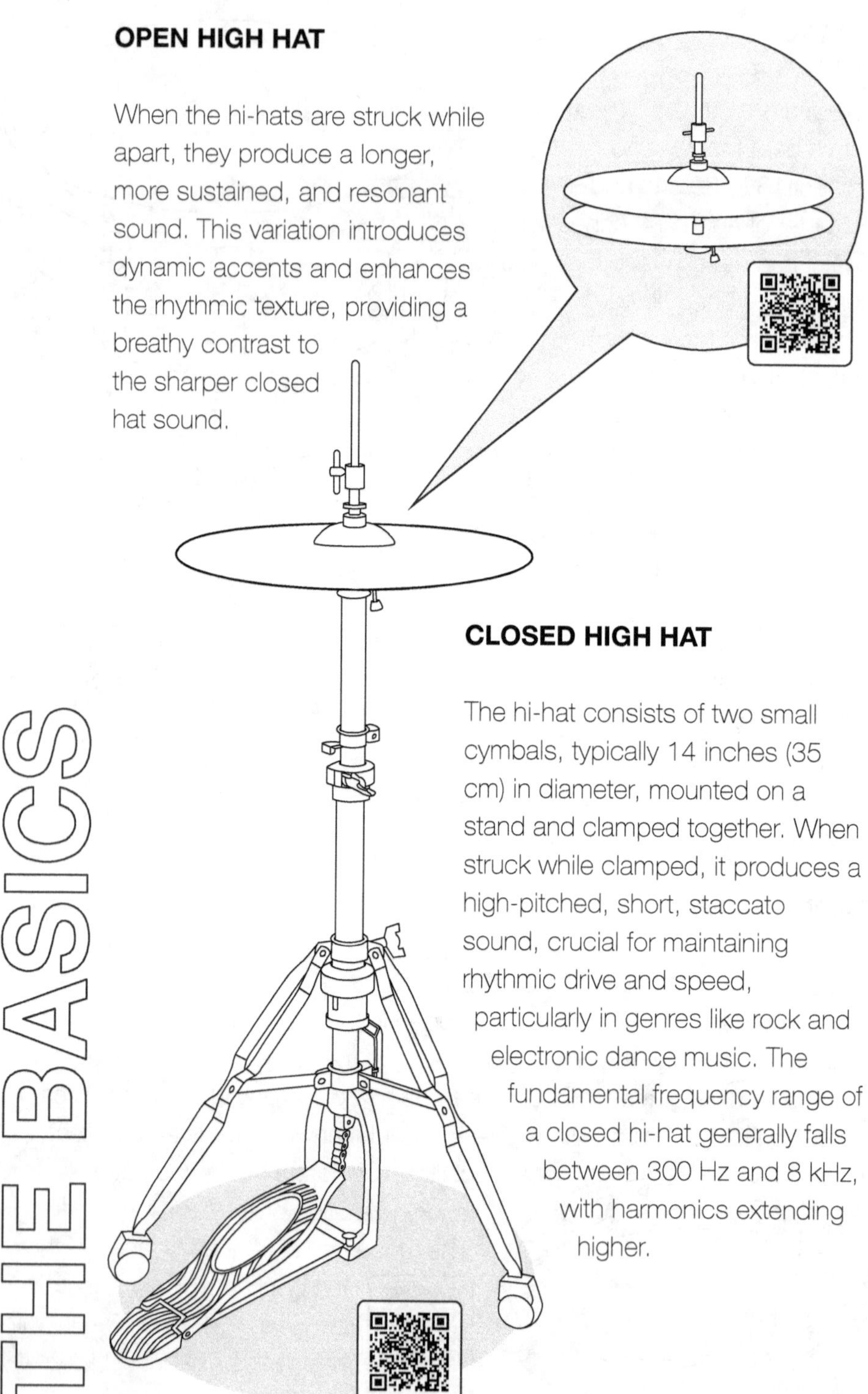

CLOSED HIGH HAT

The hi-hat consists of two small cymbals, typically 14 inches (35 cm) in diameter, mounted on a stand and clamped together. When struck while clamped, it produces a high-pitched, short, staccato sound, crucial for maintaining rhythmic drive and speed, particularly in genres like rock and electronic dance music. The fundamental frequency range of a closed hi-hat generally falls between 300 Hz and 8 kHz, with harmonics extending higher.

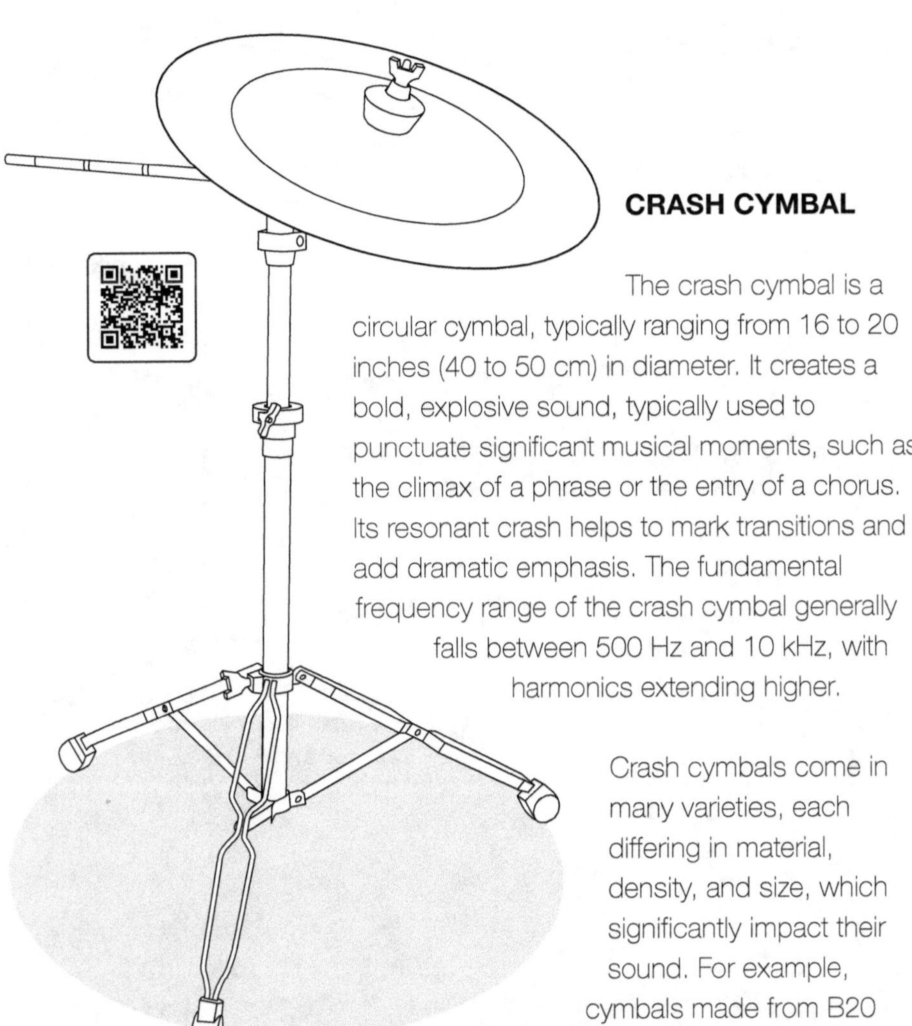

CRASH CYMBAL

The crash cymbal is a circular cymbal, typically ranging from 16 to 20 inches (40 to 50 cm) in diameter. It creates a bold, explosive sound, typically used to punctuate significant musical moments, such as the climax of a phrase or the entry of a chorus. Its resonant crash helps to mark transitions and add dramatic emphasis. The fundamental frequency range of the crash cymbal generally falls between 500 Hz and 10 kHz, with harmonics extending higher.

Crash cymbals come in many varieties, each differing in material, density, and size, which significantly impact their sound. For example, cymbals made from B20 bronze, a mix of 80% copper and 20% tin, tend to have a rich, complex sound with a wide dynamic range. In contrast, B8 bronze cymbals, made from 92% copper and 8% tin, produce a brighter, more focused sound. The density of the cymbal also affects its tone; thinner crash cymbals produce a faster, more explosive crash with quicker decay, while thicker cymbals offer a more sustained and powerful sound. Size impacts pitch and volume: larger crash cymbals (18-20 inches) generate lower pitches and greater volume, making them suitable for dramatic accents, whereas smaller crash cymbals (14-16 inches) have higher pitches and quicker responses, ideal for lighter, quicker accents.

RIDE CYMBAL

The ride cymbal is a large, circular cymbal, typically around 20 inches (50 cm) in diameter. It generates a sustained, shimmering sound that is less aggressive than a crash cymbal. It is typically used to maintain a steady, ongoing rhythmic pattern, making it indispensable in jazz and rock for carrying the groove without overshadowing other instruments. The fundamental frequency range of the ride cymbal usually falls between 200 Hz and 8 kHz, with the bell sound extending to higher frequencies around 10 kHz and beyond.

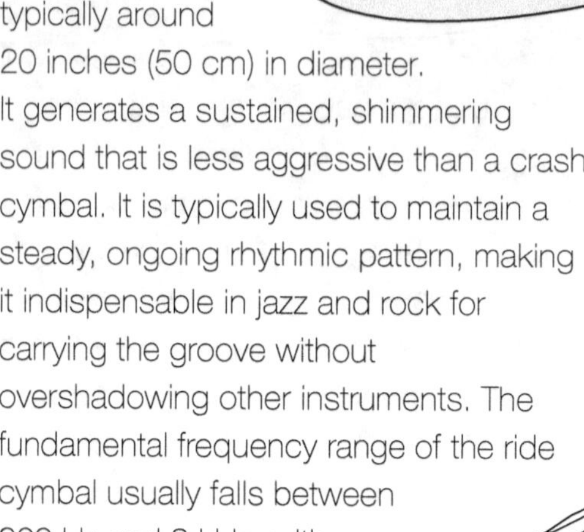

CLAVES

The clave consists of two wooden sticks, each about 8 to 12 inches (20 to 30 cm) long, that are struck together to deliver a sharp, cutting sound. It forms the rhythmic foundation of many Afro-Cuban music styles, maintaining the core rhythmic pattern.

The fundamental frequency range of the clave usually spans from 1 kHz to 4 kHz, with harmonics extending higher. Claves have also found their place in electronic music genres, offering a distinctive contrast to electronic beats and synthesized sounds.

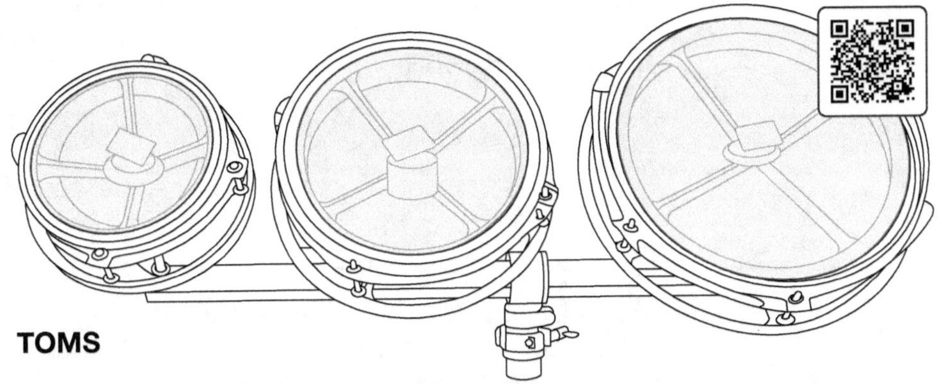

TOMS

Toms are cylindrical drums with variable diameters and depths, producing tones that range from high to deep and resonant. They are primarily used for fills and rhythmic sequences during transitions within songs, adding depth and dramatic flair to drumming patterns. The fundamental frequency range of toms varies, with small toms typically ranging from 100 Hz to 400 Hz and floor toms from 60 Hz to 200 Hz, with harmonics extending higher.

The illustration above depicts a roto-tom, a type of tom that features an open frame design. Roto-toms can be rotated to tighten or loosen the drumhead membrane, allowing for precise pitch adjustments during performance.

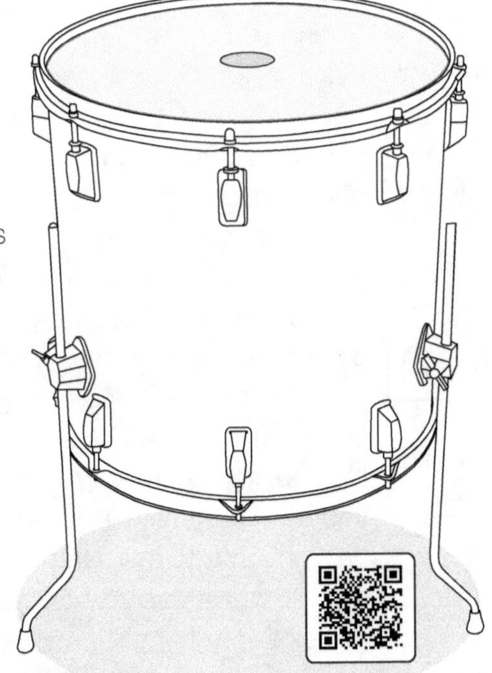

The illustration to the right shows a floor tom, which is a larger, deeper-sounding drum usually positioned on the floor with three legs for stability. Unlike the kick drum, which is played with a foot pedal the floor tom is played with sticks and used for more melodic and dynamic accents. While the kick drum anchors the beat, the floor tom adds depth and texture, often enhancing transitions and providing a resonant counterpoint to the kick's punch.

SHAKER

A shaker is a small, handheld percussion instrument, often cylindrical or egg-shaped, filled with small particles like beads or seeds. It emits a gentle, rustling sound, adding a layer of subtle texture to the music. It effectively fills the space between more prominent beats, often used in quieter or more introspective sections of a piece. The fundamental frequency range of a shaker generally spans from 3 kHz to 10 kHz, with harmonics extending higher.

808 KICK

The 808 bass drum sound originates from the Roland TR-808 drum machine, an electronic device released in 1980. Initially, the TR-808 was not commercially successful and was discontinued after only three years due to the unavailability of crucial components. The TR-808 is capable of synthesizing and sequencing a wide variety of drum and percussion sounds, including snares, hi-hats, and cymbals. Despite this versatility, it became most recognized for its ability to produce a sustained and tonal kick sound that has become a hallmark in hip-hop, trap, and electronic music. This synthesized sound is frequently used both rhythmically and melodically to support the harmonic structure of a track. The fundamental frequency range of the 808 typically spans from 20 Hz to 60 Hz, with harmonics that can extend higher.

STABS

Stabs are quick, intense bursts of sound from various instruments, such as brass, strings, or synthesized sources. They are used to dramatically punctuate parts of a track. The fundamental frequency range of stabs can vary widely depending on the instrument.

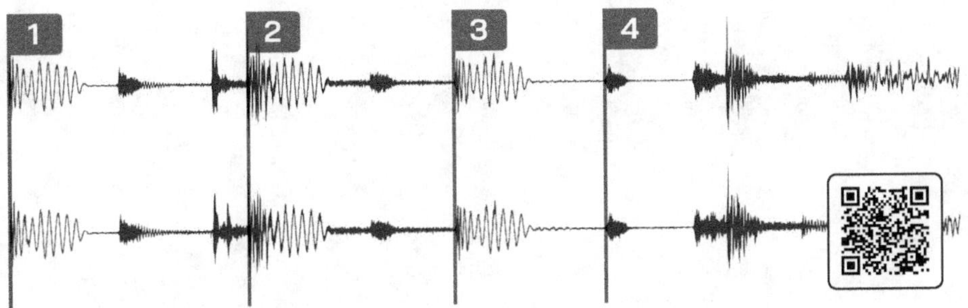

ONE-SHOTS

One shots are singular, isolated sounds that are triggered to play once each time they are activated, without looping. These sounds can encompass a wide range of percussive hits and brief melodic motifs, only limited by the user's creativity.

A one shot can also refer to a triggered sound from a "cue point" on a sample of a recording. In this context, one shots are often called "chops," where specific segments of a longer sample, such as words or short phrases, are isolated and triggered individually.

In music production and performance, especially in finger drumming setups, all drum sounds such as kicks, snares, hi-hats, toms, and cymbals are considered one shots. To determine if you are using or creating a one shot, ask yourself if the sample is looped. If it is not looped, it is a one shot.

RUDIMENTS

WHAT ARE RUDIMENTS?

Rudiments in finger drumming on a 16 pad MIDI controller are analogous to the basic building blocks or 'alphabets' of drumming language. They are fundamental patterns and techniques that form the foundation of more complex rhythms and beats. In finger drumming, mastering rudiments is crucial as they expand your range of motion on the controller.

WHY RUDIMENTS?

Skill Development: Just as in traditional drumming, rudiments develop essential skills for finger drummers. They enhance coordination, timing, speed, and dynamic control.

Versatility: Learning rudiments enables a finger drummer to play a wide range of musical styles and rhythms, providing a comprehensive toolkit for creative expression.

Finger Independence: Borrowing from piano exercises, rudiments help in developing finger independence, crucial for playing intricate patterns and maintaining a steady rhythm with one hand while executing fills or accents with the other.

Muscle Memory: Consistent practice of rudiments builds muscle memory, making complex patterns feel more intuitive and fluid during performance.

> ⚠️ *Daily practice of rudiments for at least ten minutes is suggested for steady progress. Consistency matters more than the total duration, so even short daily sessions can yield noticeable improvements within a week.*

HOW THIS SECTION IS ORGANIZED

This instructional section is thoughtfully structured to guide you through the development of finger drumming skills on a 16 pad MIDI controller. It's essential to begin with the easiest exercises and only advance when you feel comfortable performing each drill without difficulty. Here's how the progression is designed:

Start with the Basics: Begin with 'One Finger Drumming' exercises. These are the simplest and provide a solid foundation. Practice these until you can perform them smoothly and consistently.

Progressive Difficulty: As you become more adept, move on to 'Three Finger Drumming' exercises. These are moderately challenging and will build upon the skills learned in the previous section.

Advance to Complex Patterns: The 'Five Finger Rudiments' and 'Multi-finger Flams & Rolls' sections involve using more fingers simultaneously, demanding greater speed and accuracy.

Routine Warm-Ups: It's highly beneficial to use these rudiments as warm-up exercises at the start of each finger drumming session. They help in loosening up the fingers, improving coordination, and establishing a rhythmic mindset.

Foundational Beats: As you work through the exercises, you'll find they progressively lead to a set of must-know foundational beats. Mastering these beats is essential for handling a wide array of common 4/4 rhythms in popular Western music, enhancing your versatility as a finger drummer when committed to memory.

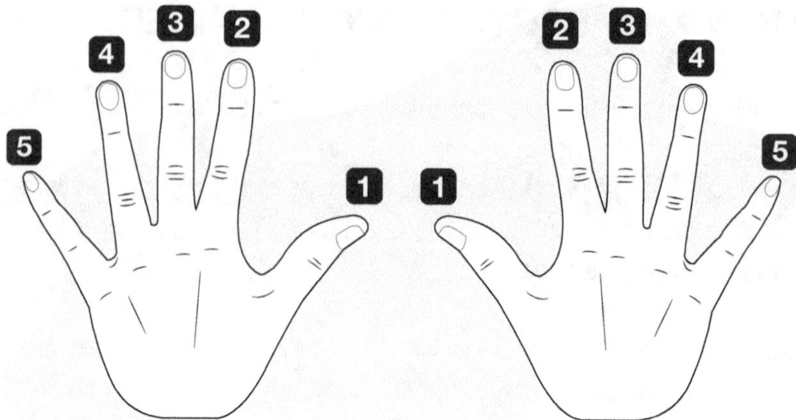

To differentiate each finger, this book assigns each finger (and thumb) a number from 1-5, respectively starting from the thumb (1), pointer fingers (2), middle fingers (3), ring fingers (4), and pinky fingers (5).

At times, a suggested hand will be indicated within a highlighted box surrounding a grid or pad. You can easily identify the corresponding hand by referring to the legend located above the pattern.

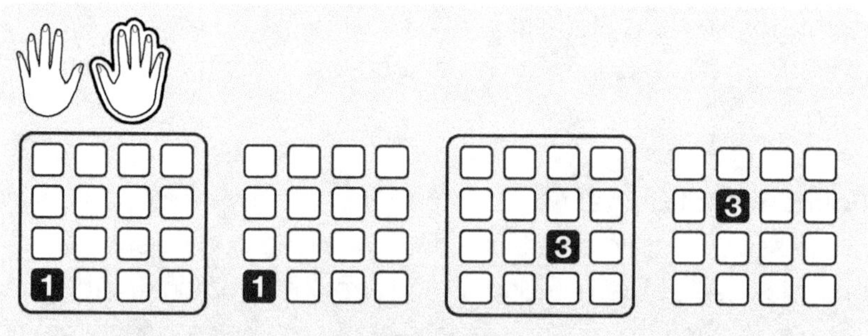

In the above example, the right hand (outlined) is suggested to trigger the pads on the first and third grids, while the left hand handles the pads on grids two and four.

Upon closer examination, you'll notice that each highlighted pad is assigned a specific finger for triggering. For instance, using finger (1) on the right hand to activate the pad on the first grid in the row.

ONE FINGER DRUMMING   (easy)

These exercises are the simplest in the set and involve using just one finger on each hand. While the pointer (2) finger is commonly used to trigger the pads, feel free to experiment with whichever finger feels most comfortable for you.

The familiar dance rhythm known as '4 on the floor' is illustrated in the grids above, each representing a 1/4 count. With your left hand, tap the pads marked with filled-in black squares (■) using your pointer finger (2). Your right hand will handle the pads outlined in the grid (▣)—use your right pointer finger (2) to trigger these pads, as shown.

120BPM

⚠ *Make it a habit to practice your rudiments with a metronome whenever you can. While mastering which pads to trigger is essential, playing steadily to the metronome's rhythm is equally crucial for refining your timing skills. If you don't have a physical metronome nearby, explore free apps available for download on your phone.*

TWO HAND POINTER
'1/8th Hats'

1/8

This variation of the '4 on the floor' rhythm features double-time hi-hats, now played as 1/8th notes. As evident from the fraction above the grid-row, each grid is now equivalent to an eighth note, making it twice as fast (or half the duration) as a quarter note.

120BPM

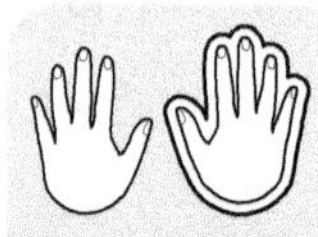

TWO HAND POINTER
'Open Hats'

1/8

Now, it's getting a bit trickier! This variation of the '4 On The Floor' rhythm introduces 1/8th note hats with an alternating pattern, incorporating both open and closed hi-hats.

120BPM

RUDIMENTS

SWITCH HANDS
'Four On The Floor'

1/4

Back to 1/4 note grids, here's the '4 On The Floor' rhythm once more, but this time with a hand switch. Now, your right hand sets the beat with the kick drum, while your left hand, slightly crossed over the right, alternates between the clave and clap.

120BPM

SWITCH HANDS
'1/8ths'

1/8

The 1/8th note pattern with hand switching serves as an excellent exercise for evenly developing strength on both sides. While this pattern utilizes claves and claps, feel free to explore different pad selections as you become proficient with the pattern. For instance, try using the tambourine with your left hand instead of the claves.

120BPM

ROCK YOU
'1/4 Hats'

An uncomplicated yet impactful rhythm showcasing a recognizable kick and clap combination, accompanied by quarter note hats.

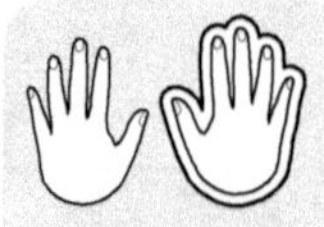

ROCK YOU FASTER
'1/8 Hats'

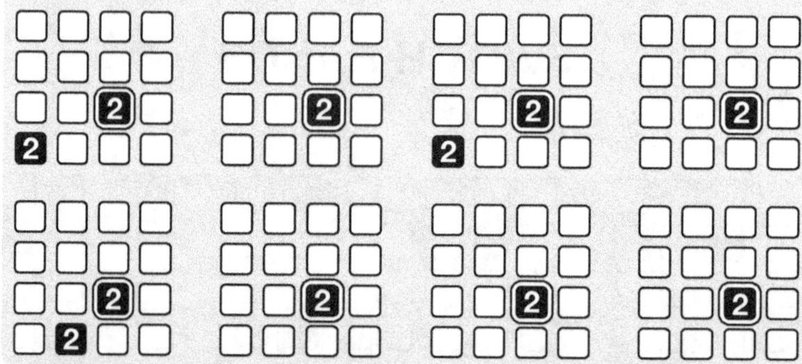

Now feeling a bit faster, this exercise introduces double-time hats layered over the 'Rock You' kick and clap pattern.

80BPM

Feeling too easy? Why not jump to the 'Three Finger Drumming' exercises next?

RUDIMENTS

SYNCOPATION
'Dotted Eighth Kicks'

1/16

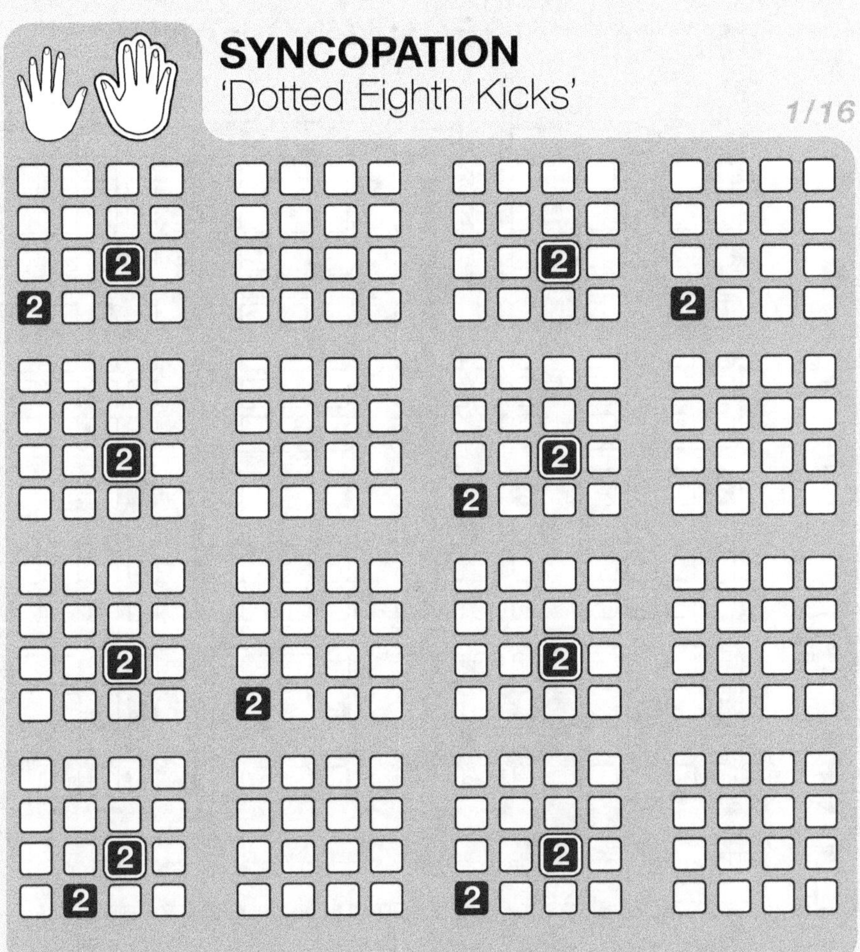

Up to now, you've been honing your ability to move your hands together smoothly. In this exercise, you'll be playing a closed hat at 1/8th note intervals while the kick drum follows a "Dotted Eighth" pattern.

100BPM

In traditional music notation, a dotted note increases the duration of the note by half of its original value.

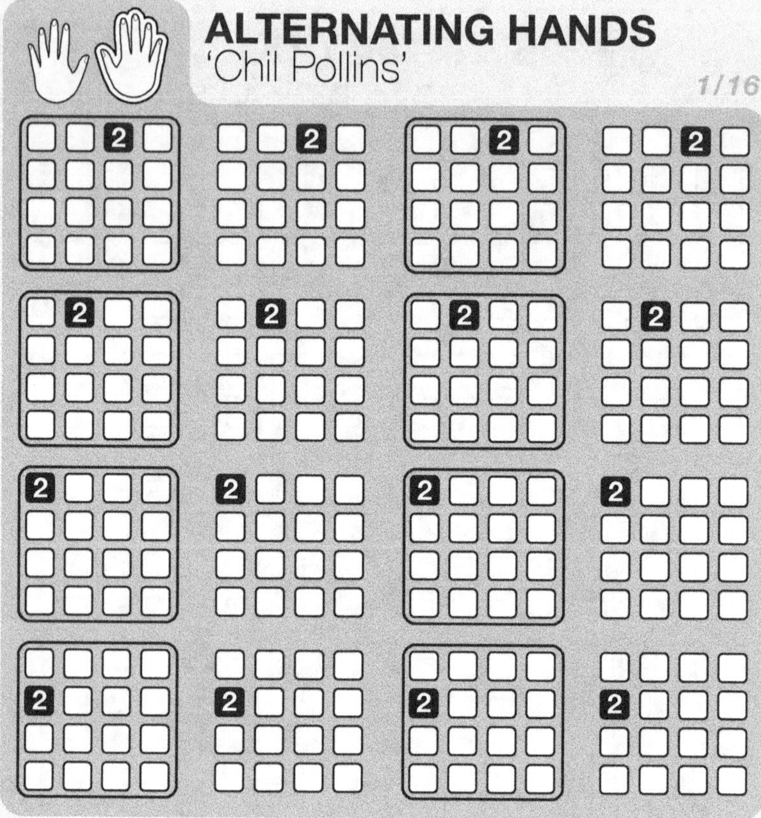

RUDIMENTS

This classic tom-drum fill is included not only for its iconic sound but also for its requirement of consistent hand alternation, now at a 1/16th note count. This exercise is designed to enhance accuracy as you transition between pads and maintain a steady pulse.

120BPM

A fill is an embellishment or flourish, often used to transition between different sections of a musical piece, such as moving from a verse to a chorus. It's a short sequence that adds excitement, intensity, or variation to the music.

THREE FINGER DRUMMING   (moderate)

Approaching the form you'll use for more intricate patterns, the following rudiments engage up to three digits on each hand. While each rudiment is initially presented for individual hands, you're encouraged to progress to practicing with both hands simultaneously once you've mastered the pattern on each hand separately.

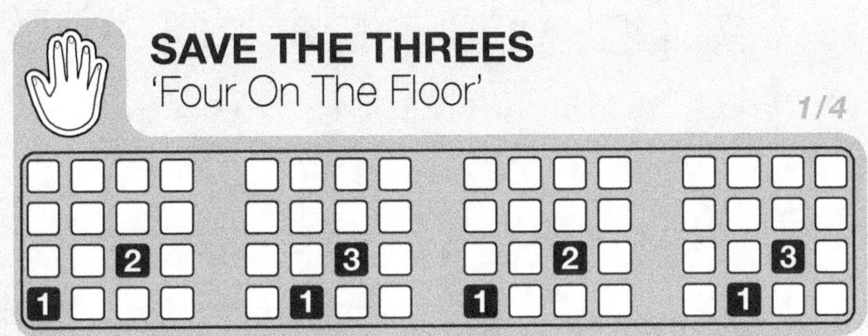

Use only your right hand for the pattern above, noting that the pointer (2) and middle (3) fingers alternate for each 1/4 note step.

Try playing this mirrored pattern with your left hand, ensuring that the pointer (2) and middle (3) fingers alternate, then **attempt with both hands simultaneously after mastering each individually.**

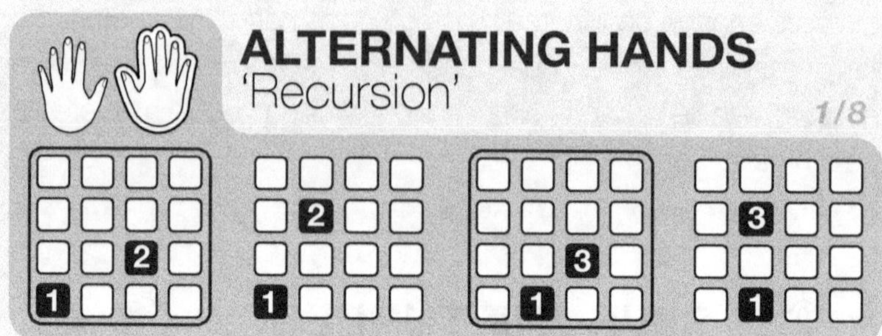

ALTERNATING HANDS
'Recursion'

1/8

Employ your right hand for grids one and three, and your left for the others. Start with your second finger, then proceed to the third to maintain order (2)(3)(2)(3).

120BPM

NOT GARAGE
'It's Garidge, Mate'

1/8

Here's a simplified Garage-style rhythm with offbeat hats, arguably one of the most versatile patterns to master. It sounds great at any tempo and pairs seamlessly with variations on the kick and snare/clap.

130BPM

RUDIMENTS

HIP HOP
'Slow Trap'

1/8

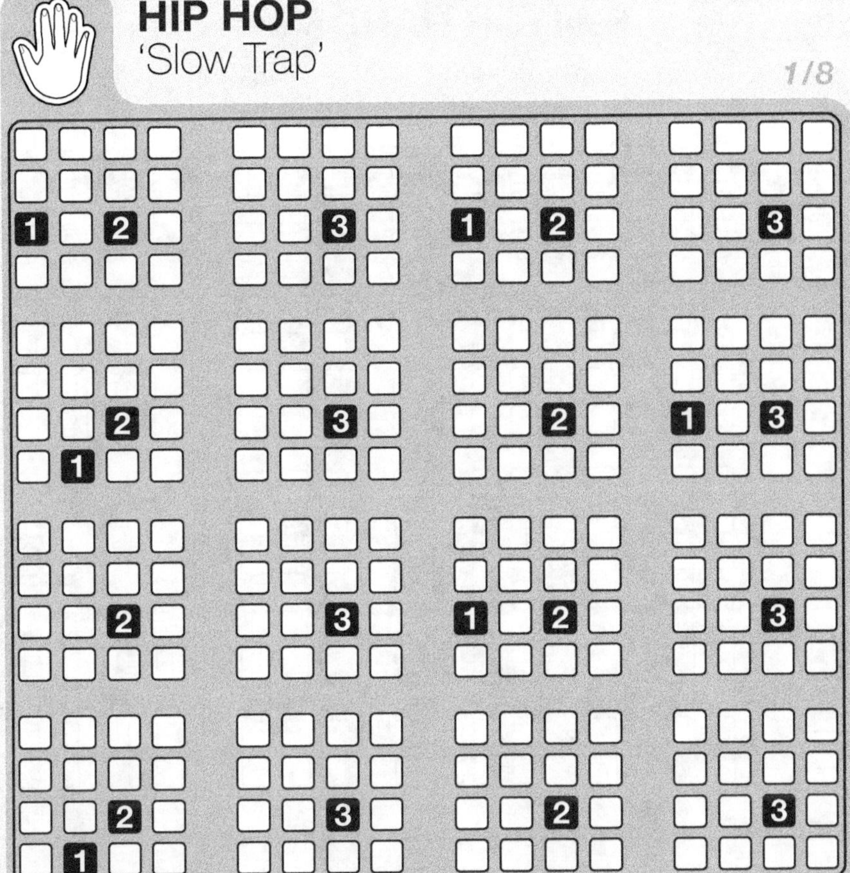

This leisurely Trap/Hip-Hop rhythm aims to enhance the strength of your pointer (2) and middle (3) fingers, as well as your thumb independence. Initially, the tab instructs you to trigger the 808 bass with your thumb (1), but once you've mastered the pattern, feel free to experiment with transitioning between the kick and 808.

80BPM

SWITCH HANDS
'Hip Hop'

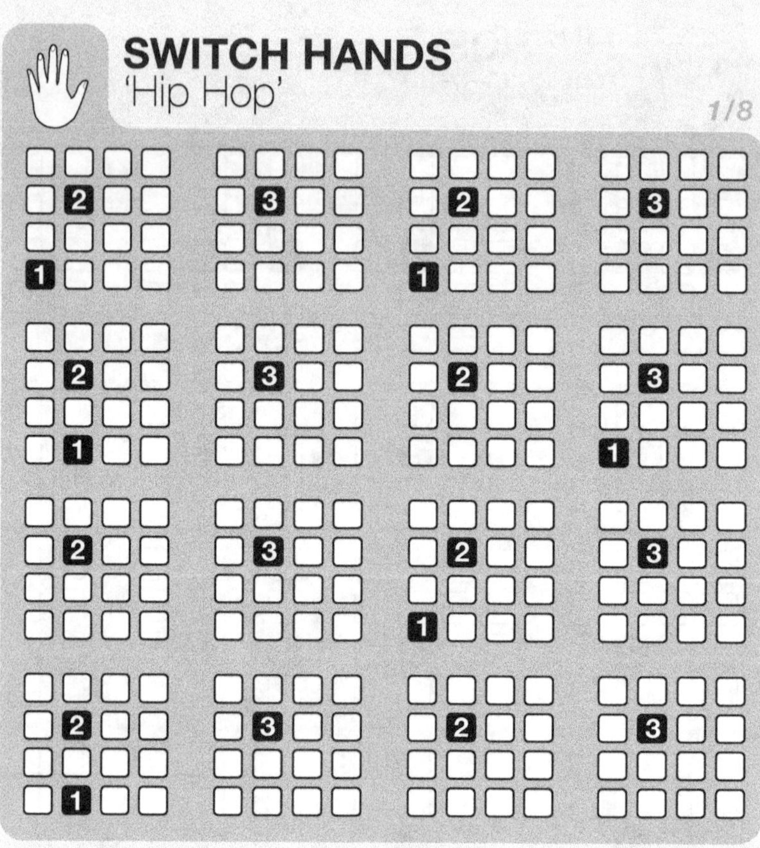

Presenting the Hip Hop beat once again, this time with a tweak specifically for the left hand. Difficulty in playing with your non-dominant hand, regardless of whether you're right or left-handed, signifies a chance for growth in strength and skill. Embrace challenging practice to break through learning plateaus!

80BPM

RUDIMENTS

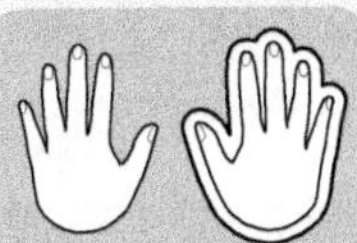

ALTERNATING HANDS
'Is There An Echo In Here?'

1/16

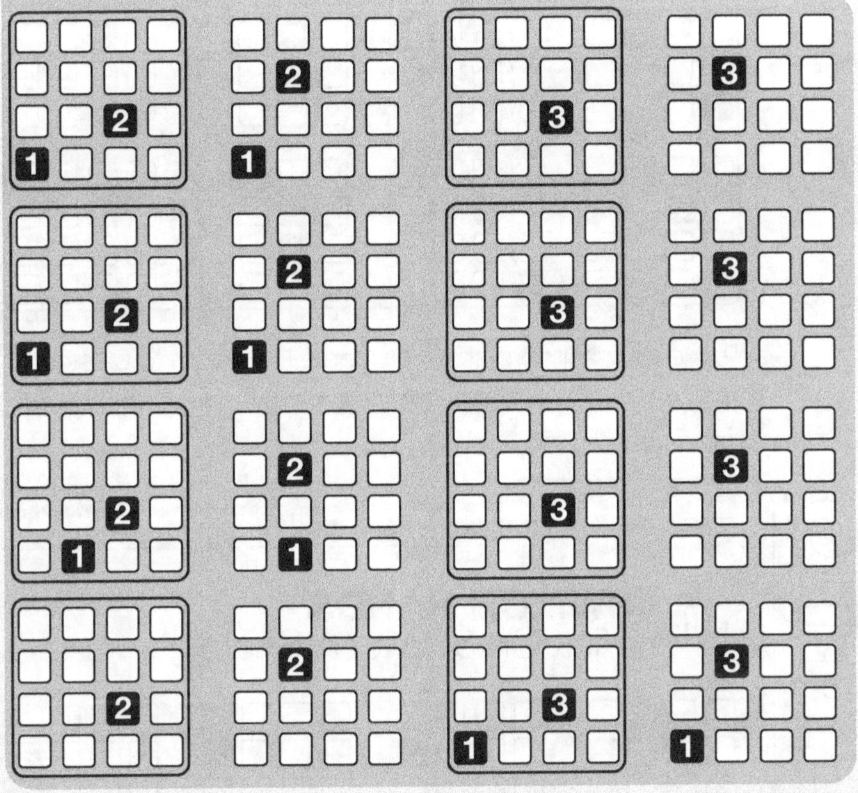

This combines the Hip Hop pattern with both hands, but note how the highlighted grids indicate alternating between hands. Keep the (2)(3) sequence consistent on both sides! Remember to practice with your metronome. While the tempo remains unchanged, you'll now be triggering pads as 1/16th notes.

80BPM

KICK ON '&'
'With A Little Stretch'

1/8

This exercise incorporates a double kick drum to bolster your accuracy and speed during transitions between pads using your thumb.

80BPM

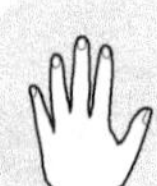

SWITCH HANDS
'Kick On & (With A Stretch)'

1/8

Now, utilizing your left hand, this exercise integrates a double kick drum and widens the gap between pads.

80BPM

RUDIMENTS

ROLLING RIGHT
'A Personal Favourite'

1/16

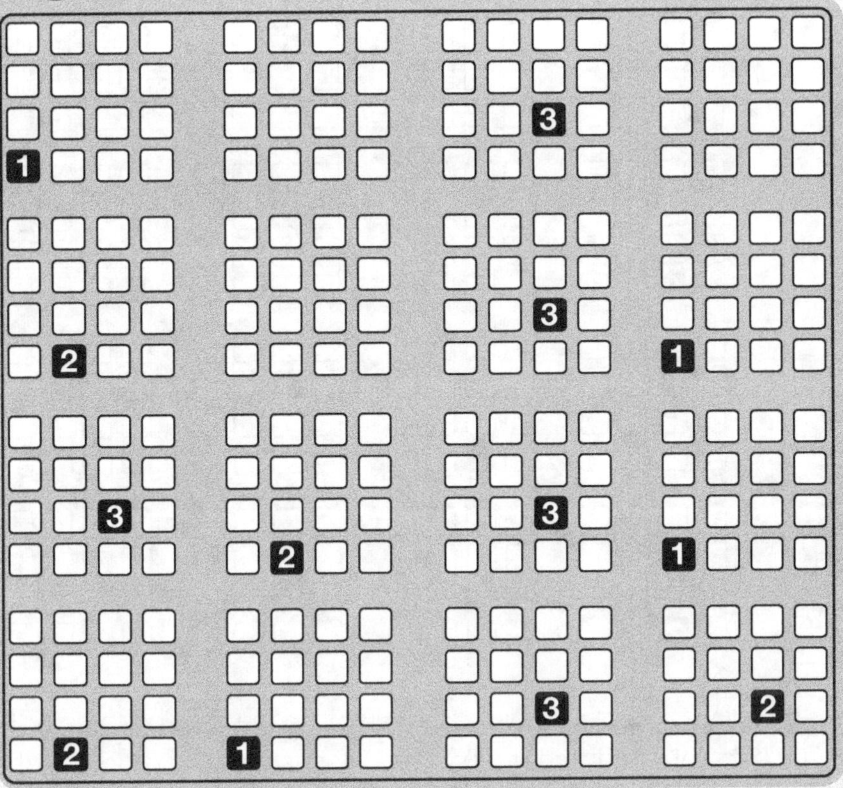

This pattern is incredibly satisfying to master, as it demands both independent finger control and quick execution. When everything clicks, it's exhilarating to watch your fingers glide through what feels like an intricate rhythm. This pattern serves as a solid foundation to explore and adapt across various styles and tempos. Don't forget to practice with your metronome to keep your timing sharp!

85BPM

ROLLING LEFT
'Switch Those Hands'

1/8

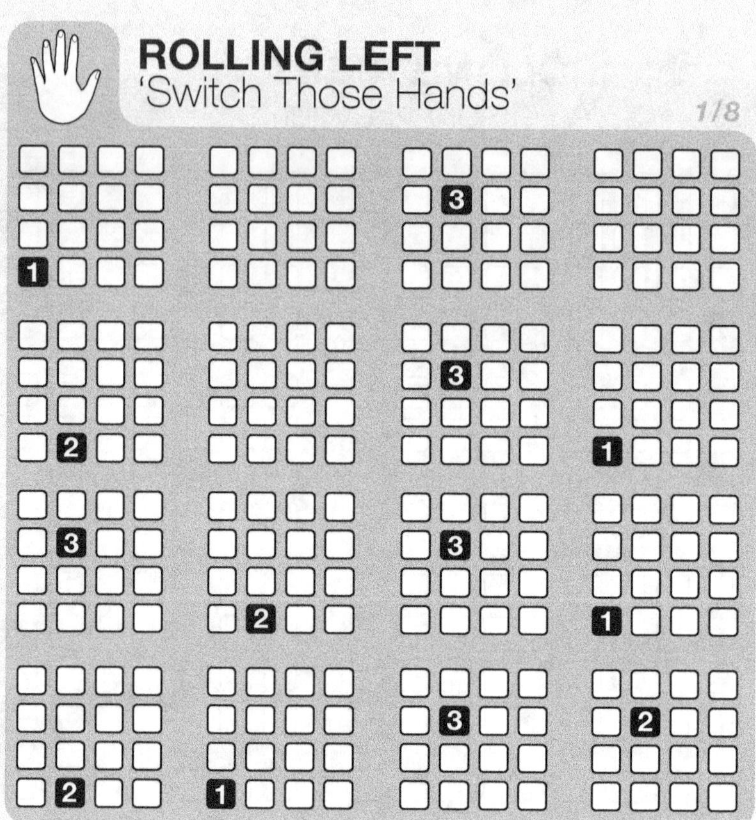

If you aren't left-hand dominant, this one is going to be a burn! Which means it's more important than ever to take the time to practice it over and over until you nail it! Just imagine the complexity you can add to this with your right hand once you've got this committed to memory. Try high-hat and percussion flourishes, or even triggering other melodic one-shots and loops with your right hand. You've got this!

85BPM

FIVE FINGER DRUMMING   (harder)

Getting a bit tougher now! These next rudiments use all five fingers and are similar to some of the strength-building exercises in the book. The added challenge is hitting the right pads accurately while you practice. It's a fun way to build up your precision and control!

> ⚠ If you're feeling any signs of mental or physical fatigue, take a break! Rest for a while, do some light stretches, stay hydrated, and come back to it later. Taking care of yourself will help you perform better in the long run.

1, 3, 2, 4, 3, 5, 2, 4
'5 digits'

1/4

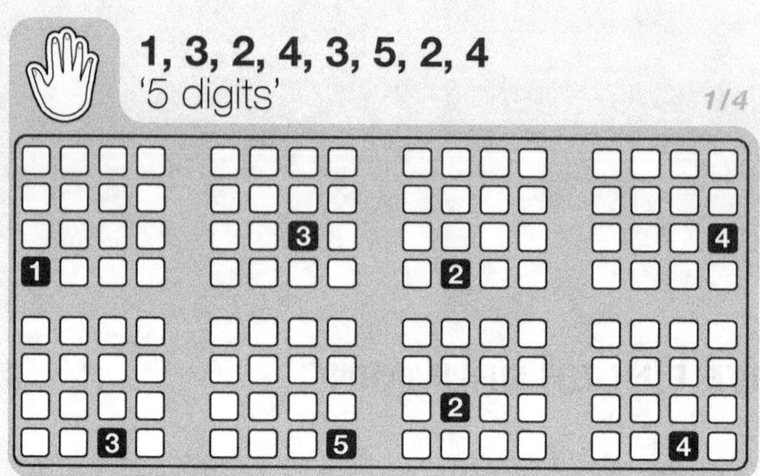

This sequence might not sound the prettiest, but it's fantastic for building finger independence and accuracy. I love using this exercise to warm up before a jam session.

80BPM

1, 3, 2, 4, 3, 5, 2, 4
'Left Side'

1/4

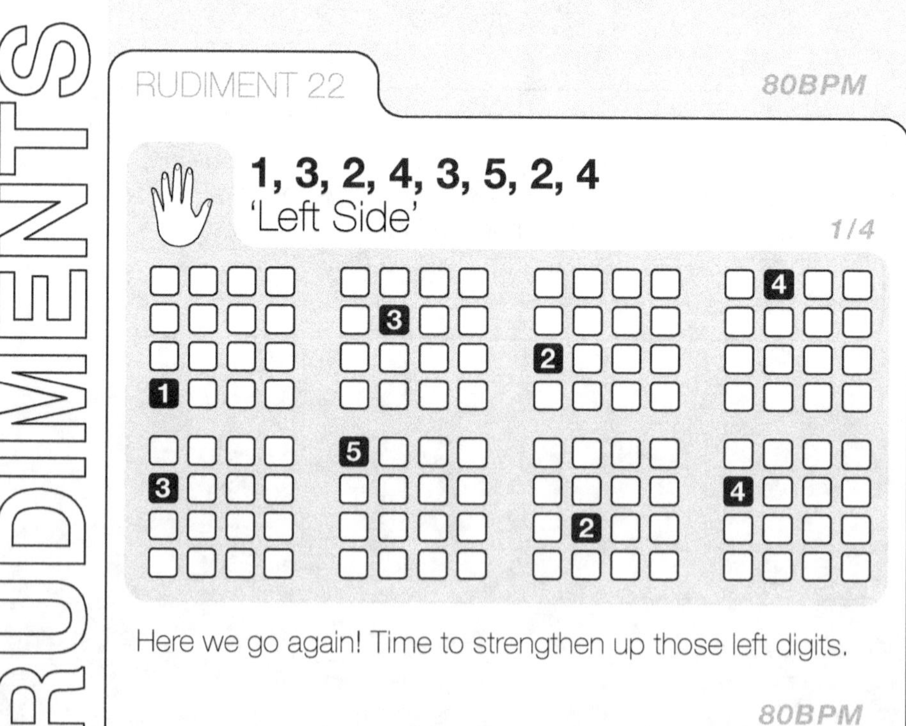

Here we go again! Time to strengthen up those left digits.

80BPM

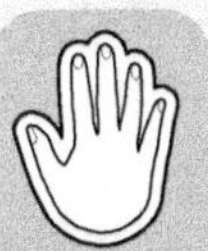

5 FINGER POLY-RHYTHM
'A Tik-Tok Sensation'

SPEED ROLL
'Snare, Toms, Percs'

1/16

Among the most important skills to master in finger drumming is the multi-finger roll. This technique can be more challenging on smaller pads but is nonetheless a valuable addition to your skill set. Start with your dominant hand, using your third finger followed by your second finger on a pad, then mirror the pattern with your opposite hand on the same pad. The pattern is: R3, R2, L3, L2. Practice with a metronome and focus on consistency.

RUDIMENT 25

TRIPLES
'A Triple Roll'

1/16

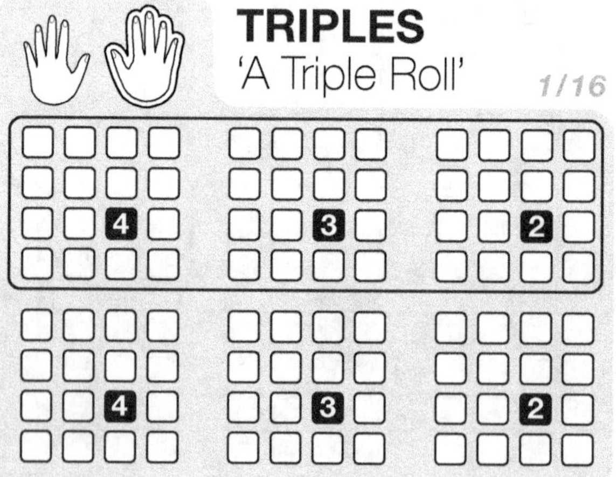

This roll is a great way to introduce more speed and groove into a rhythm. The pattern is: R4, R3, R2, L4, L3, L2.

FLAMS
'What the heck is a flam?'

A flam is a drumming technique characterized by playing two drum strokes nearly at the same time; the first, called the grace note, is played slightly earlier and softer than the second, which is the main, louder note.

Practicing flams can be akin to practicing drum rolls. One effective approach is to use your middle finger (3) to gently tap a pad, quickly followed by a forceful strike on the same pad with your index finger (2). Achieving the correct velocity and volume for the grace note might be challenging, but consistent practice will aid in mastering the technique.

Alternatively, for easier execution, consider using two pads instead of one. Set one pad to a lower volume or sensitivity, and strike the pads in quick succession—one with each finger.

FOUNDATIONAL RHYTHMS

FOUNDATIONAL

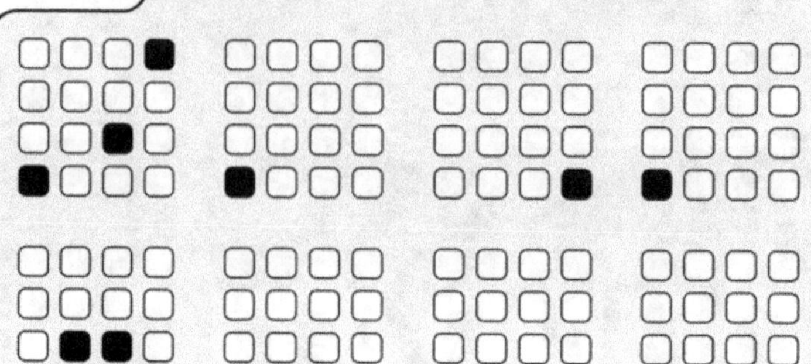

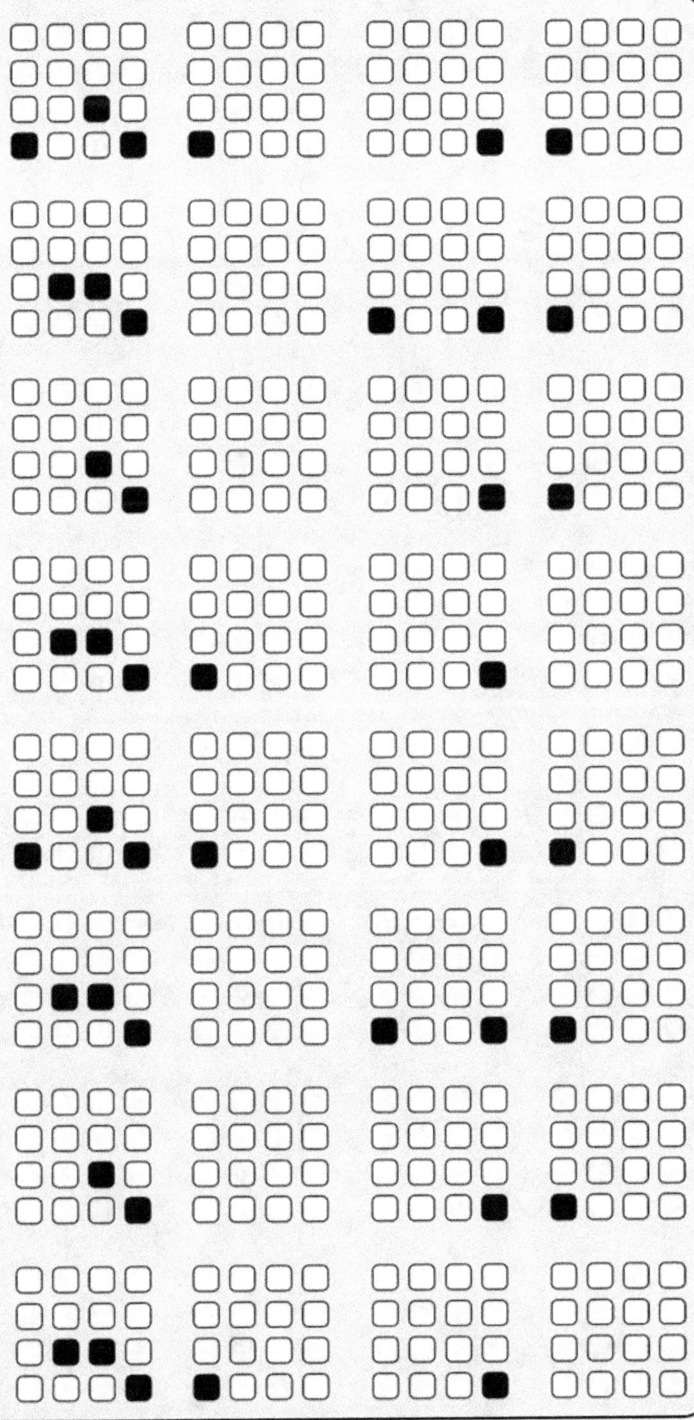

ALTERNATIVE ROCK

16

100BPM

FOUNDATIONAL

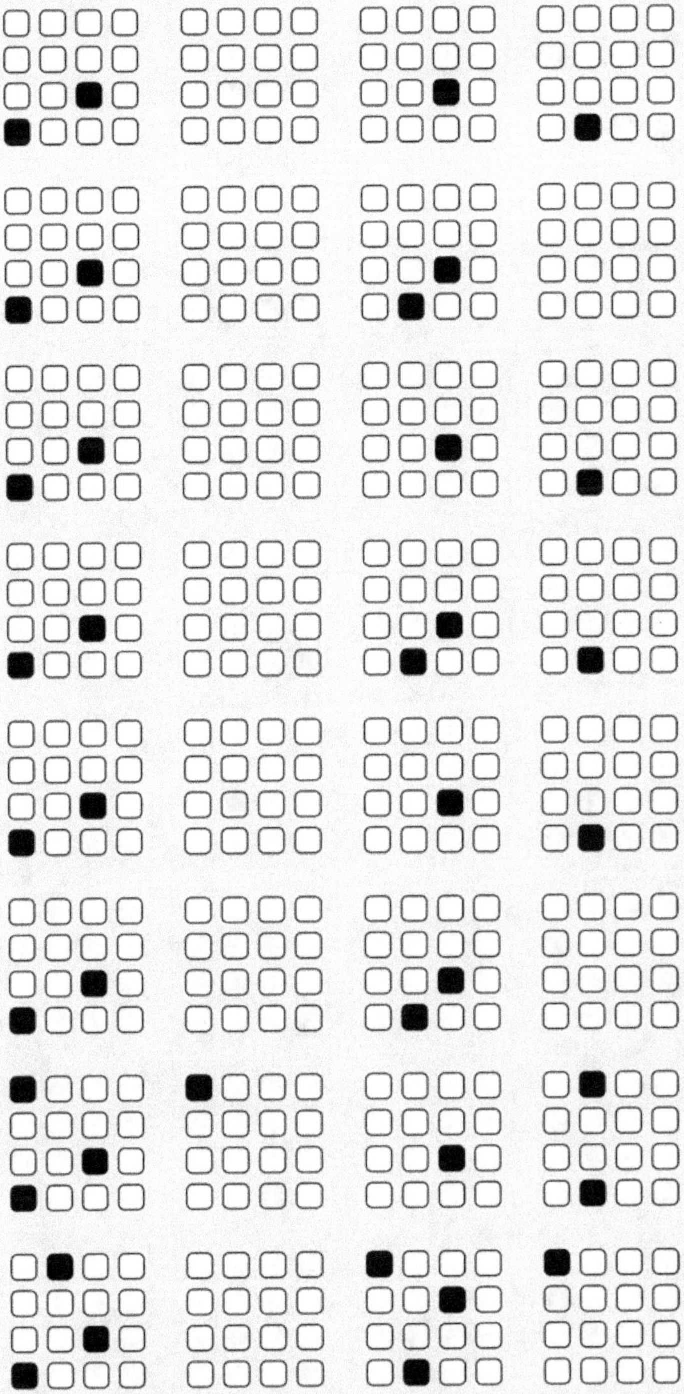

FOUNDATIONAL

120BPM

16

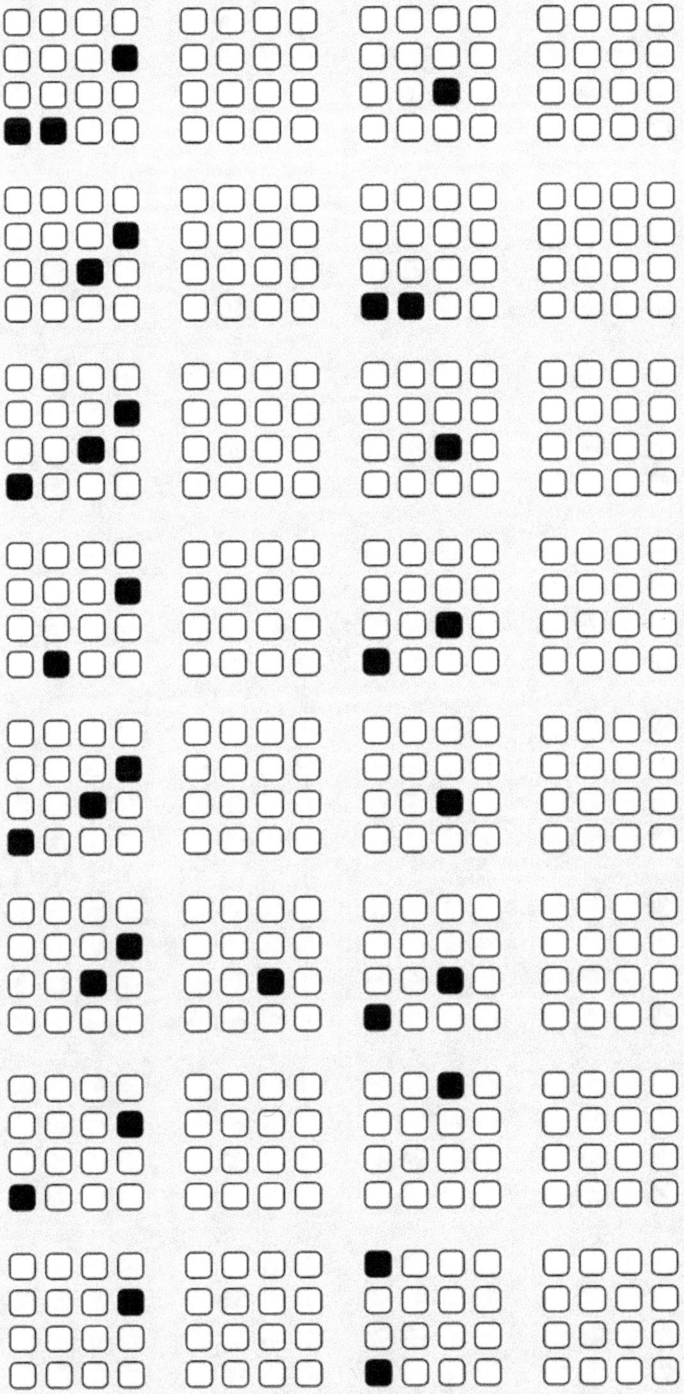

BOSSANOVA

DANCEHALL (DEMBOW) 1/2

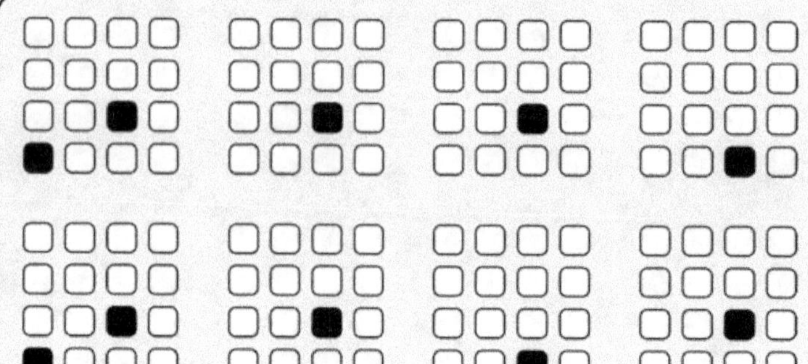

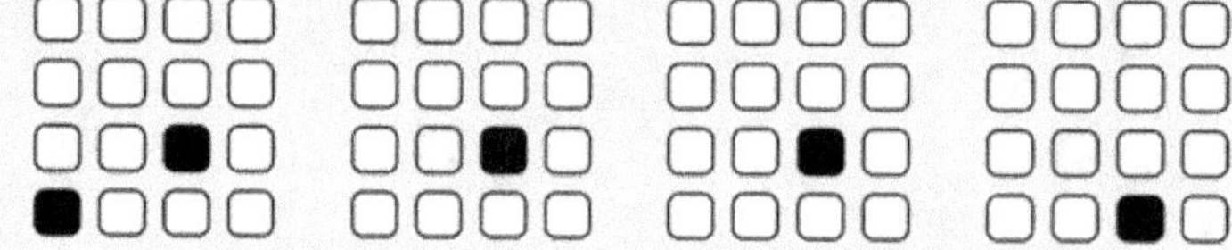

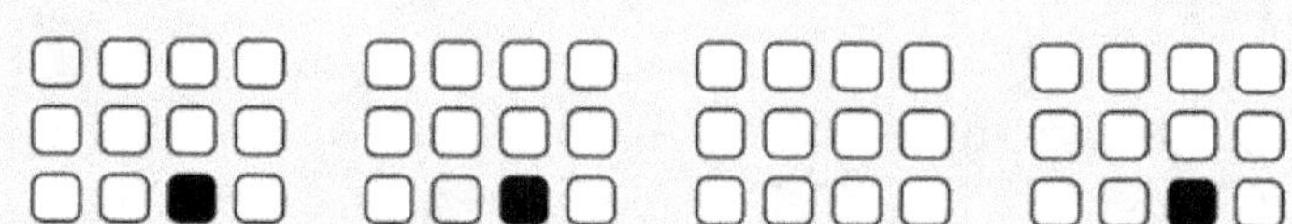

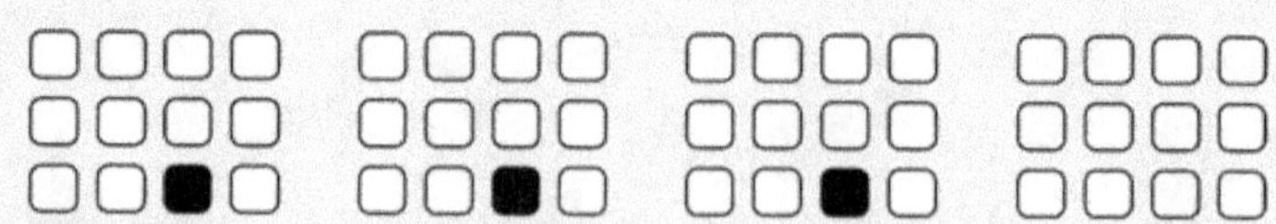

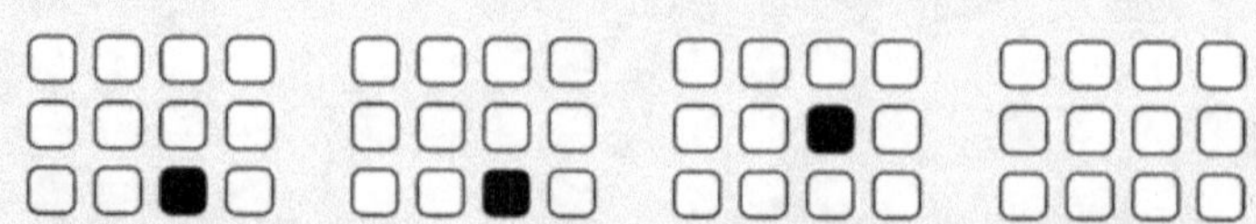

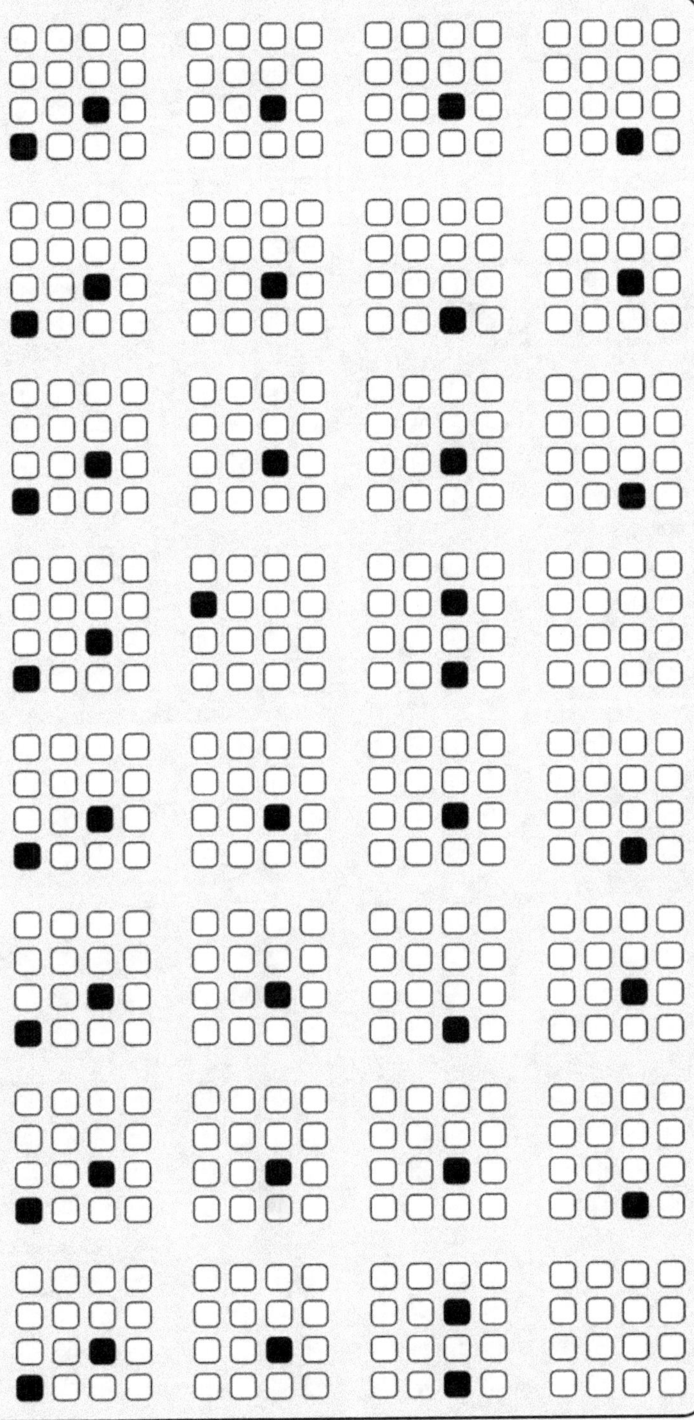

DANCEHALL

DUBSTEP 1/2
16
135BPM
FOUNDATIONAL

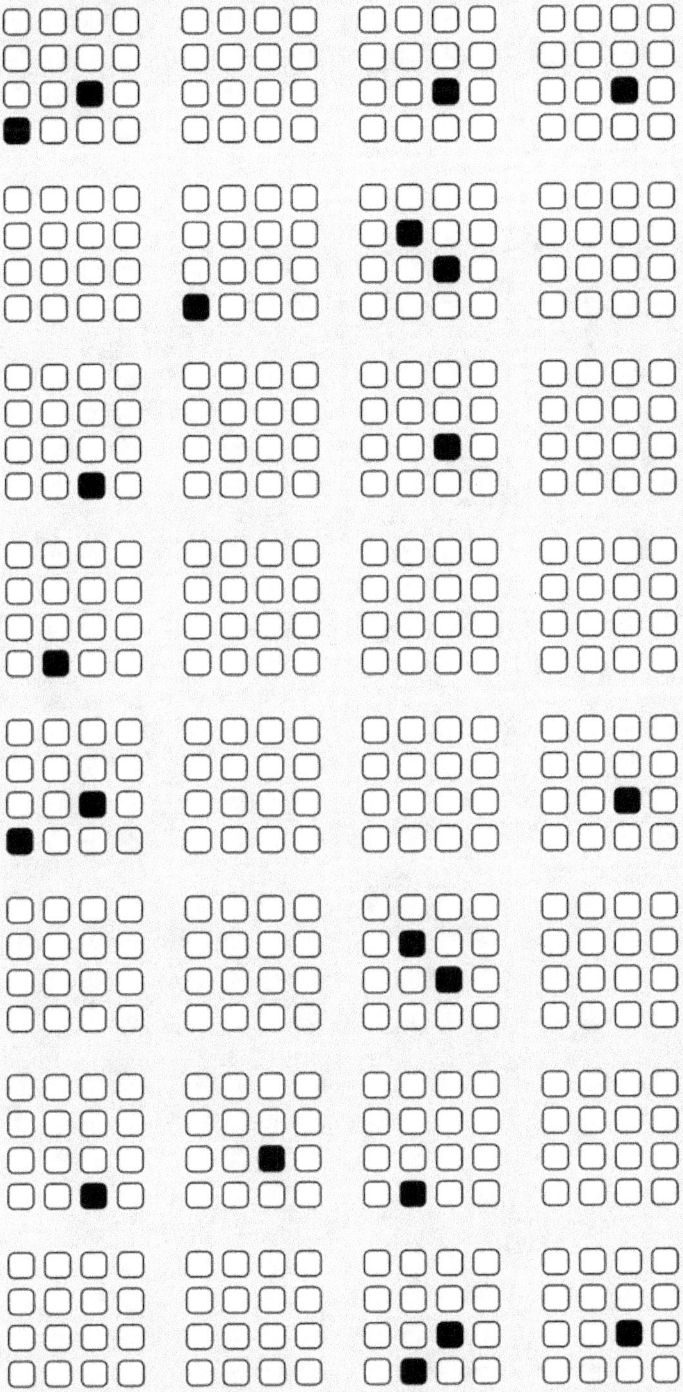

FOUNDATIONAL
90BPM
16

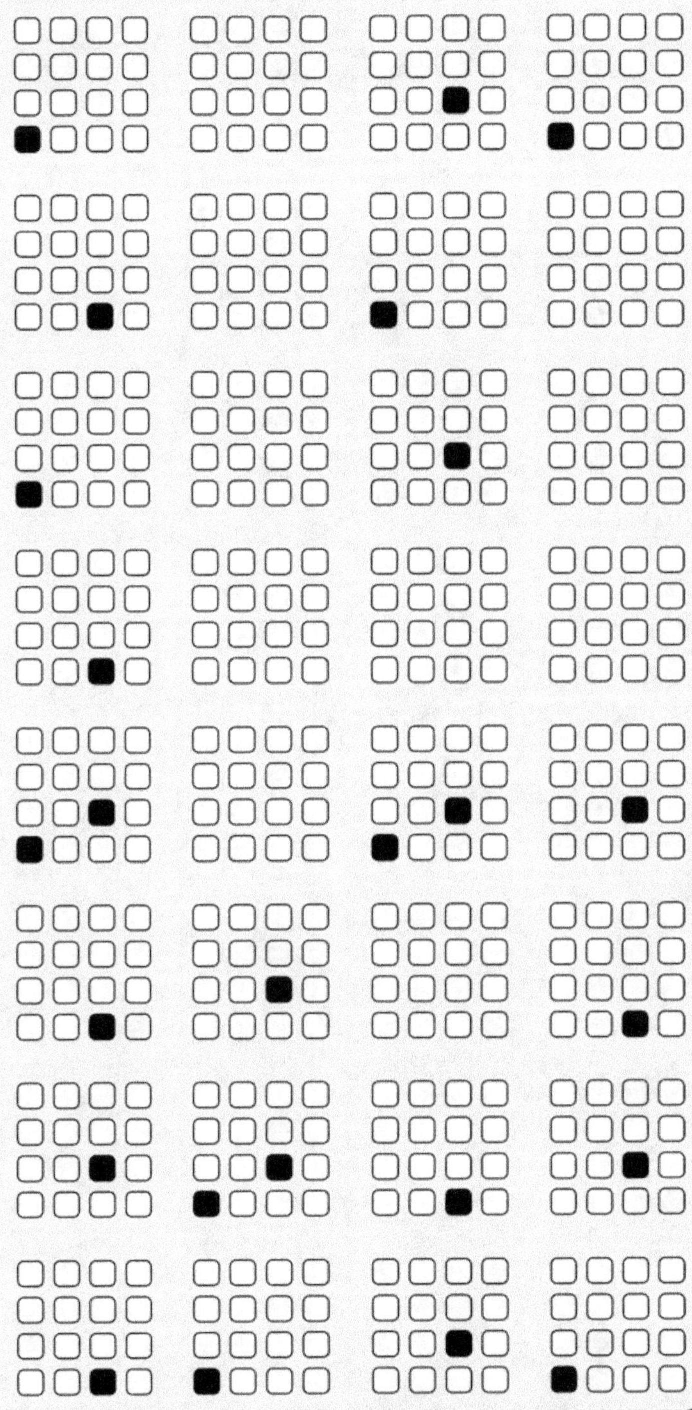

FOUNDATIONAL

110BPM

16

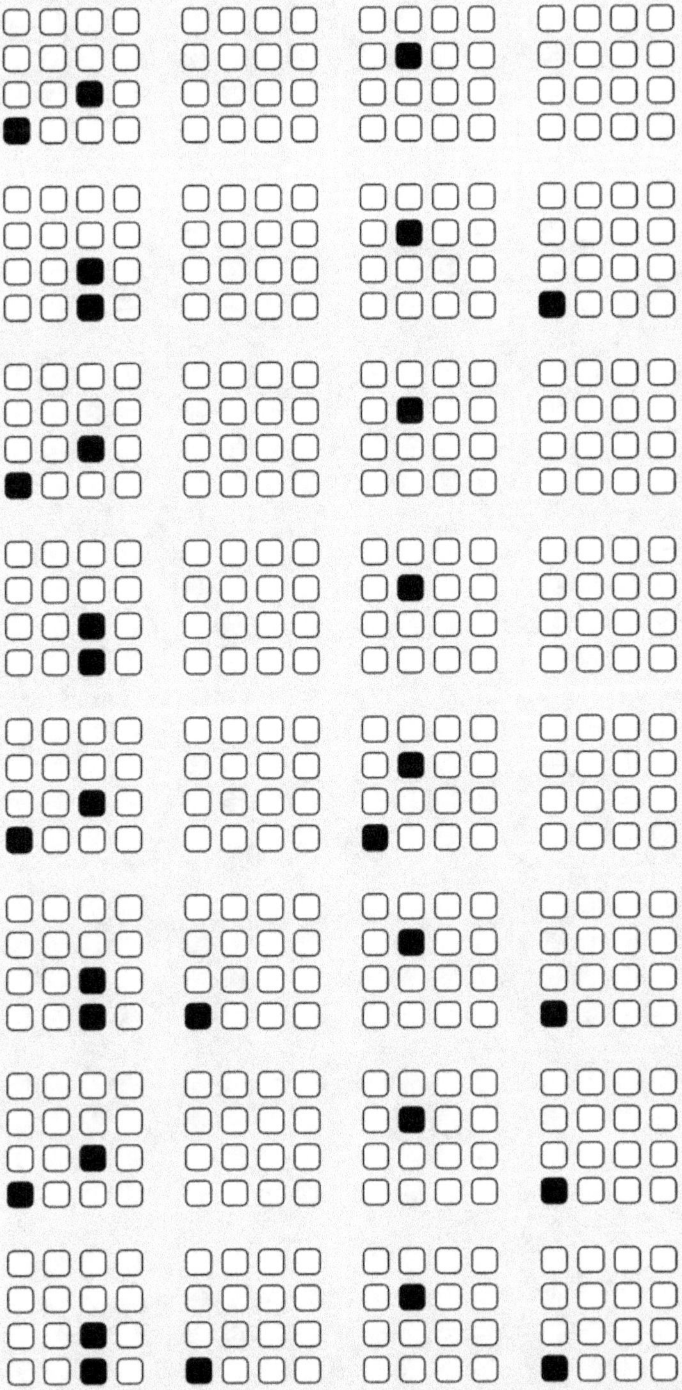

FOUNDATIONAL

130BPM

16

GARAGE

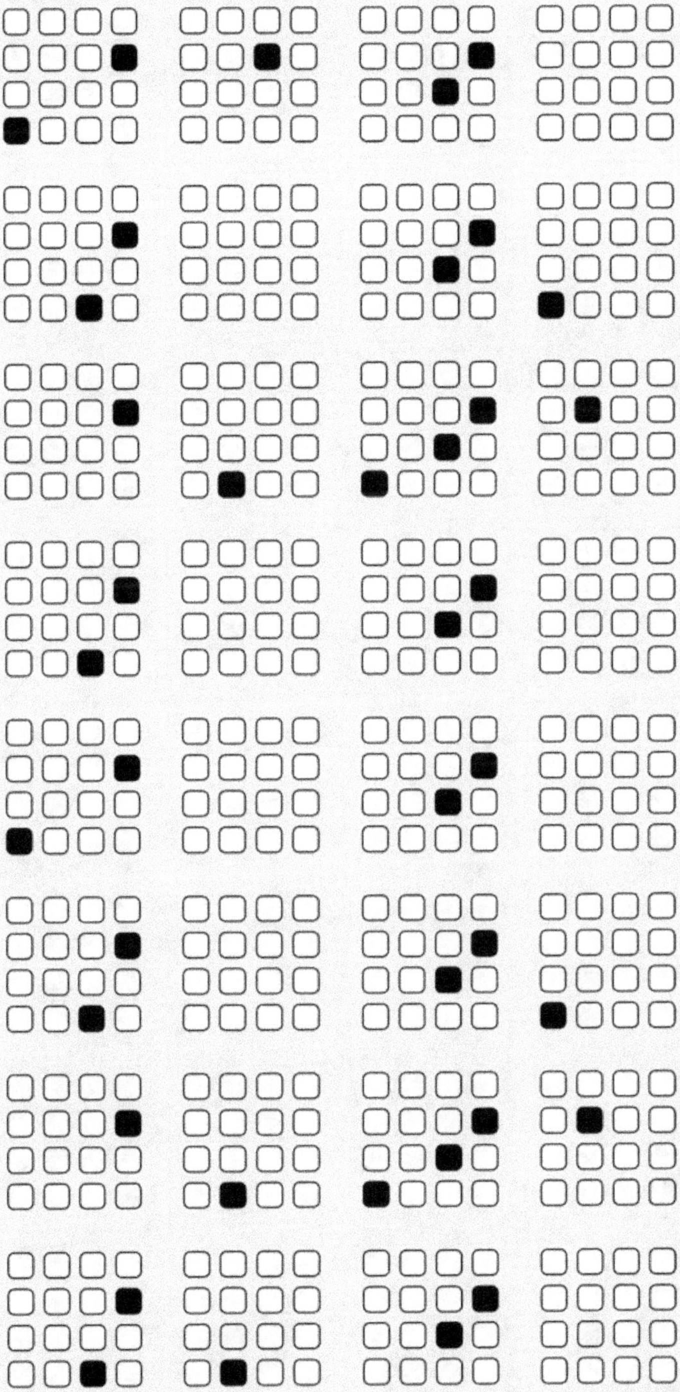

16

90BPM

FOUNDATIONAL

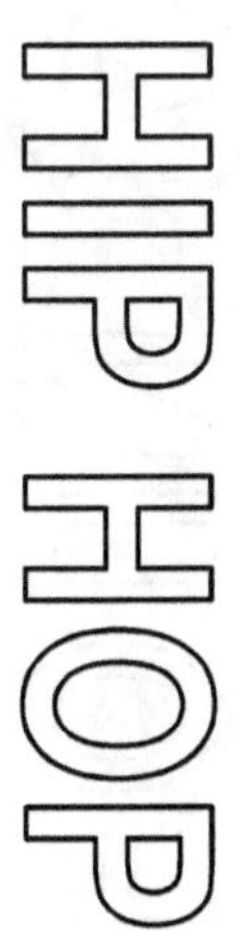
HIP HOP

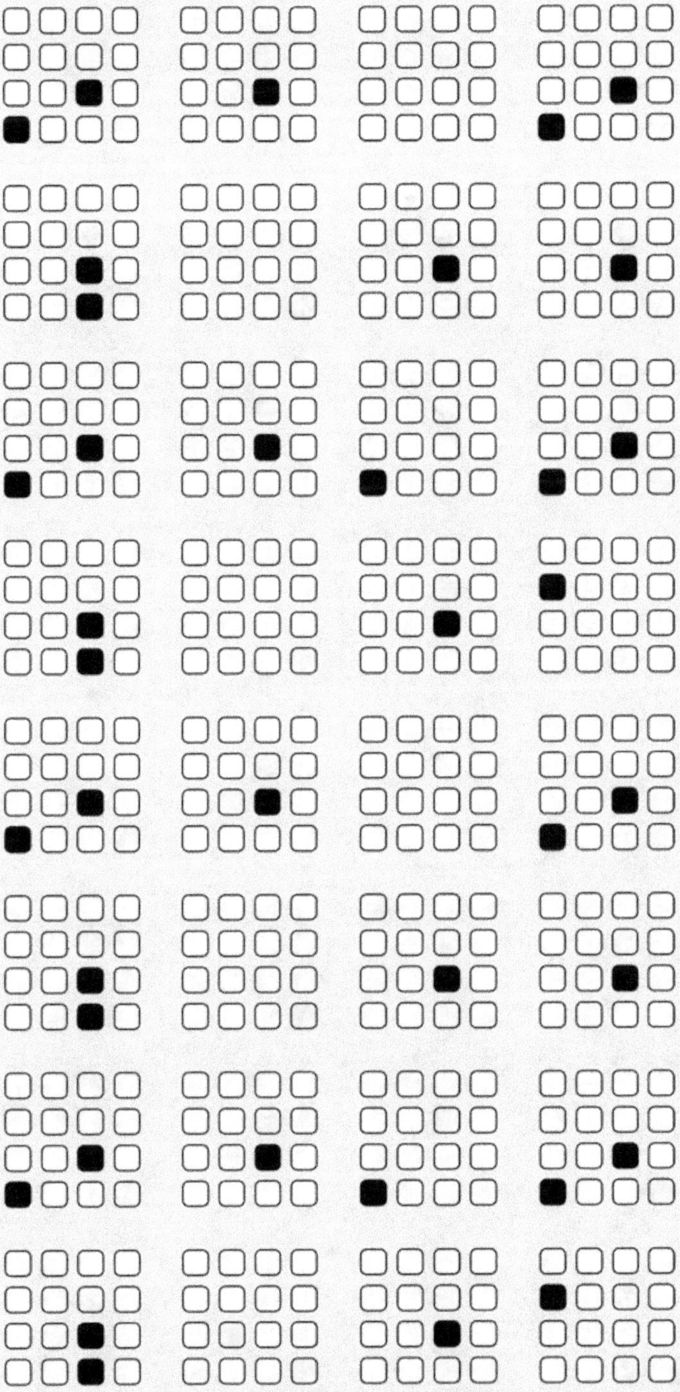

FOUNDATIONAL

120BPM

16

HOUSE

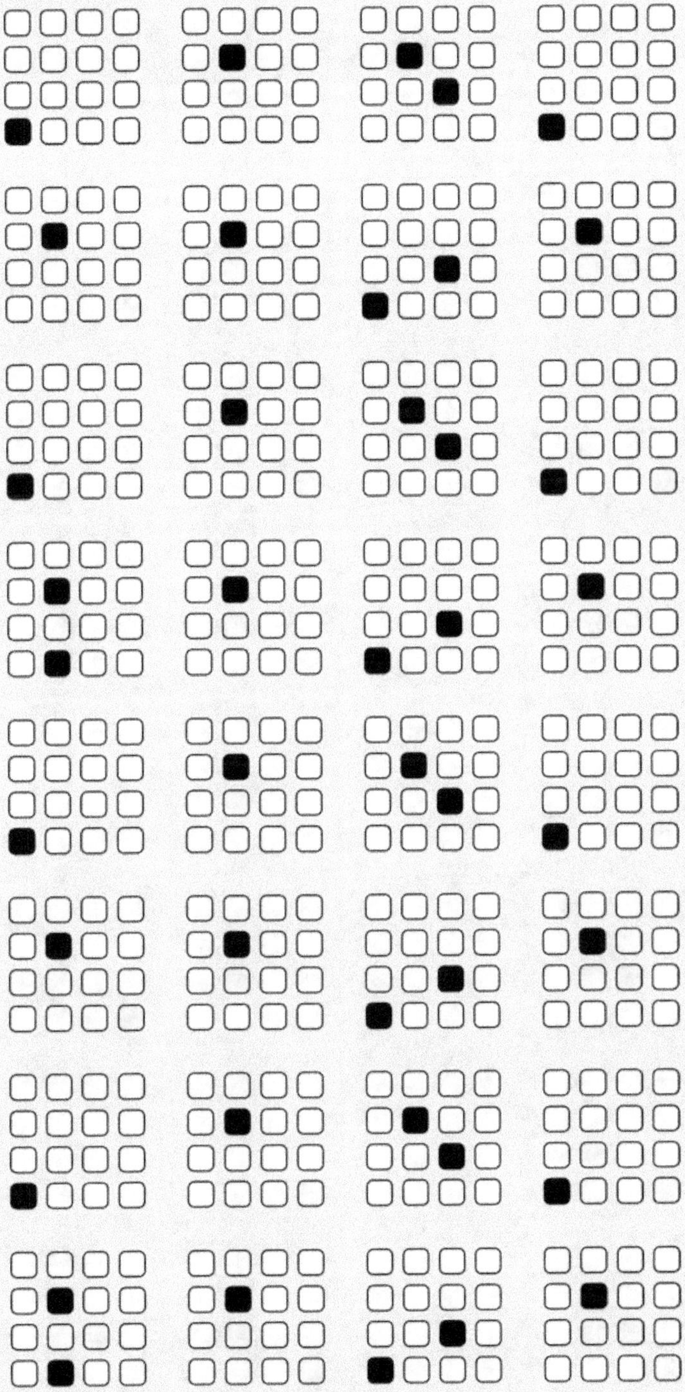

16

96BPM

FOUNDATIONAL

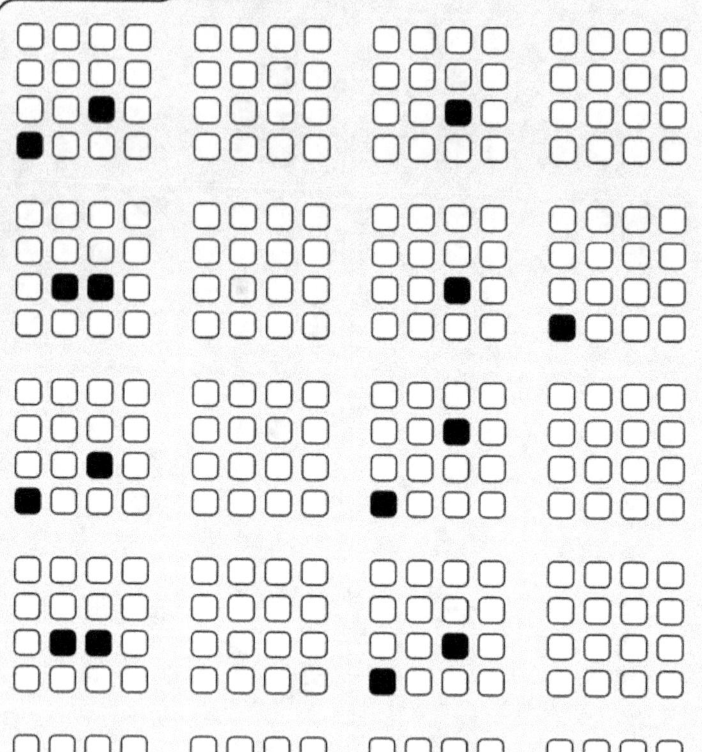

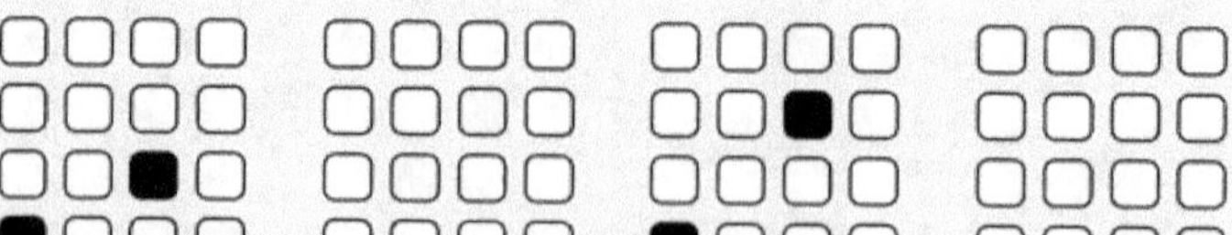

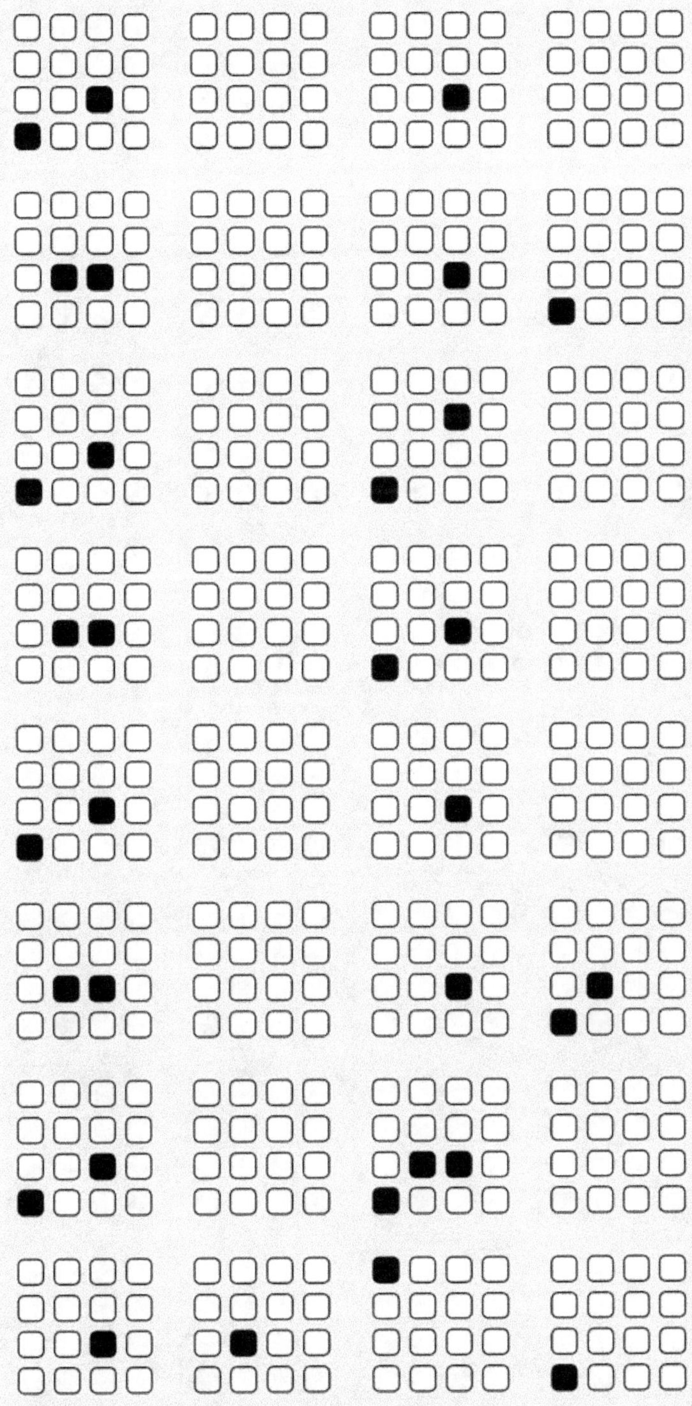

16

140BPM

FOUNDATIONAL

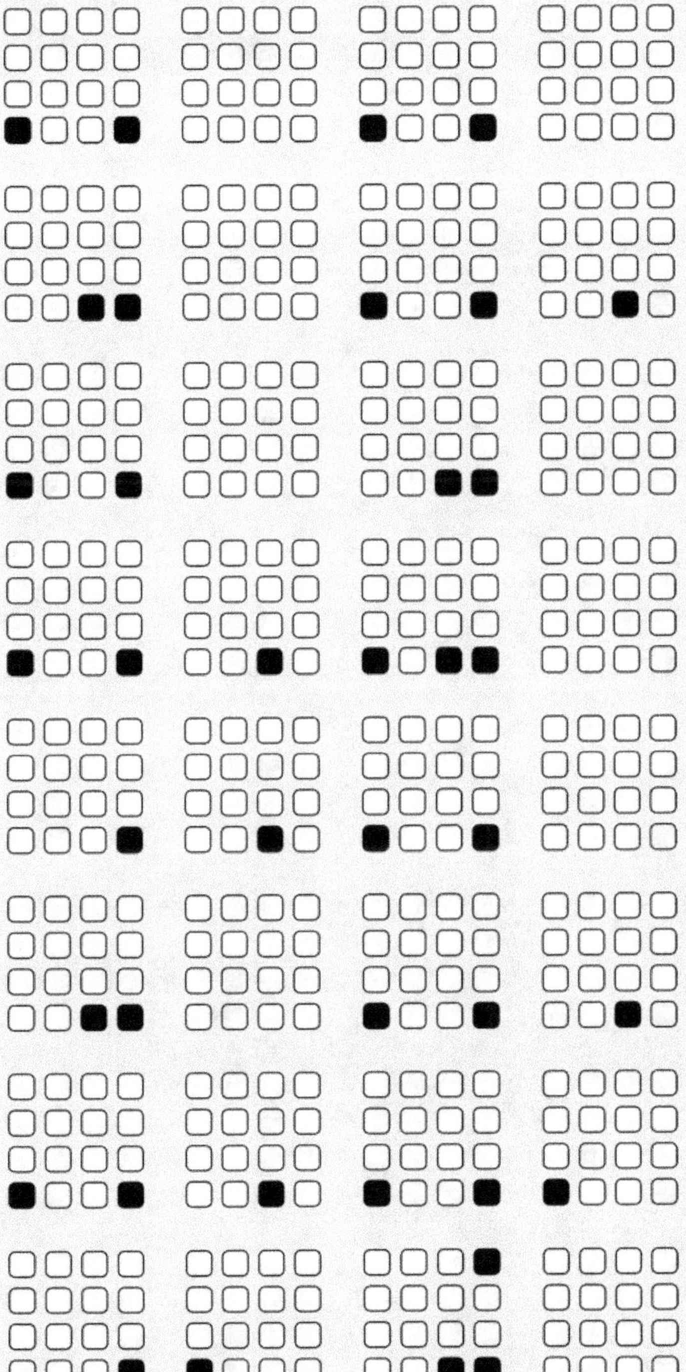

16

90BPM

FOUNDATIONAL

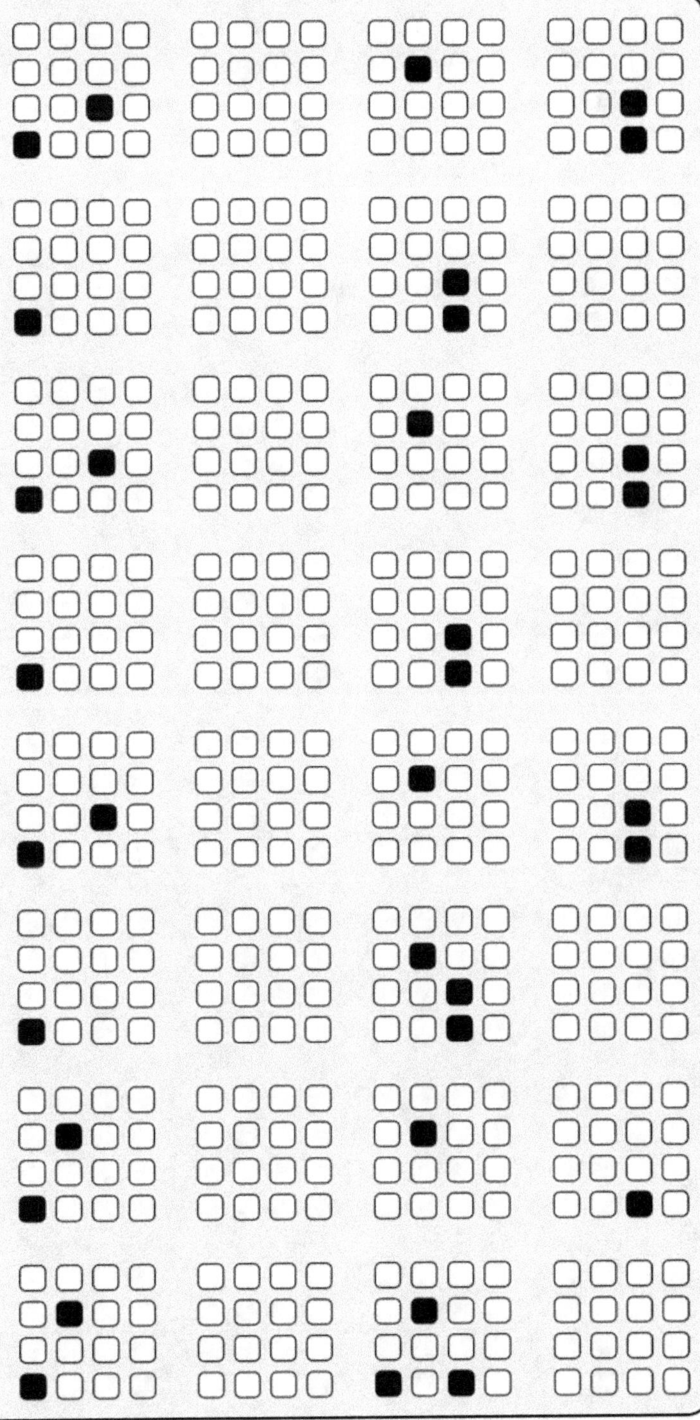

16

170BPM

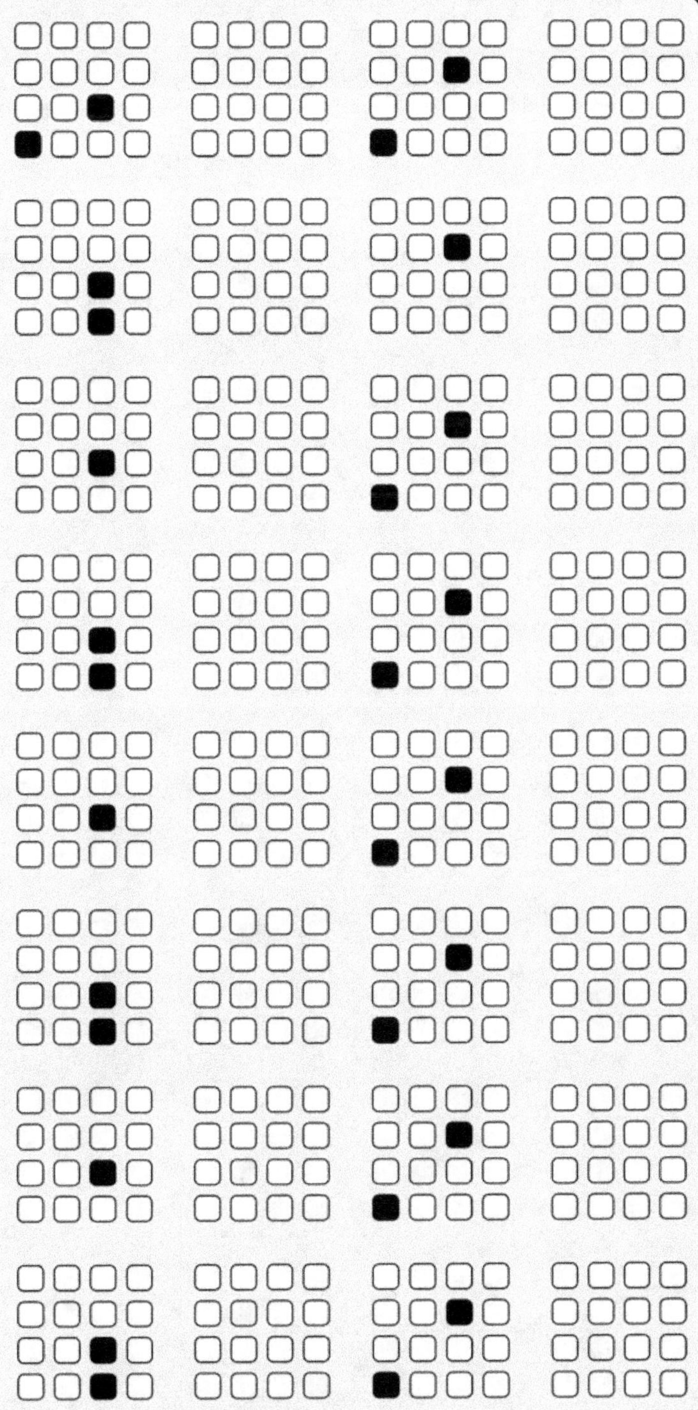

PUNK ROCK

FOUNDATIONAL

100BPM

16

R&B 1/2

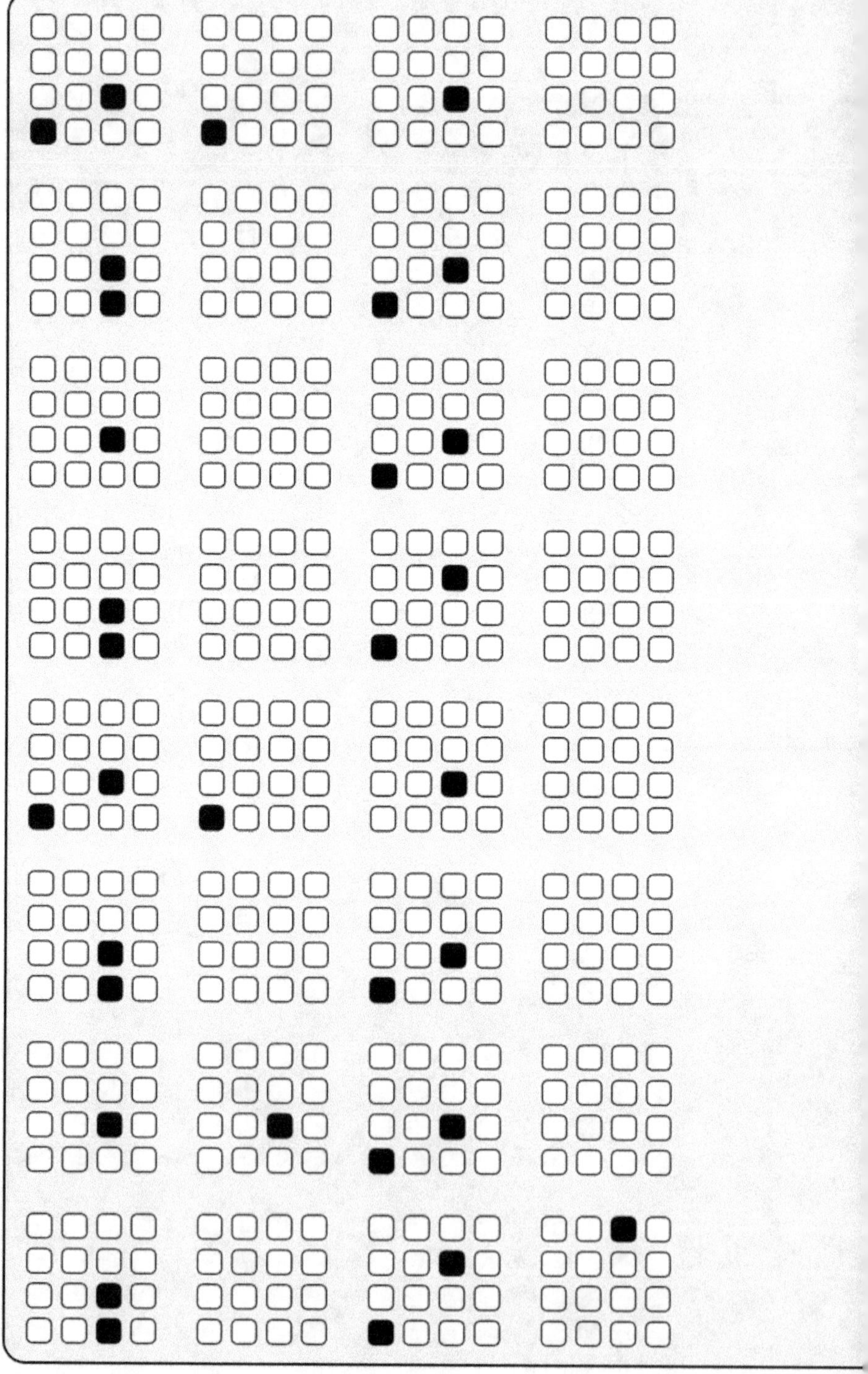

FOUNDATIONAL

100BPM

16

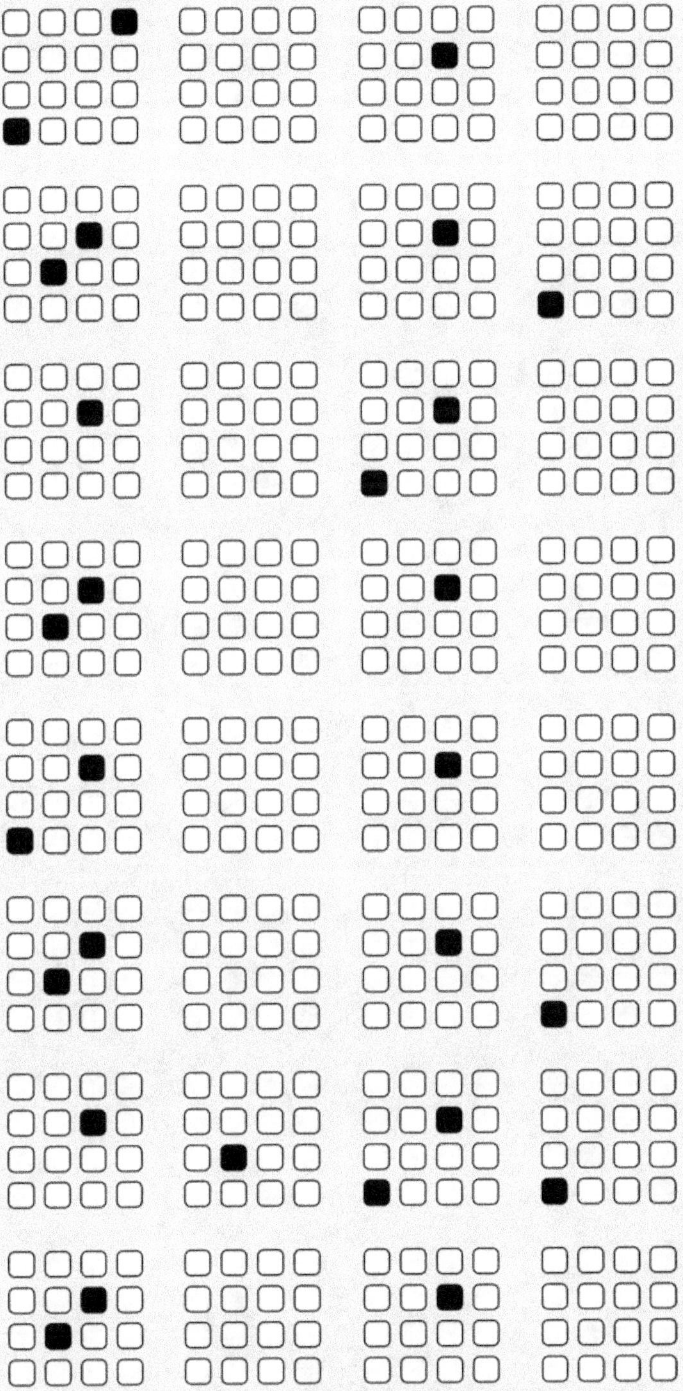

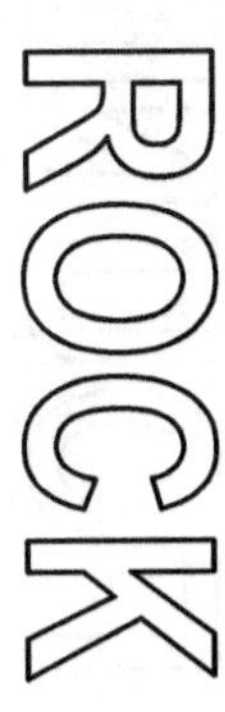

16

150BPM

FOUNDATIONAL

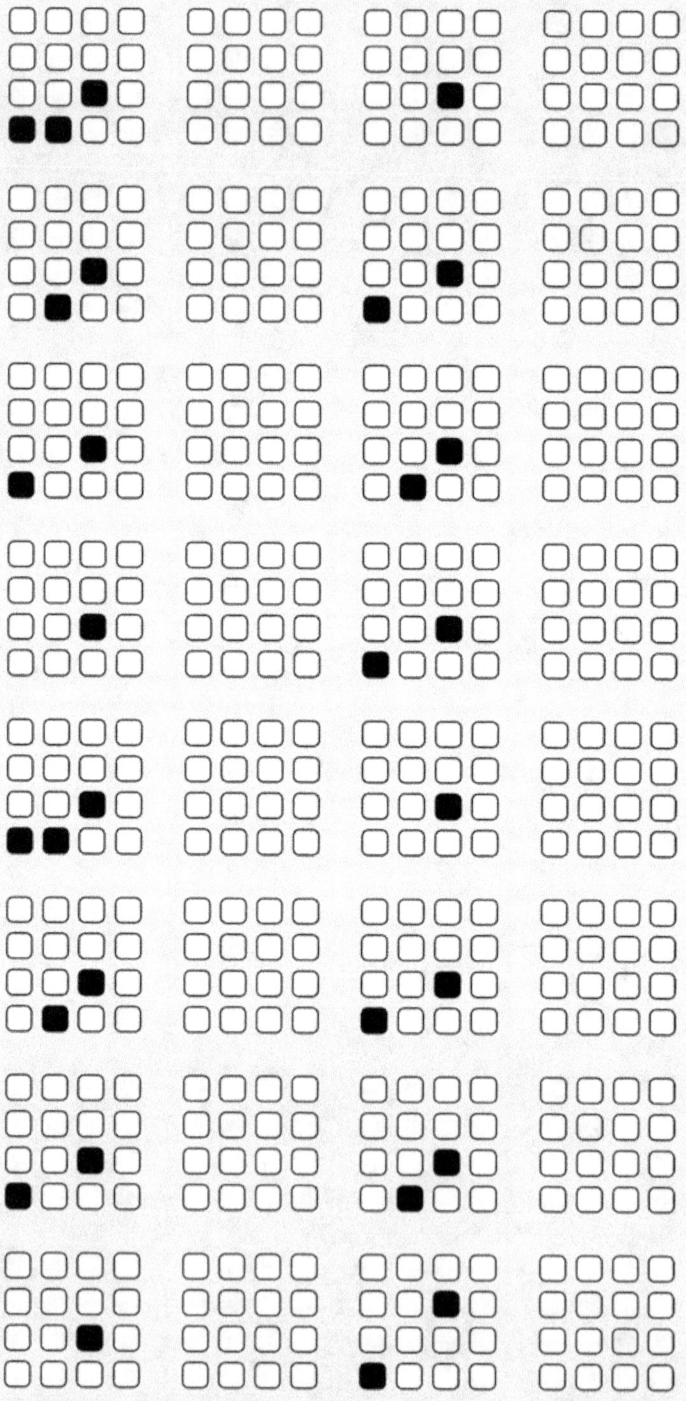

SALSA

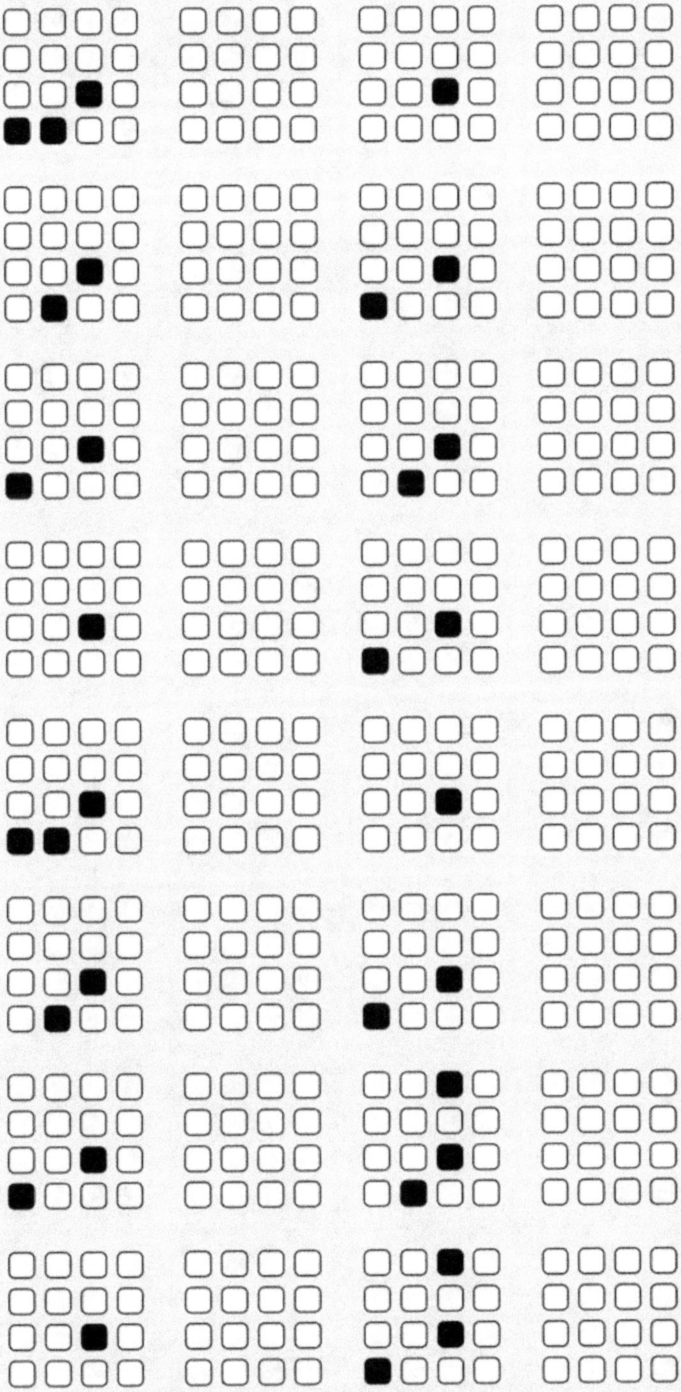

16

FOUNDATIONAL

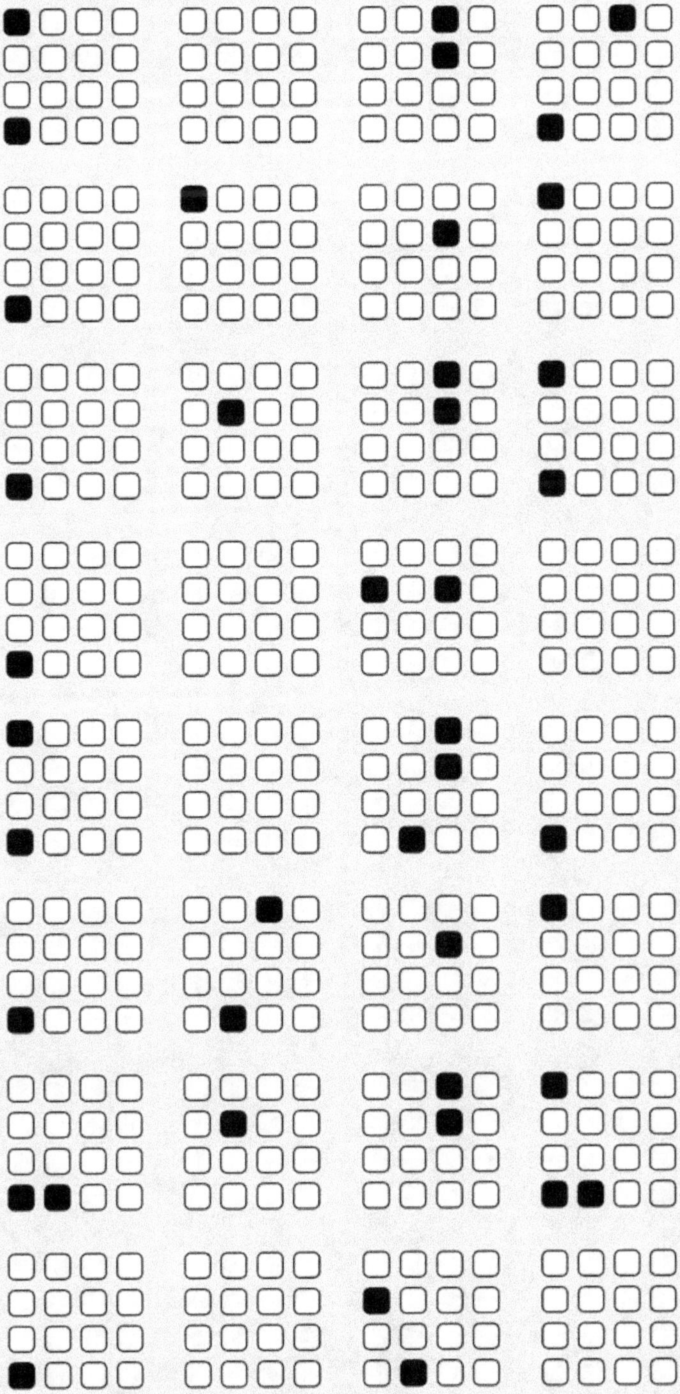

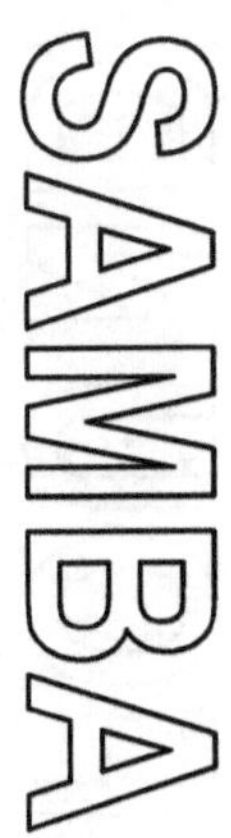
SAMBA

16

120BPM

FOUNDATIONAL

SWING

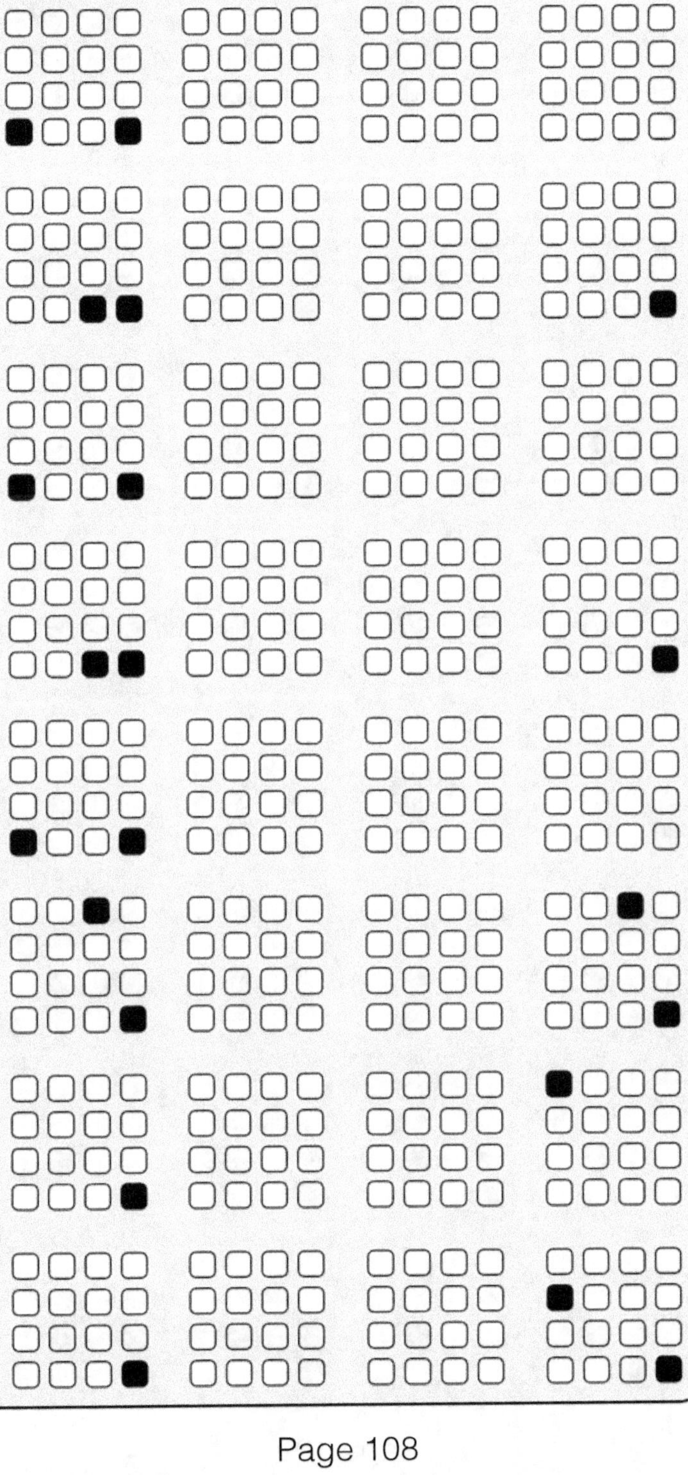

90BPM

16

FOUNDATIONAL

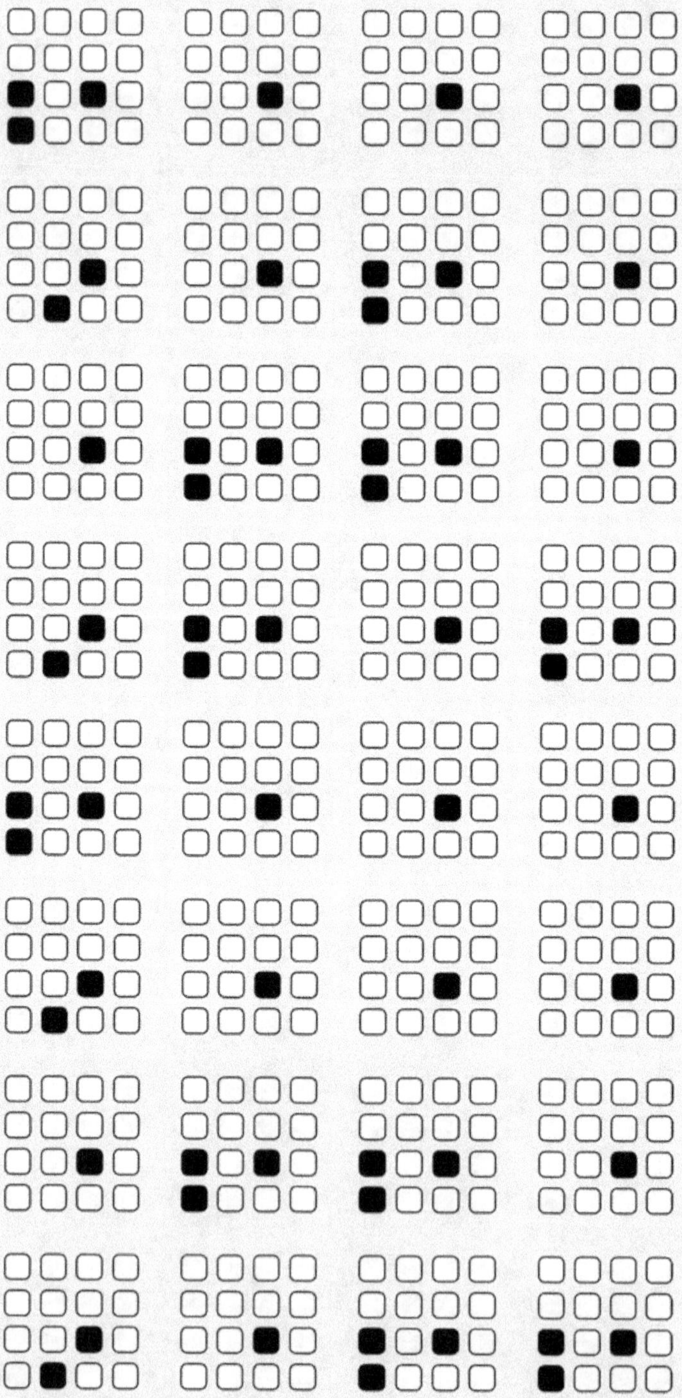

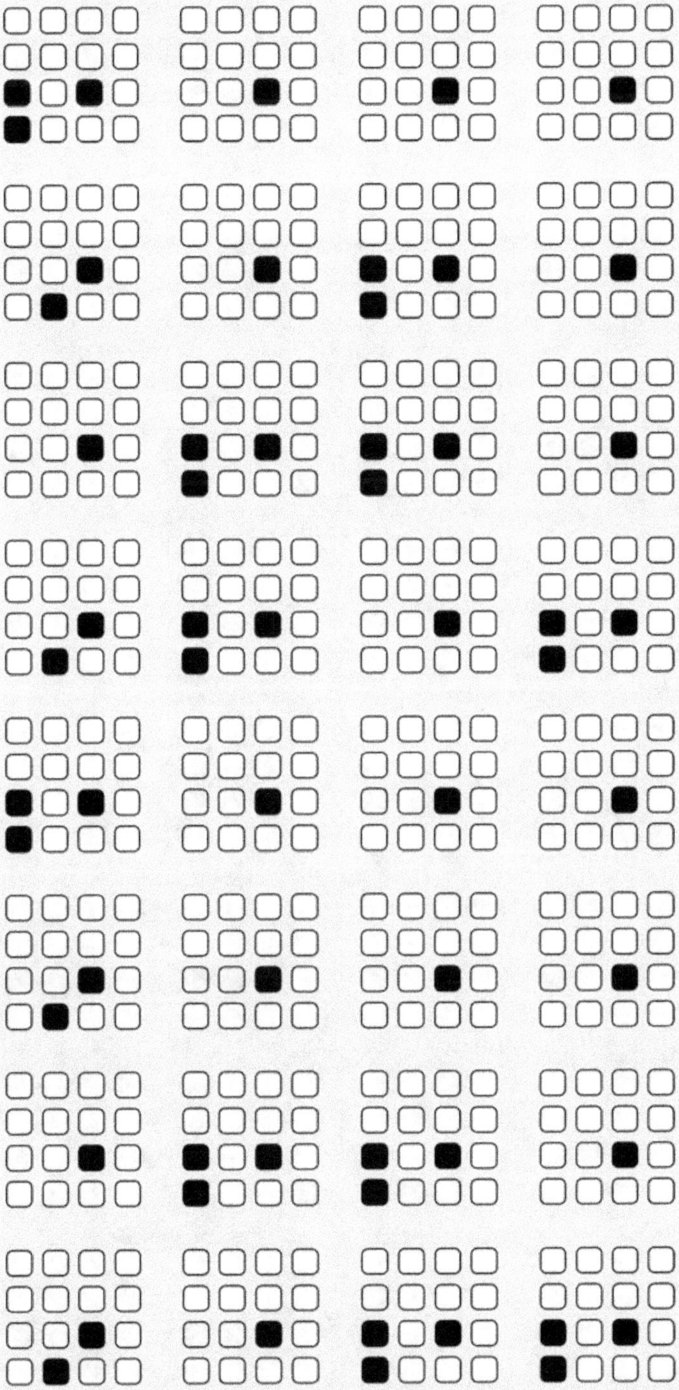

16

150BPM

FOUNDATIONAL

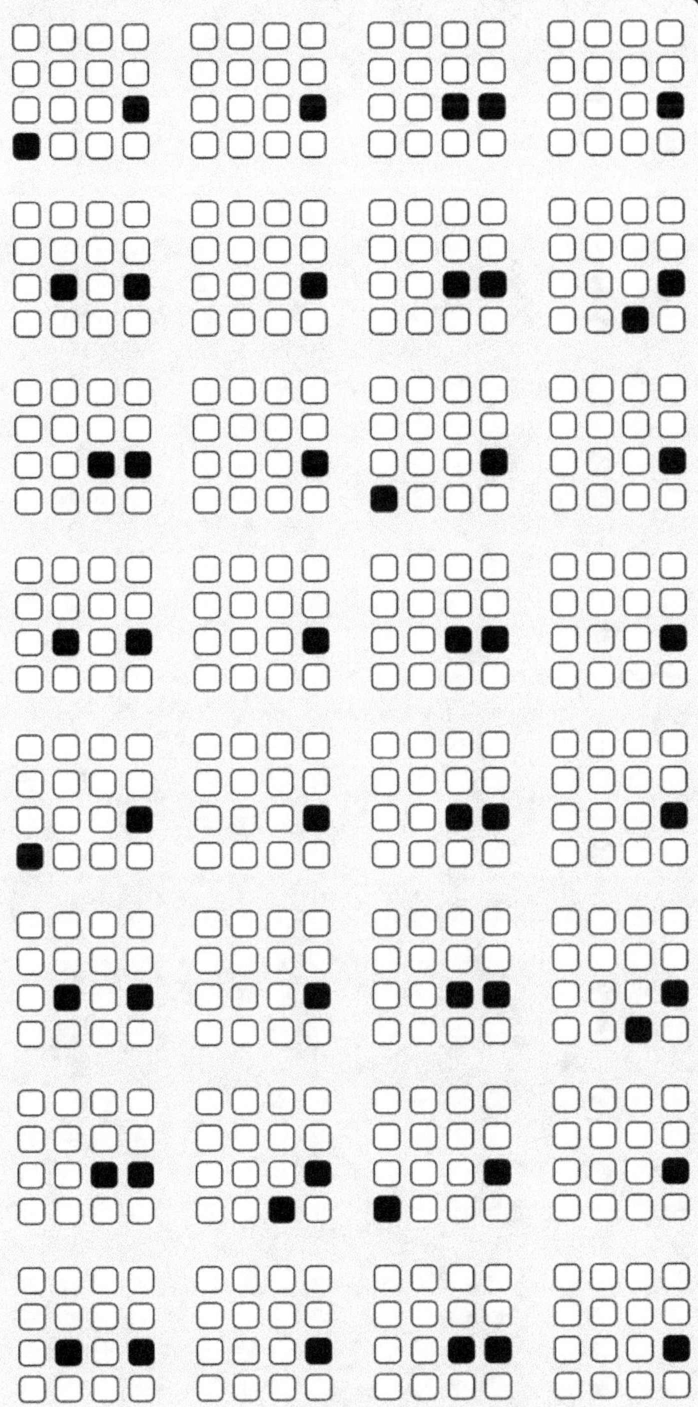

TWO STEP

16

115BPM

FOUNDATIONAL

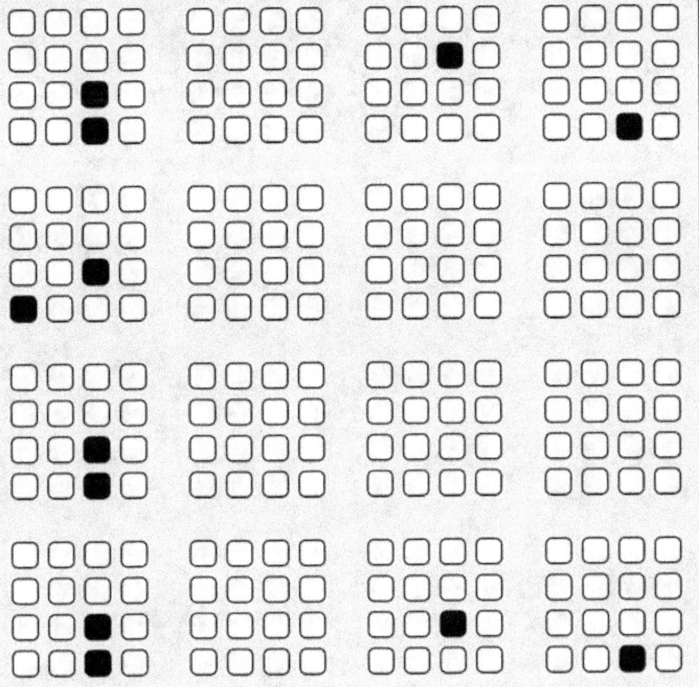

WALTZ

WHAT IS SAMPLE MUSIC?

Sample music involves using segments of pre-existing recordings in new compositions. These segments, or "samples," can be anything from a single drum hit to a full melodic phrase. Sampling is a foundational technique in many genres, especially hip-hop, electronic music, and pop. This technique allows producers to incorporate unique sounds, textures, and elements from other recordings to create new, innovative music.

WHAT IS SAMPLING?

Sampling is the process of taking a portion of a sound recording and reusing it in a different song or piece of music. This can include snippets of another artist's music, sounds from movies or TV shows, or even everyday noises recorded in the environment. For example, a producer might sample a classic funk drum break to add a vintage feel to a modern hip-hop track.

LEGALITIES OF SAMPLING

Using samples from other artists requires obtaining the correct permissions, a process known as "clearing" the sample. Without these permissions, sampling another artist's work is not permitted and can lead to legal action, including lawsuits and financial penalties. A common misconception is the "5-second rule," which suggests that using a sample shorter than 5 seconds is permissible without clearance. This is incorrect; any use of an uncleared sample, regardless of its length, is illegal and can result in significant legal repercussions. It is crucial for sample musicians to ensure they have the necessary rights to use any sampled material to avoid these issues

COPYRIGHT-FREE SAMPLE RESOURCES

To avoid legal issues, consider using royalty-free samples. These samples are pre-cleared and can be used without additional permissions or fees. Many websites offer extensive libraries of royalty-free sounds for various genres and purposes. Examples include Splice, Loopmasters, and FreeSound.org. These platforms often categorize samples by genre, instrument, or mood, making it easy to find the perfect sound for your project.

AI MUSIC GENERATORS

AI music generators can create original samples that are free of copyright restrictions. These tools can produce unique sounds and sequences tailored to your needs, providing an innovative way to source samples. Examples include SUNO, AIVA, and Jukedeck. These AI tools can generate custom loops, melodies, and even entire compositions that you can use freely in your music. As companies and technologies evolve, it is crucial to review the terms and conditions of these platforms regularly. This ensures that you have the correct permissions to use the generated music in your own songs, avoiding any potential legal issues.

SAMPLING OTHER ARTISTS

If you choose to sample other artists' work, ensure you go through the proper channels to get the samples cleared. This often involves contacting the record label and/or the artist and negotiating the terms of use. For instance, if you want to use a vocal snippet from a popular song, you would need to reach out to the song's copyright holders and possibly pay a licensing fee.

HOW TO USE SAMPLES

BACKING TRACKS

Samples can be used as backing tracks to provide a foundation for your music. AI stem-splitting tools can help isolate different elements of a track, allowing you to create custom backing tracks. For example, you can use a stem-splitting tool to remove the drum track from a song and use it as a foundation for your own rhythms.

MUSIC ONE-SHOTS

One-shot samples & Chops are single non-looping snippets. These can include drum hits, vocal exclamations, or instrument notes, and are often used to create new melodic and percussive sequences.

MULTI-LAYER PADS

Nearly every DAW and sampling hardware can be configured to trigger multiple samples with a single pad hit. The potential applications of this technique are limited only by your creativity. It is often used to create more dynamic and organic-sounding sequences, utilizing the following methods:

LAYERING

Triggering multiple sounds simultaneously can create a very appealing result. For example, a kick drum can be layered with an 808 bass boom, or perhaps a snare drum layered with the sound of gravel impacting the ground. Layering is a surefire way to create a unique result you'll be proud to call "your sound." Just be sure to consider the mixture of overlapping frequencies between each layer to avoid clipping, muddiness, and other unwanted distortions by using EQs, side-chaining, and/or volume envelopes.

ROUND ROBIN SEQUENCES

Round robin sequencing involves cycling through a set of samples with each trigger, creating a more natural and less repetitive sound. This technique is often used for drum hits, basslines, melodies, and even acapella sequences. For example, instead of triggering the same snare drum sample each time, a round robin sequence can cycle through multiple snare samples to give the illusion of a live drummer.

RANDOM VARIATION

In contrast to the Round Robin configuration, where different samples are cycled through linearly, using a randomize parameter will trigger a different sound upon each pad hit. Introducing random variation in your samples can make your music sound more organic. This can be particularly effective with drum one-shots, where slight variations in each hit can mimic the natural differences in live drum performance. For instance, you can use a random function to select between different hi-hat samples, giving your drum pattern a more human feel.

VELOCITY VARIATION

Using velocity-sensitive pads can trigger different samples based on how hard the pad is hit. This technique can add expressiveness to your performance, allowing for soft, medium, and hard hits to produce distinct sounds, beyond mere changes in amplitude. For example, lightly tapping a pad might trigger a soft piano note, while hitting it harder could produce a more intense, fortissimo sound.

BE CREATIVE!

Depending on the software and hardware at your disposal, there are virtually limitless configurations for your finger drumming setup. I encourage you to experiment and explore unique combinations of routing, devices, envelopes, and effects to create a setup that truly inspires you!

HISTORY OF SAMPLE MUSIC

ORIGINS AND EARLY INNOVATIONS

The practice of sampling has its roots in the early 20th century with the advent of musique concrète, a form of experimental music developed in the 1940s by French composer Pierre Schaeffer. He used recorded sounds as raw material and manipulated these sounds through techniques like splicing, looping, and speed changes to create new compositions, using tape recorders and turntables (Producertech Blog, 2020; Kadenze Blog, 2020).

THE 1960s AND 1970s: BIRTH OF MODERN SAMPLING

Modern sampling began to take shape in the late 1960s and 1970s with the rise of electronic music. Innovators such as the BBC Radiophonic Workshop and artists like The Beatles used tape manipulation to incorporate samples into their music. The Beatles' song "Revolution 9" from the "White Album" is a notable example, featuring a collage of tape loops and sound effects (Producertech Blog, 2020; Kadenze Blog, 2020).

The Mellotron, developed in the early 1960s, was an early sample-based keyboard instrument that used tape loops to reproduce orchestral sounds, allowing musicians to "sample" pre-recorded sounds and play them back using a keyboard (Producertech Blog, 2020).

THE 1980s: SAMPLING GOES MAINSTREAM

Sampling became mainstream in the 1980s, driven by advancements in digital technology. Key developments included the introduction of affordable and accessible sampling equipment like the E-MU Emulator, Akai S900, and the Fairlight CMI. These digital samplers allowed musicians to record, manipulate, and play back samples with unprecedented ease (t.blog, 2020).

Hip-hop emerged as a genre heavily reliant on sampling during this period. Early hip-hop DJs and producers like Grandmaster Flash and Afrika Bambaataa used turntables to loop breakbeats from funk and soul records, creating new tracks by mixing these loops with raps and other sounds. The Akai MPC (Music Production Center) revolutionized hip-hop production, enabling producers to create intricate beats and tracks by sampling and sequencing sounds (Kadenze Blog, 2020; Icon Collective, 2020).

THE 1990s AND BEYOND: SAMPLING IN ALL GENRES

By the 1990s, sampling had permeated nearly every genre of music, from electronic dance music to rock and pop. Artists like The Prodigy, Fatboy Slim, and Moby became known for their extensive use of samples, blending elements from various musical styles into their work. The advent of digital audio workstations (DAWs) and software samplers democratized sampling, allowing anyone with a computer to access and manipulate samples (t.blog, 2020; uDiscover, 2020).

KEY FIGURES IN SAMPLING HISTORY

PIERRE SCHAEFFER

As the pioneer of musique concrète, Schaeffer's experiments with tape manipulation in the 1940s and 1950s laid the foundation for modern sampling techniques (Producertech Blog, 2020; Kadenze Blog, 2020).

THE BEATLES

The Beatles' innovative use of tape loops and studio effects in the 1960s, particularly on tracks like "Revolution 9" and "Tomorrow Never Knows," showcased the creative potential of sampling in popular music (Kadenze Blog, 2020; t.blog, 2020).

GRANDMASTER FLASH AND AFRIKA BAMBAATAA

These hip-hop pioneers used turntables and early samplers to create new tracks by looping and manipulating breakbeats, setting the stage for the genre's sampling-based production style (Icon Collective, 2020).

AKAI AND ROGER LINN

Roger Linn, the designer of the Akai MPC series, created one of the most influential samplers in music history. The MPC's user-friendly interface and powerful features made it a staple in hip-hop and electronic music production (t.blog, 2020; Icon Collective, 2020).

THE PRODIGY, FATBOY SLIM, AND MOBY

These artists popularized the use of sampling in electronic dance music in the 1990s, blending diverse musical elements into their tracks and achieving mainstream success. The Prodigy's "Smack My Bitch Up," Fatboy Slim's "Praise You," and Moby's "Play" album are prime examples of how sampling can be used to create innovative and commercially successful music. These artists utilized samples from a wide array of sources, including soul, funk, and blues records, and integrated them into modern electronic music, showcasing the versatility and creative potential of sampling (t.blog, 2020; uDiscover, 2020).

HOW SAMPLING WAS DONE

EARLY TECHNIQUES

In the early days of sampling, artists used analog tape recorders to splice and loop tape segments manually. This labor-intensive process required precise cutting and splicing of tape to create loops and effects. Pierre Schaeffer and other early experimenters in musique concrète used these techniques to manipulate recorded sounds (Producertech Blog, 2020; Kadenze Blog, 2020).

TURNTABLES AND VINYL

Hip-hop DJs in the 1970s and 1980s used turntables to loop breakbeats from vinyl records. By manipulating the records manually, DJs could extend short drum breaks into continuous loops, providing the rhythmic foundation for raps and other elements. Techniques such as backspinning and scratching were developed to enhance these performances (Icon Collective, 2020).

DIGITAL SAMPLERS

The introduction of digital samplers in the 1980s revolutionized sampling. These devices allowed users to record audio samples digitally, edit them with precision, and trigger them using pads or keyboards. The Akai MPC series, designed by Roger Linn, became synonymous with hip-hop production, enabling producers to create complex beats and compositions by sampling and sequencing sounds. The Fairlight CMI and E-MU Emulator were also significant in making sampling more accessible and versatile (t.blog, 2020; uDiscover, 2020).

MODERN SAMPLERS AND DAWS

Today, sampling is largely done using software and digital audio workstations (DAWs). Programs like Ableton Live, FL Studio, and Logic Pro offer powerful sampling tools that allow users to record, edit, and manipulate samples with ease.

MUSIC CHOPS
MUSIC CHOPS
MUSIC CHOPS
MUSIC CHOPS
MUSIC CHOPS
MUSIC CHOPS
MUSIC CHOPS
MUSIC CHOPS
MUSIC CHOPS
MUSIC CHOPS
MUSIC CHOPS

CHOPPED CHICKEN

This is an engaging and catchy demonstration of what can be achieved with an AI music generator, enhanced with a few creative techniques to make it stand out!

The track was generated from a prompt for a funky song featuring vocals composed entirely of the word "Chicken." These vocals were subsequently removed using an AI stem splitter like "The Ultimate Vocal Remover." After the stems were separated, the vocal sections were distributed across the second row of pads

The instrumental parts, minus the drums and percussion (also separated using an AI splitter), were chopped and arranged sequentially across the top row of pads. The drum one-shots were then processed to enhance their punch and loudness and allocated across the lower pads.

CHOPPED CHICKEN LAYOUT

DOWNLOAD ALL KITS:

MUSIC CHOPS

100BPM

16

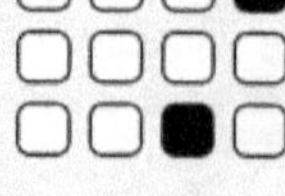

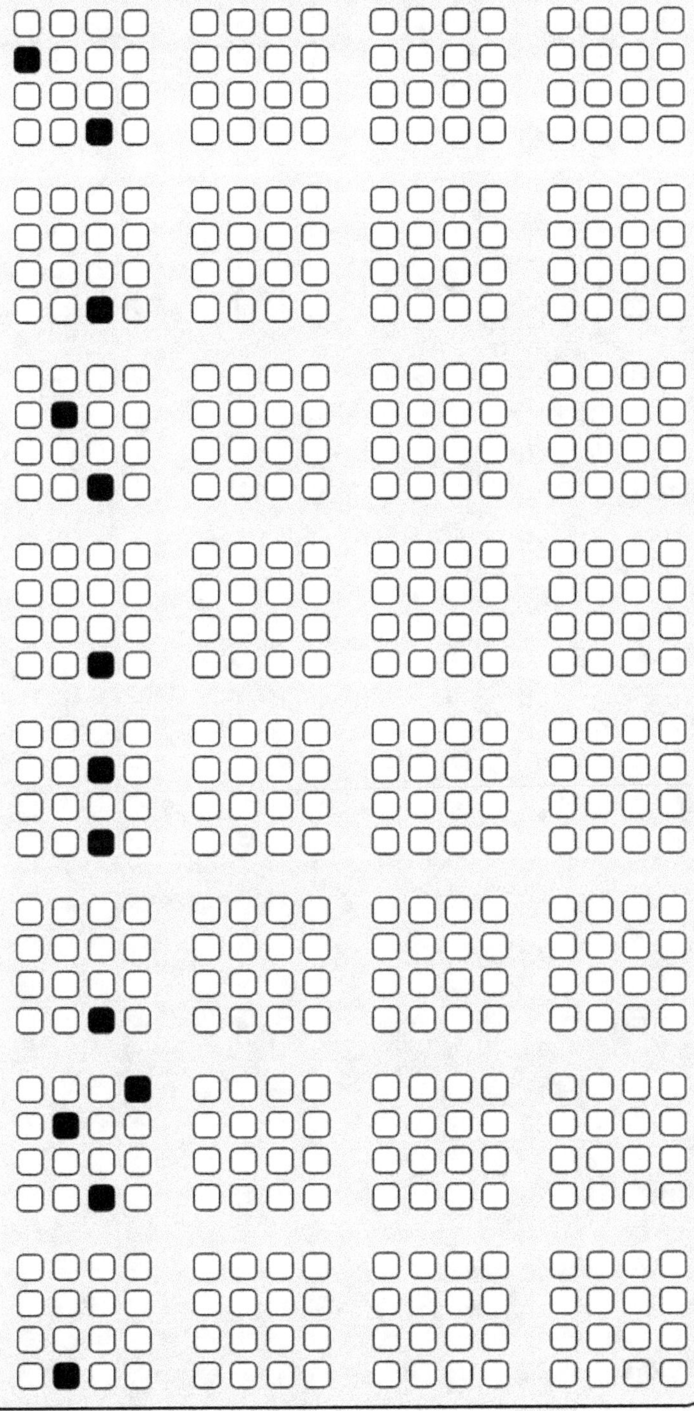

CHOPPED CHICKEN

CHOPPED CHICKEN 3/8

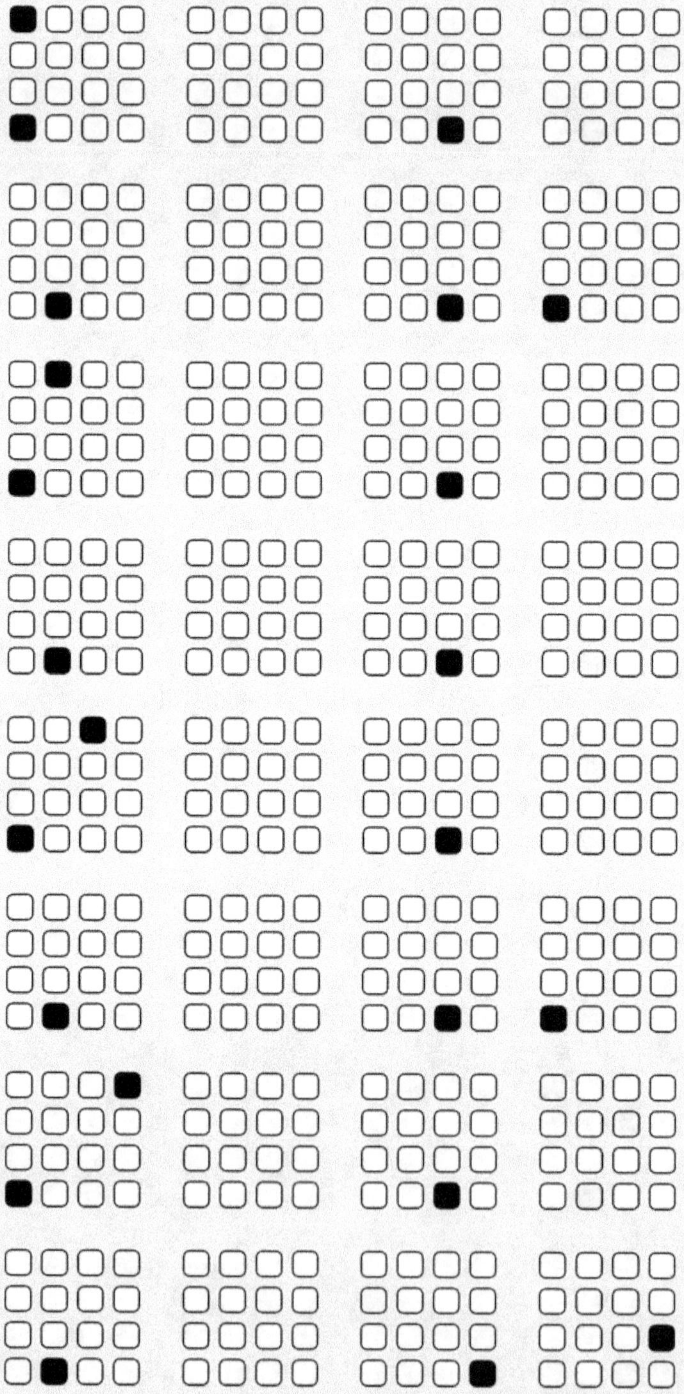

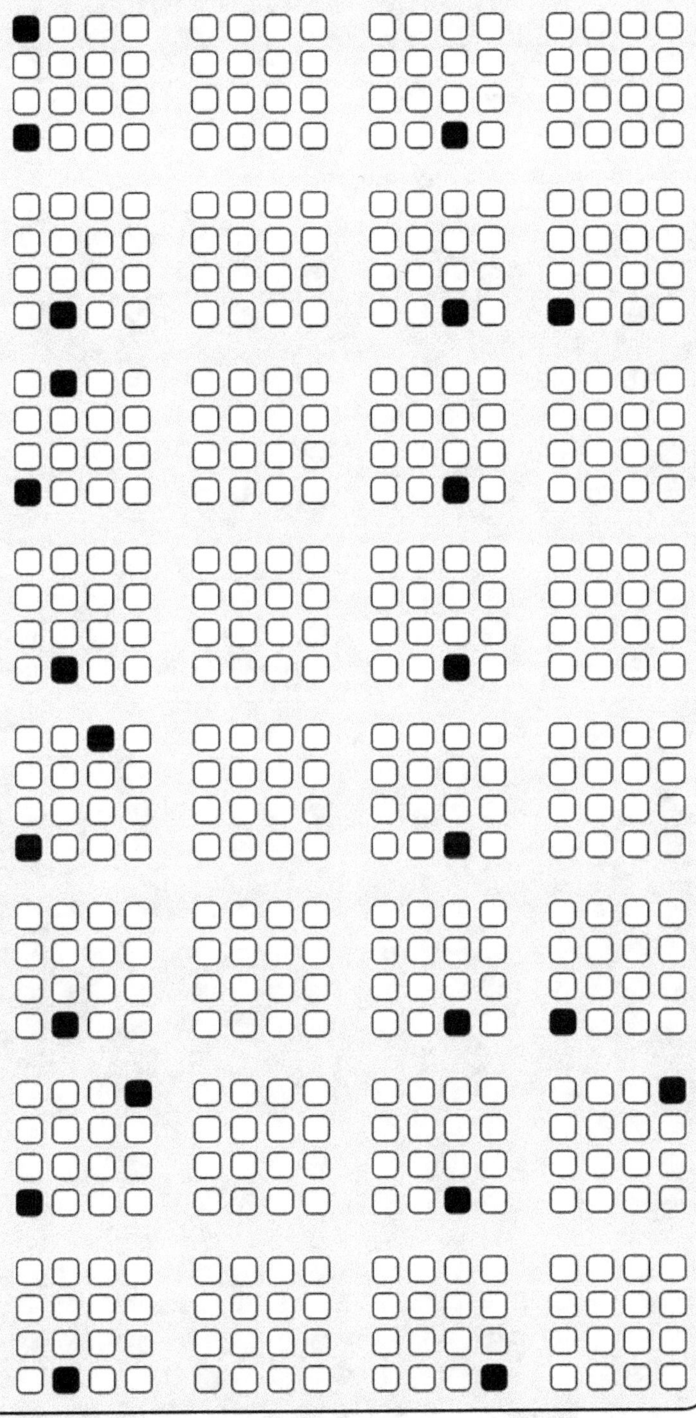

100BPM CC

MUSIC CHOPS

CHOPPED CHICKEN 5/8

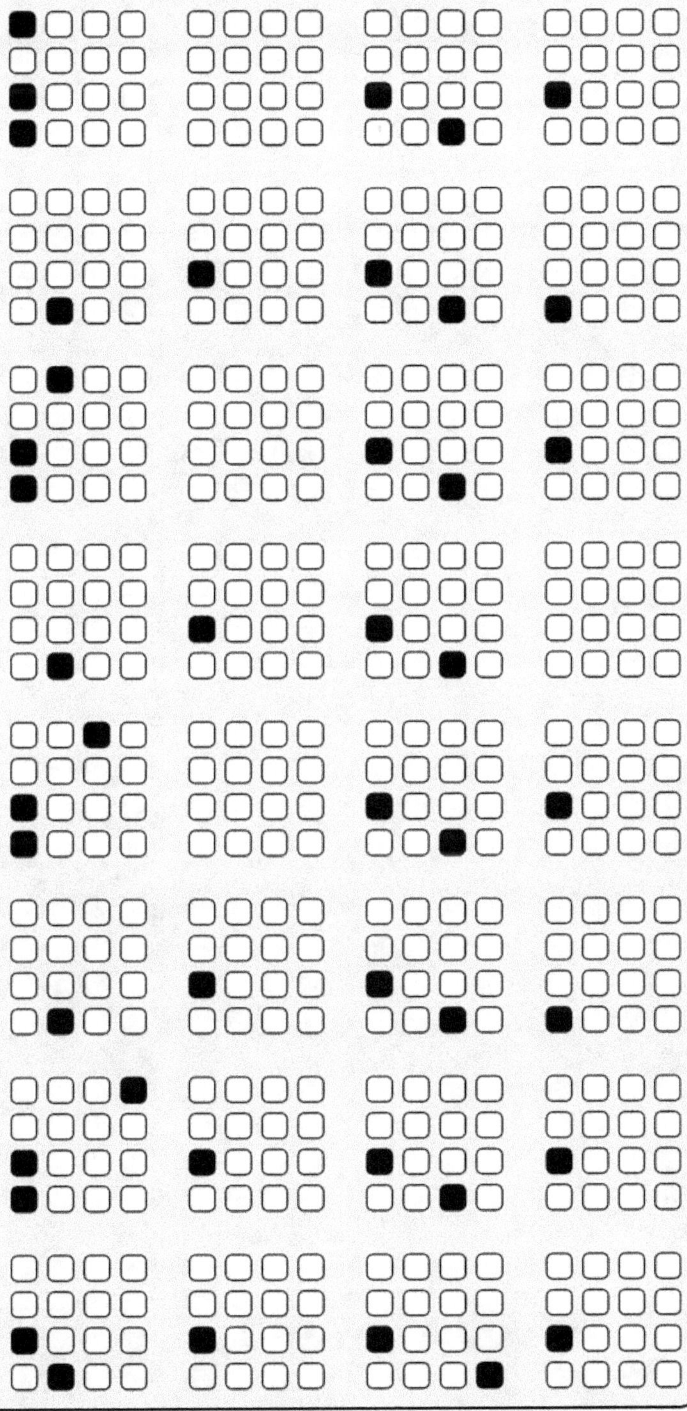

CHOPPED CHICKEN

CHOPPED CHICKEN 7/8

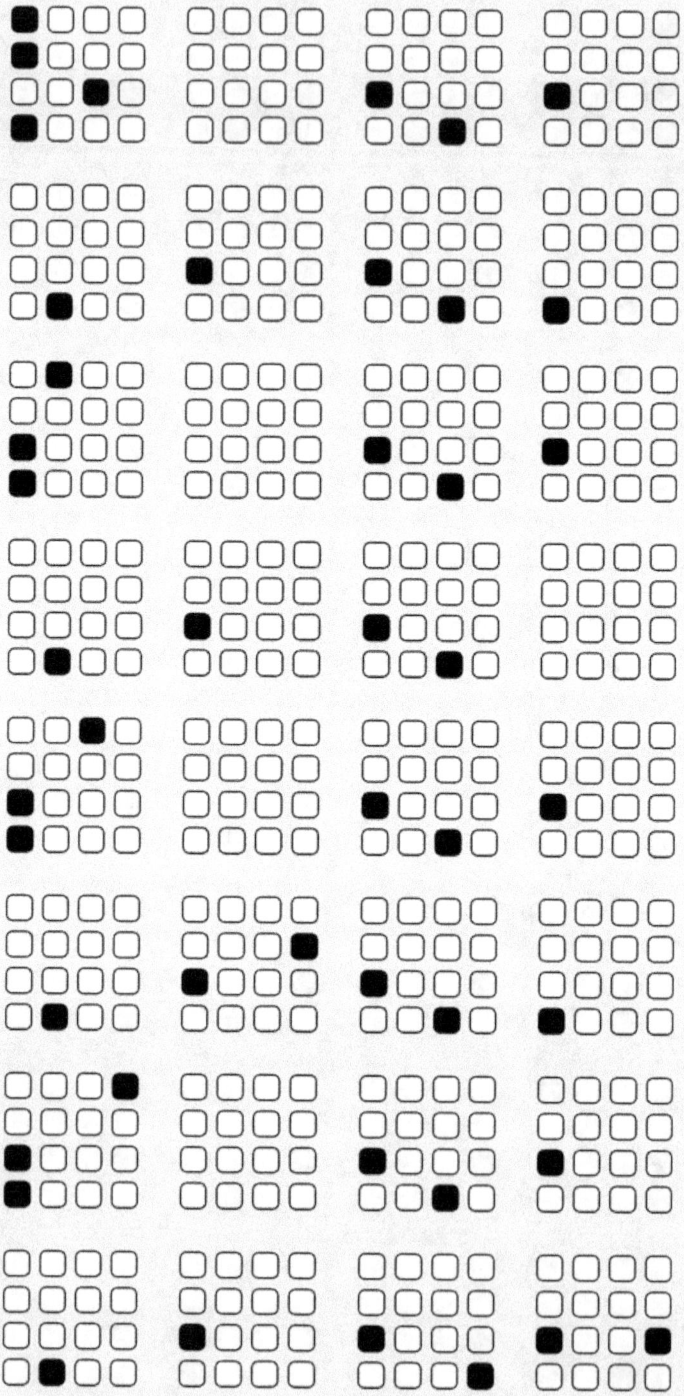

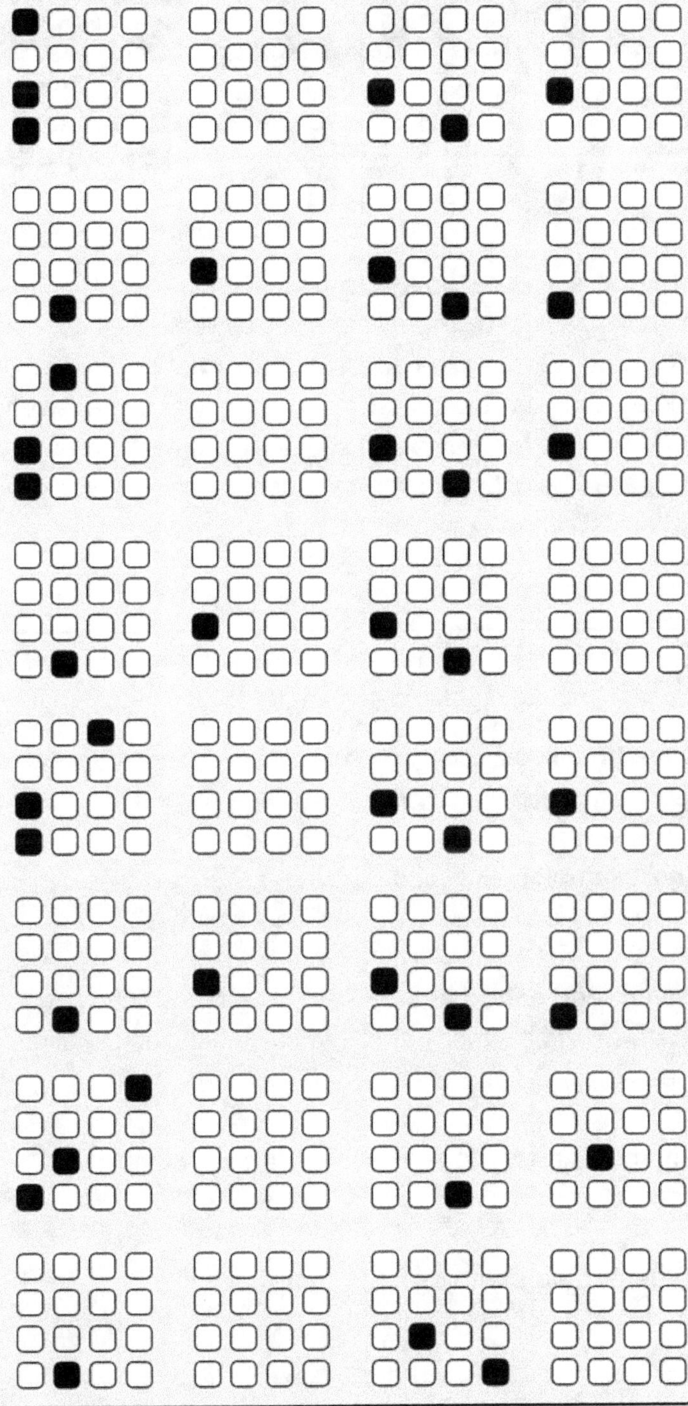

CHOPPED CHICKEN

CHILL FUNK

"Chill Funk" is a smooth blend of minimalist funk, employing one-shot slices derived from another AI-generated song. This laid back groove leans into the concept of one-shots by primarily using extremely short samples of guitar and bass riffs. Some reverb and echo effects are applied to add space around each one-shot to prolong the vibe of each sample, resulting a minimal yet extremely groovy music chop example.

IDEAS:

One-shot slices - Use one-shot slices from other songs, especially AI-generated ones, for unique sounds.

Short samples - Focus on extremely short samples of guitar and bass riffs to create a minimalist funk groove.

Reverb and echo effects - Apply reverb and echo to add space around each one-shot and smooth out abrupt sample releases.

Minimalist approach - Embrace a minimalist approach to create a smooth, groovy vibe.

AI-generated samples - Incorporate AI-generated samples for more control and a modern twist.

CHILL FUNK LAYOUT

GUITAR 1 13	BASS 1 14	GUITAR 2 15	BASS 2 16
GUITAR 3 9	GUITAR 4 10	GUITAR 5 11	GUITAR 6 12
FLOOR TOM 5	SNARE 2 6	CRASH 7	MID TOM 8
KICK 1	SNARE 1 2	HAT 1 3	HAT 2 4

DOWNLOAD ALL KITS: 

MUSIC CHOPS

80BPM CF

16

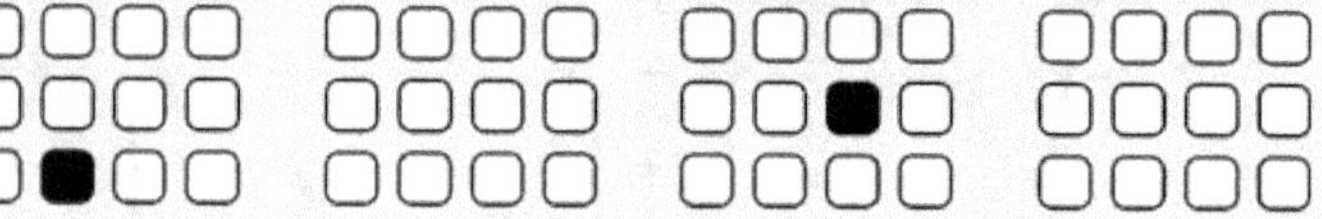

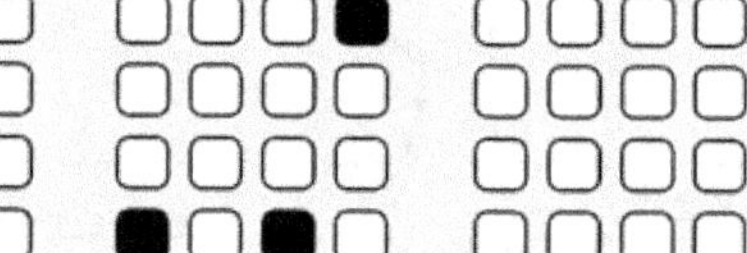

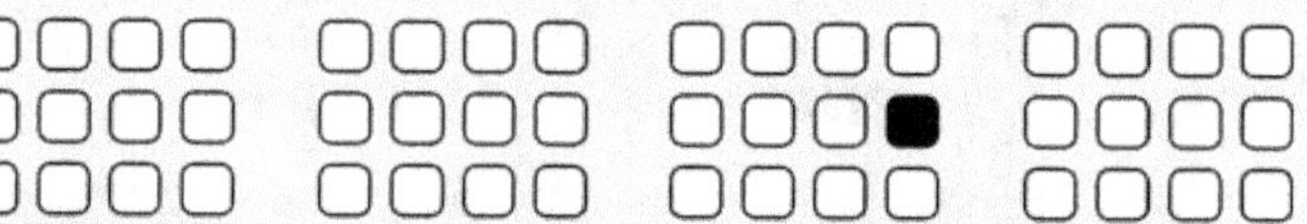
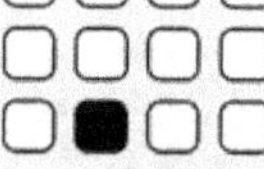
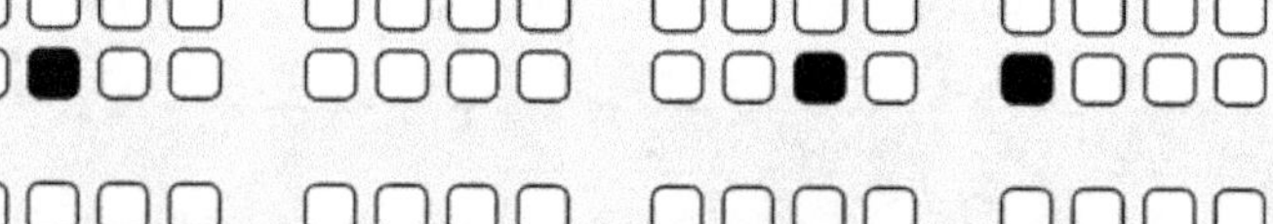
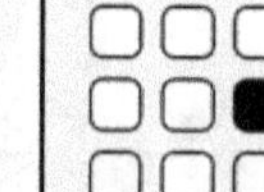
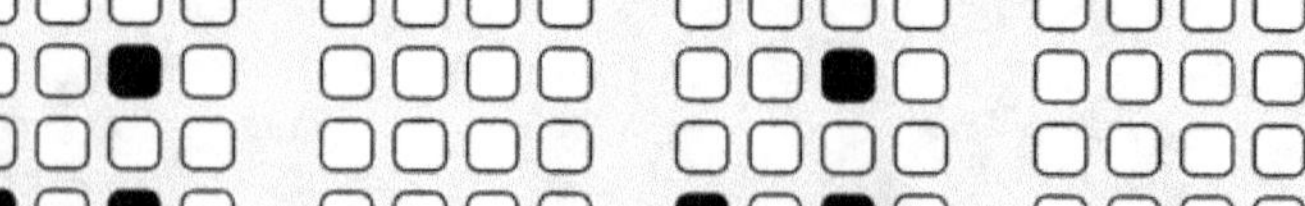
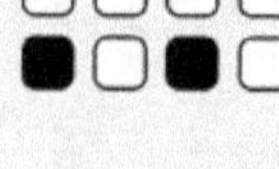

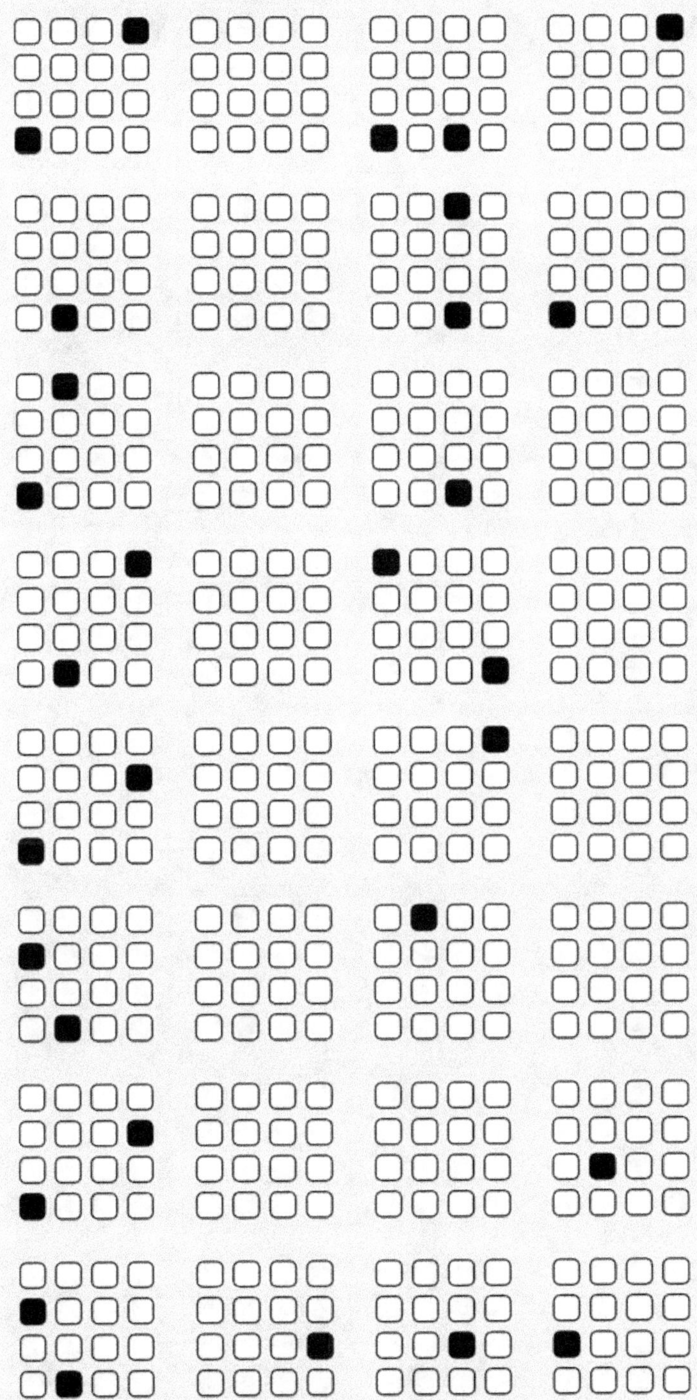

80BPM

CF

MUSIC CHOPS

CF

CHILL FUNK 5/8

MUSIC CHOPS

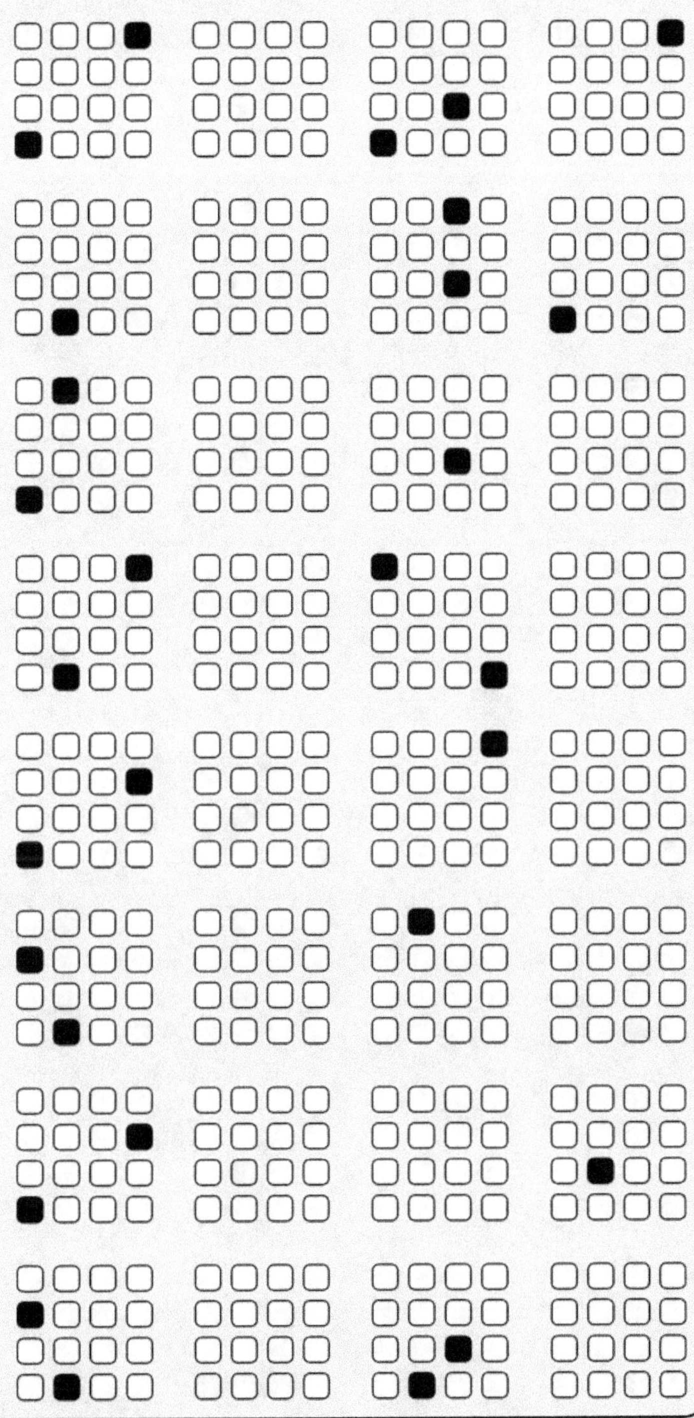

CHILL FUNK

CF

80BPM

MUSIC CHOPS

CHILL FUNK 7/8

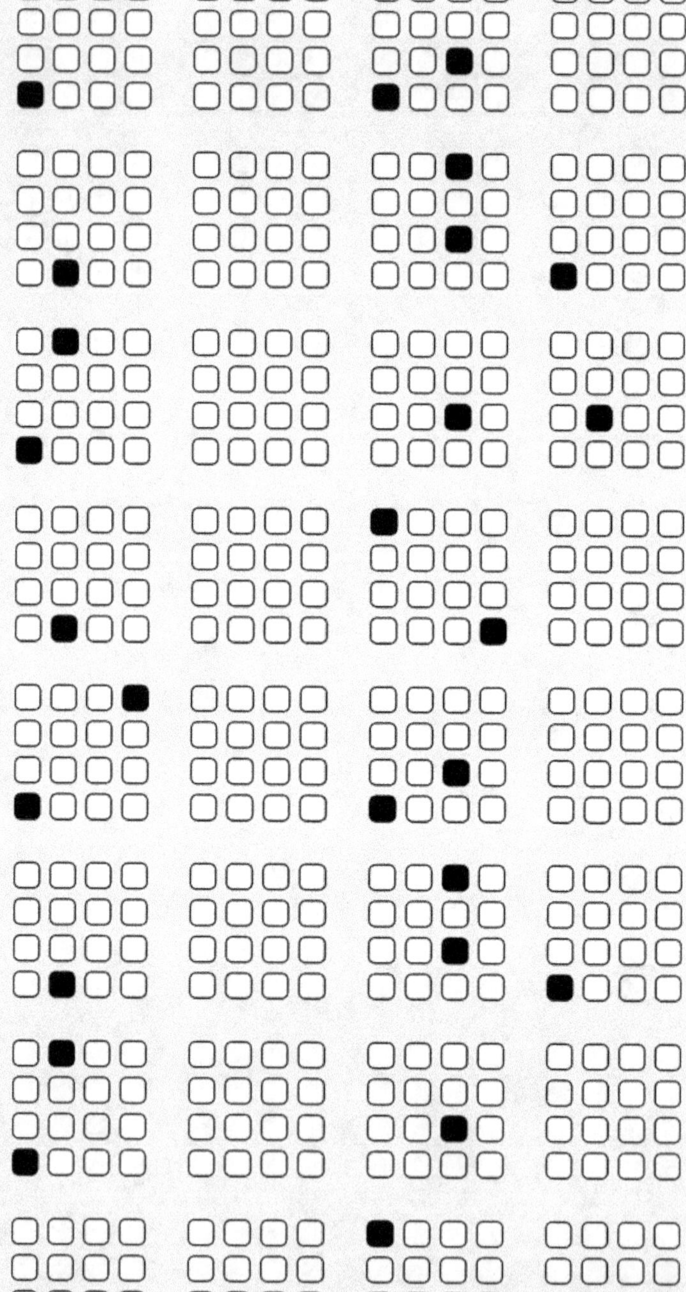

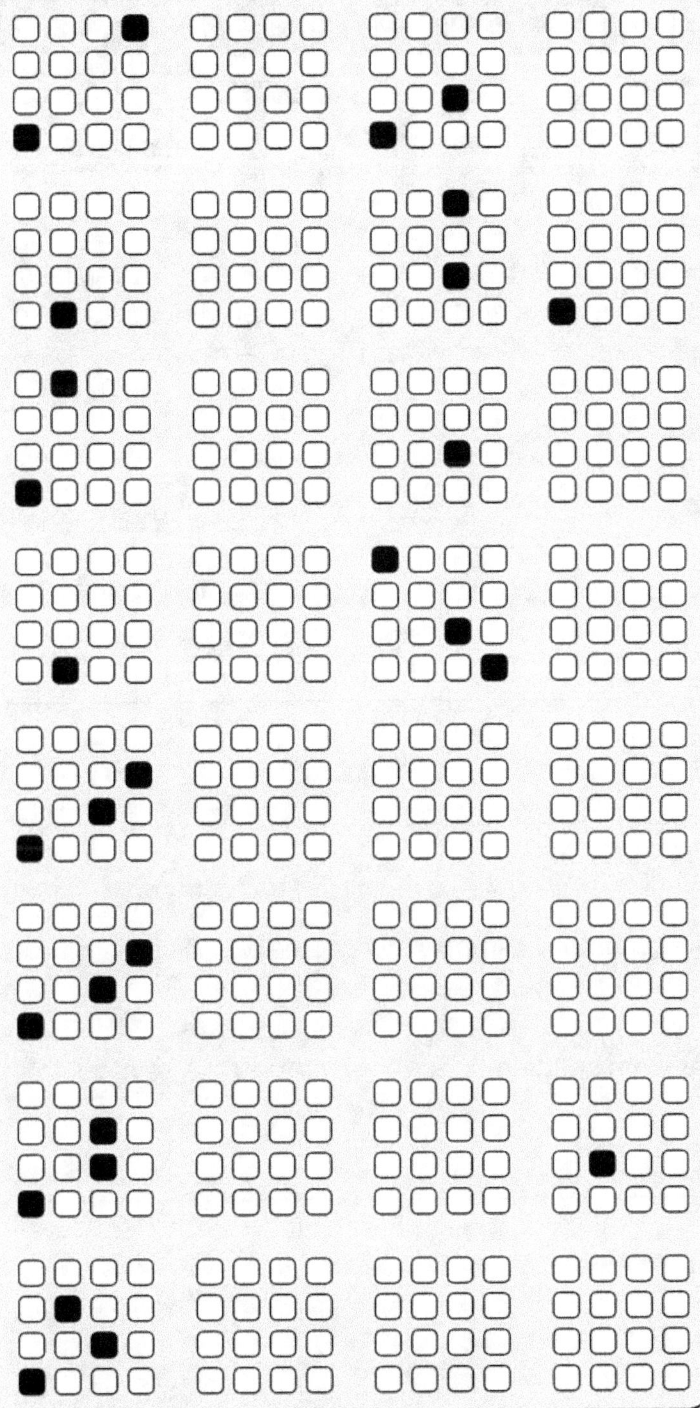

CHILL FUNK

THAT'S RIGHT

This 1980s-style example features a classic Boom Bap drum pattern, brass one-shots, and an emulated vinyl scratch. The original sample was generated using an AI music generator. The vocals were separated using an AI stem splitter and distributed across the pads.

The vinyl scratching effect was created through pitch modulation, with the modulation amount controlled by an LFO. This sound was resampled and assigned to a pad equipped with a randomizer to play a different slice with each hit.

IDEAS:

Emulated vinyl scratch - Add an emulated vinyl scratch for authenticity.

AI-generated samples - Use AI music generators for unique sample creation.

AI stem splitting - Separate vocals using AI stem splitters and distribute them across the pads.

THAT'S RIGHT LAYOUT

"THAT'S RIGHT" 13	BRASS 3 14	BRASS 2 15	BRASS 1 16
STAB 1 9	HIGH PLUCK 10	"MAINTAIN THE FLOW" 11	"HEY EVERY TIME" 12
STAB 2 5	STAB 3 6	SNARE 2 7	VINYL SCRATCH 8
KICK/BASS 1	SNARE 1 2	HAT 1 3	HAT 2 4

DOWNLOAD ALL KITS: 

MUSIC CHOPS
110BPM
TR
16
THAT'S RIGHT 1/8
Page 149

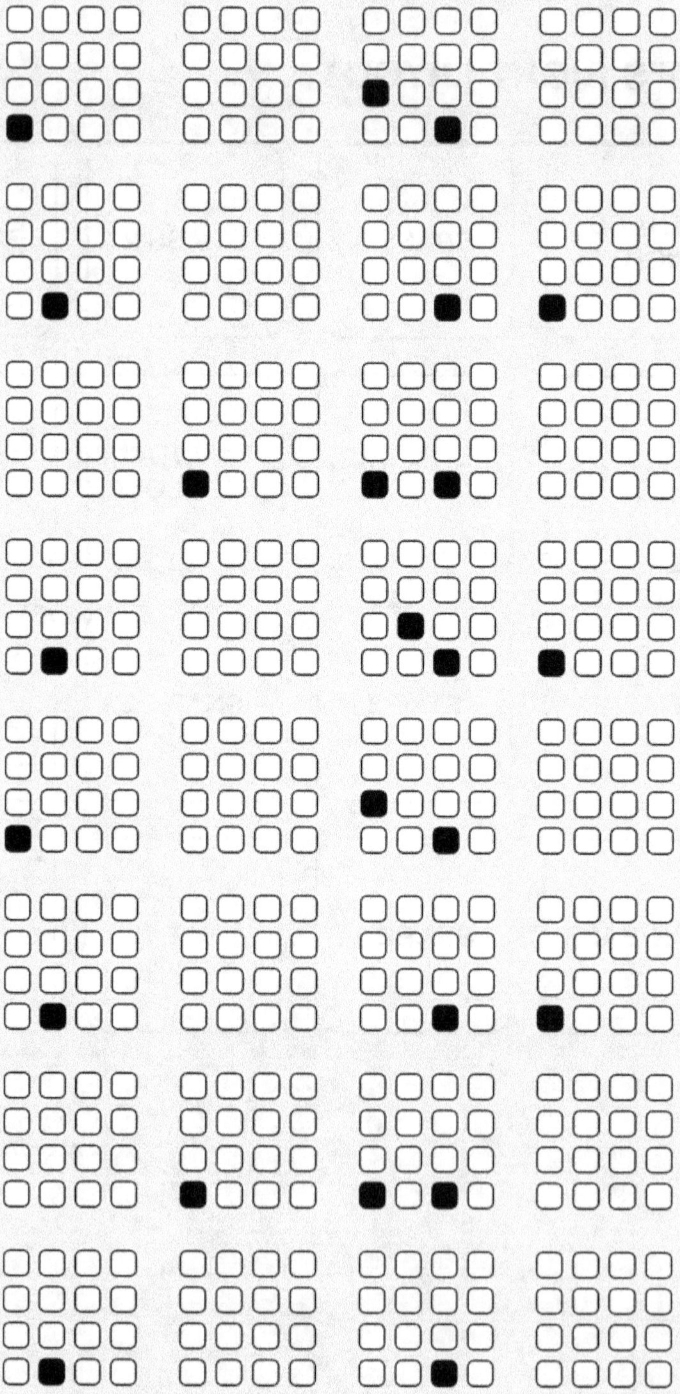

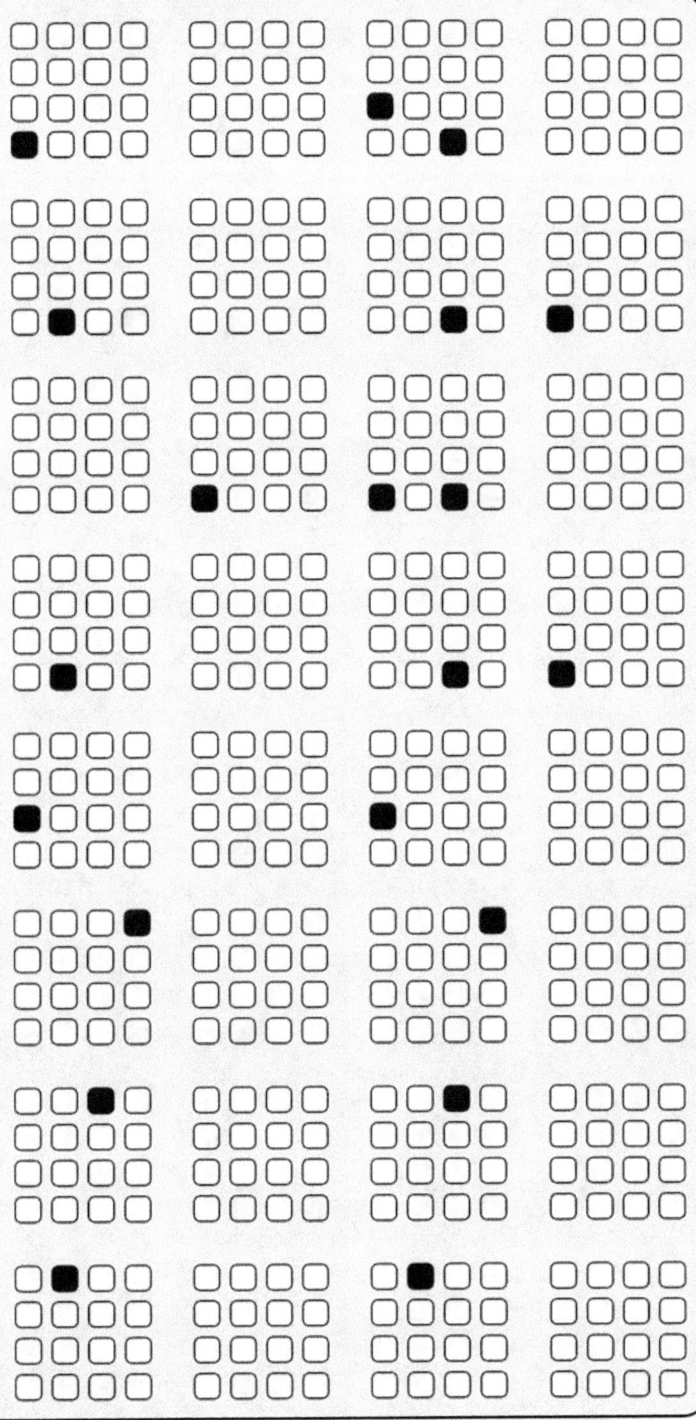

THAT'S RIGHT

16

TR

110BPM

MUSIC CHOPS

THAT'S RIGHT 5/8

THAT'S RIGHT

TR

THAT'S RIGHT 7/8

MUSIC CHOPS

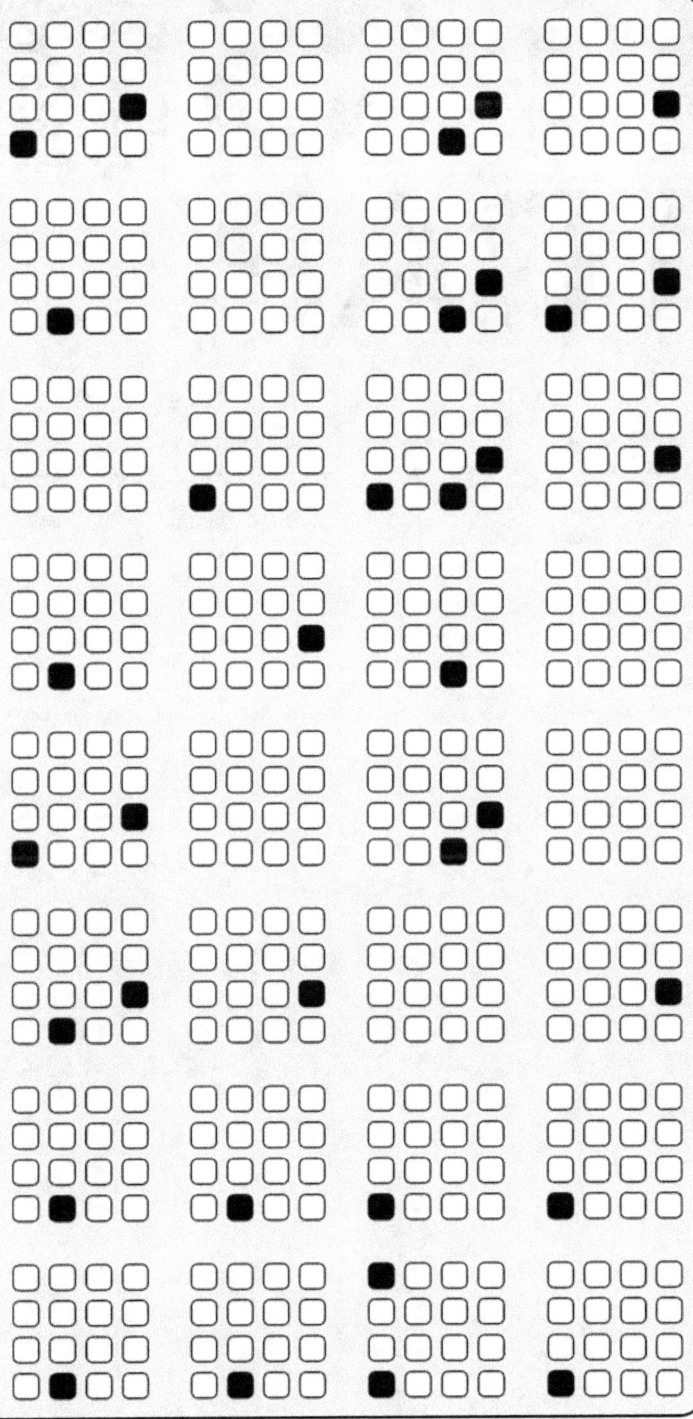

THAT'S RIGHT

IT'S TRAP

This heavy-hitting example features orchestral stabs, dark and otherworldly plucks, and a deep, distorted 808 bass. The sounds were composed in a DAW and adapted for the pads. Composing specifically for a 16-pad layout allows for creative limitations, preventing over-production and maintaining simplicity.

MUSIC CHOPS

IT'S TRAP LAYOUT

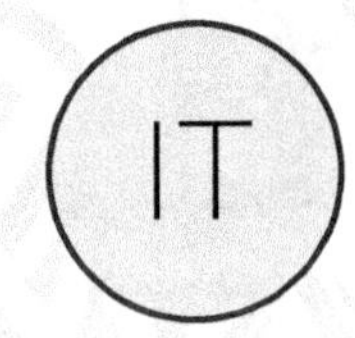

PLUCK 3 13	PLUCK 2 14	PLUCK 1 15	"IT'S TRAP" 16
PLUCK 6 9	PLUCK 5 10	PLUCK 4 11	HARSH PERC 12
BASS 5	STAB 3 6	STAB 2 7	STAB 1 8
KICK 1	SNARE 2	RIDE 3	CYMBAL 4

MUSIC CHOPS

138BPM IT 16

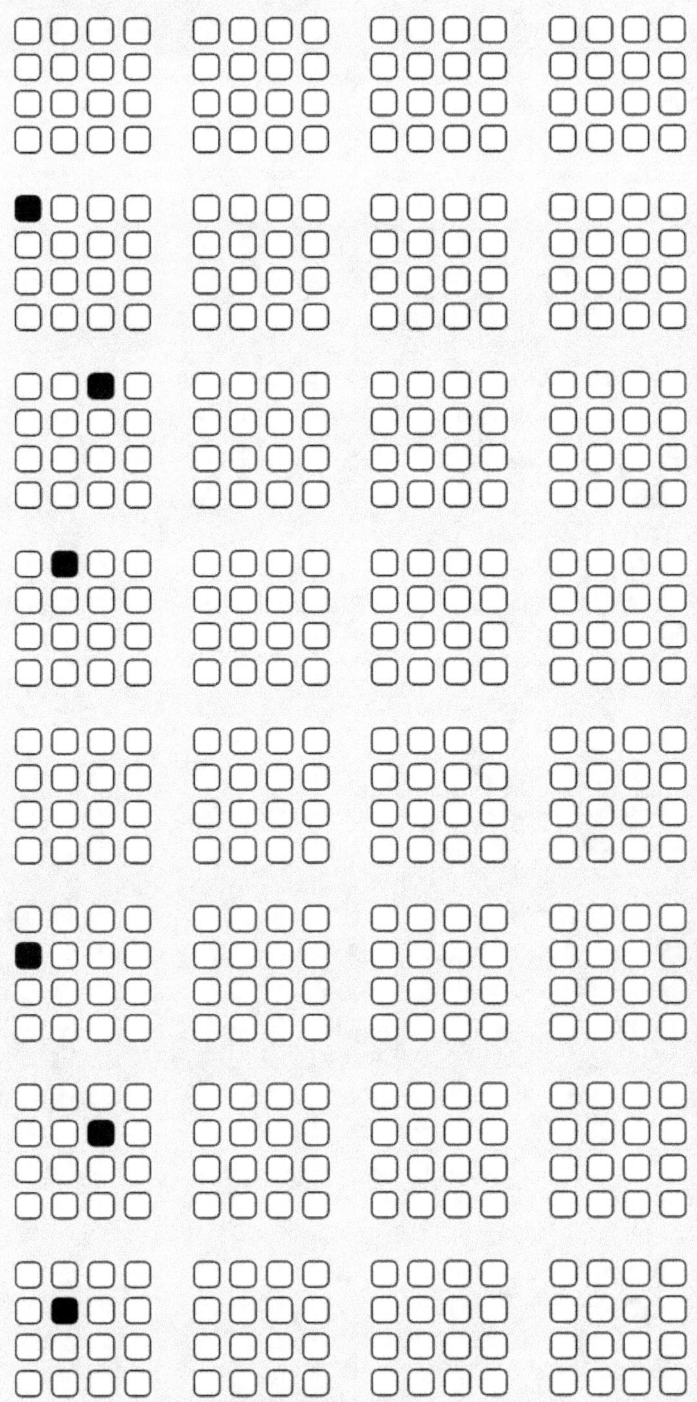

IT'S TRAP

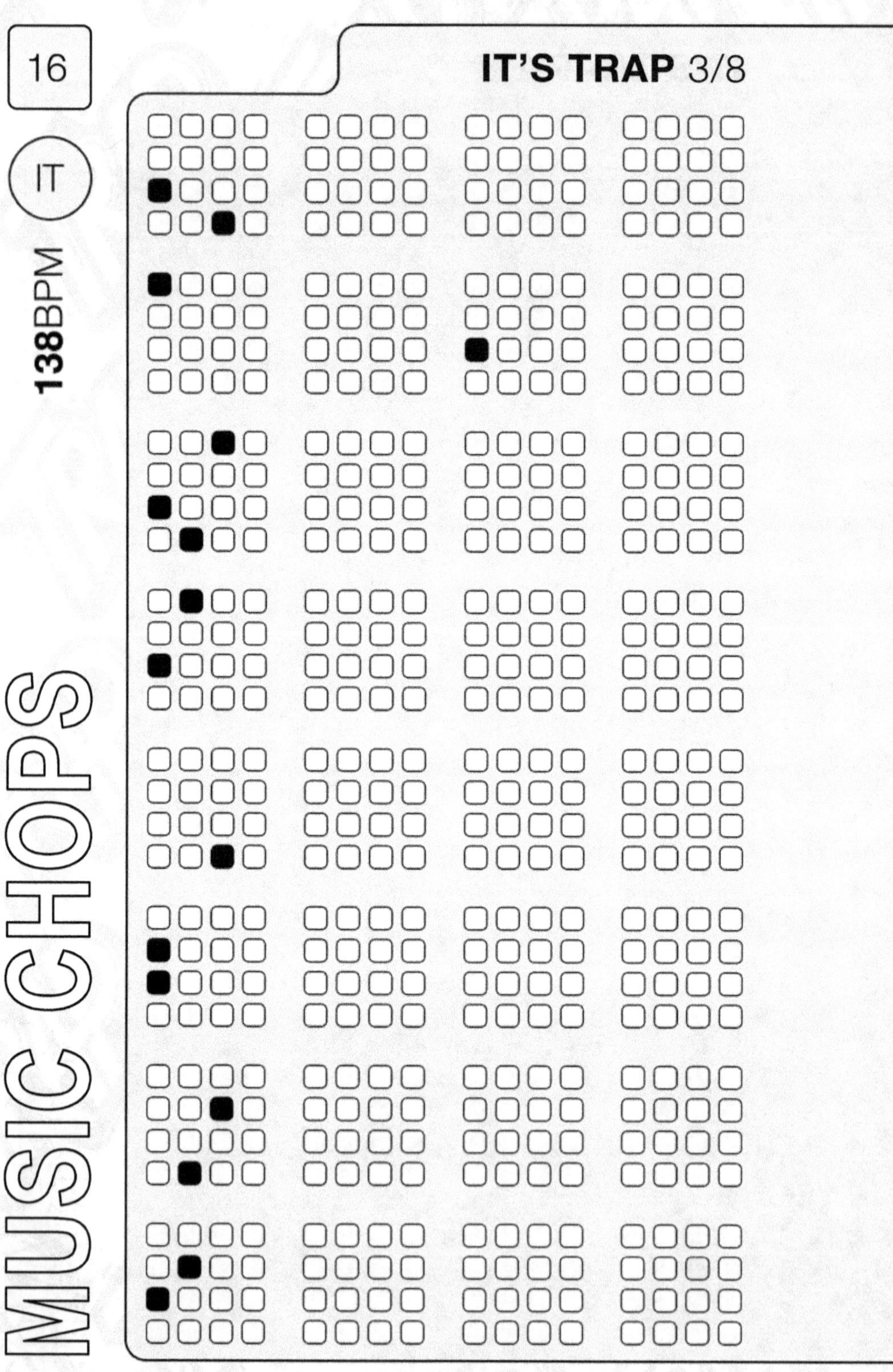
138BPM
MUSIC CHOPS
IT'S TRAP 3/8

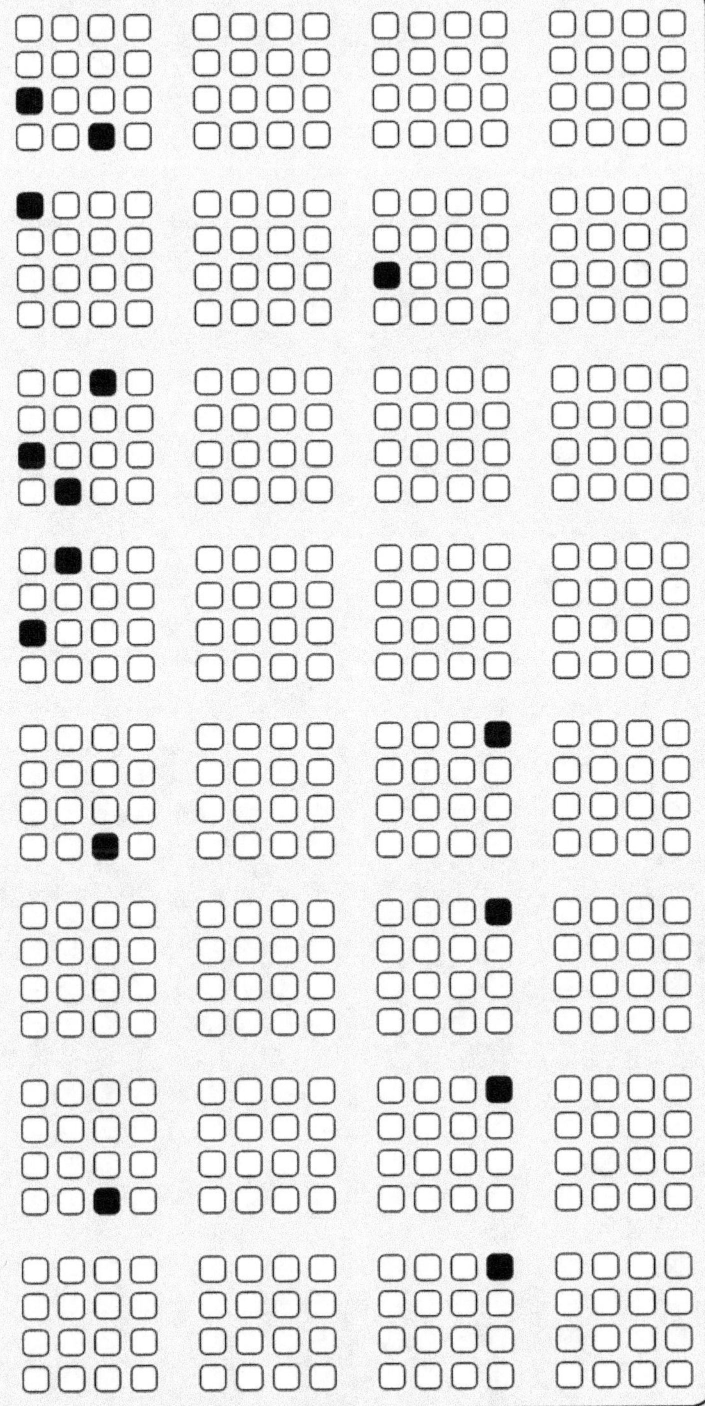

138BPM IT

MUSIC CHOPS

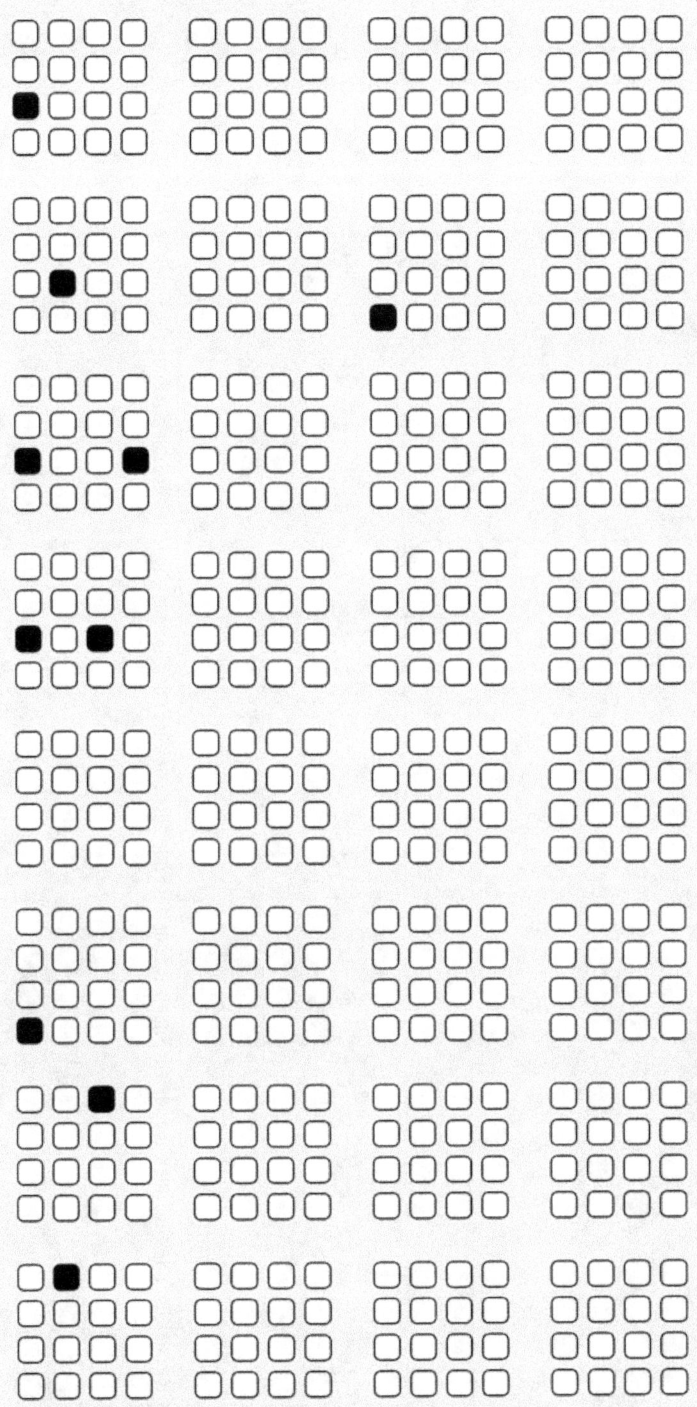

138BPM IT

IT'S TRAP 7/8

MUSIC CHOPS

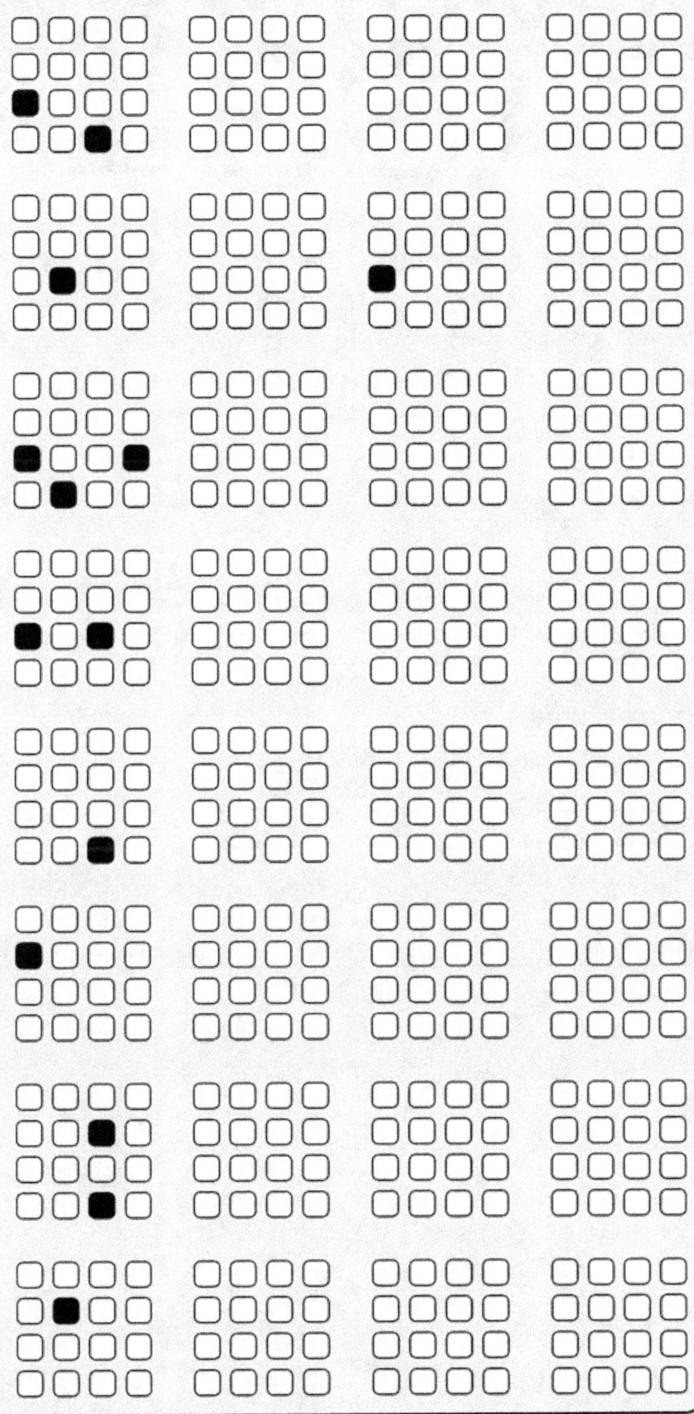

MOMENTS PASS

This dreamy chill-hop sequence features vocal chops layered on ethereal, time-stretched piano textures. As always, all chops are grouped using the same choke/mute group to prevent unwanted muddiness and dissonance. A liberal amount of reverb is applied to each sample to enhance the dreamy vibe.

IDEAS:

Vocal chops - Layer vocal chops on top of other textures.

Ethereal time-stretched piano - Use time-stretching on piano samples to create an ethereal texture.

Liberal reverb - Apply a generous amount of reverb to enhance the dreamy vibe.

MUSIC CHOPS

MOMENTS PASS LAYOUT

CHOP 4 13	CHOP 3 14	CHOP 2 15	CHOP 1 16
CHOP 7 9	CHOP 6 10	CHOP 5 11	"MOMENTS PASS" 12
CRASH 5	SNARE ROLL 6	HAT CLOSED 7	HAT ROLL 8
KICK 1	SNARE 2	HAT LID 3	SHAKER 4

DOWNLOAD ALL KITS: 

MUSIC CHOPS
85BPM
16
MP
MOMENTS PASS 1/8

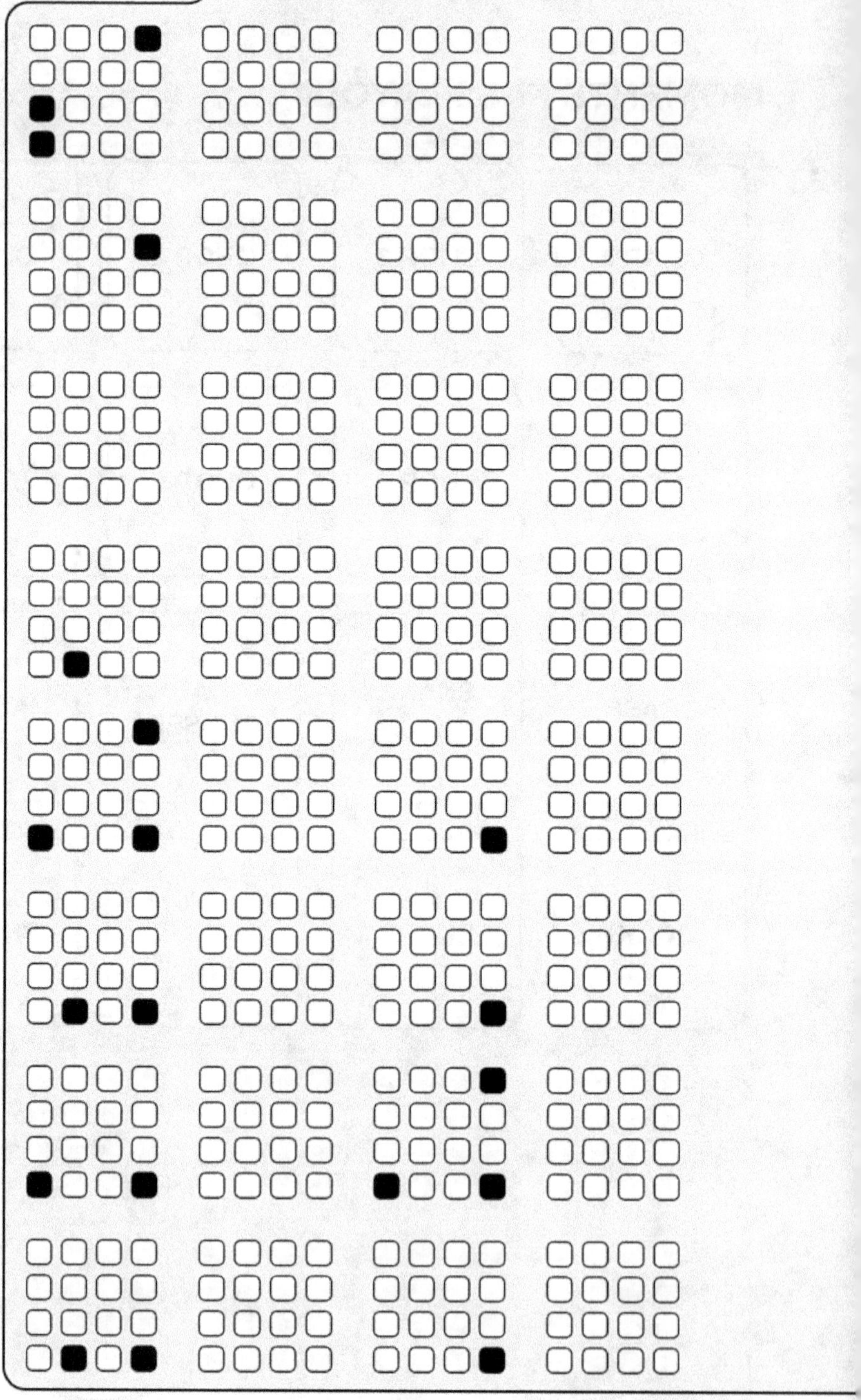

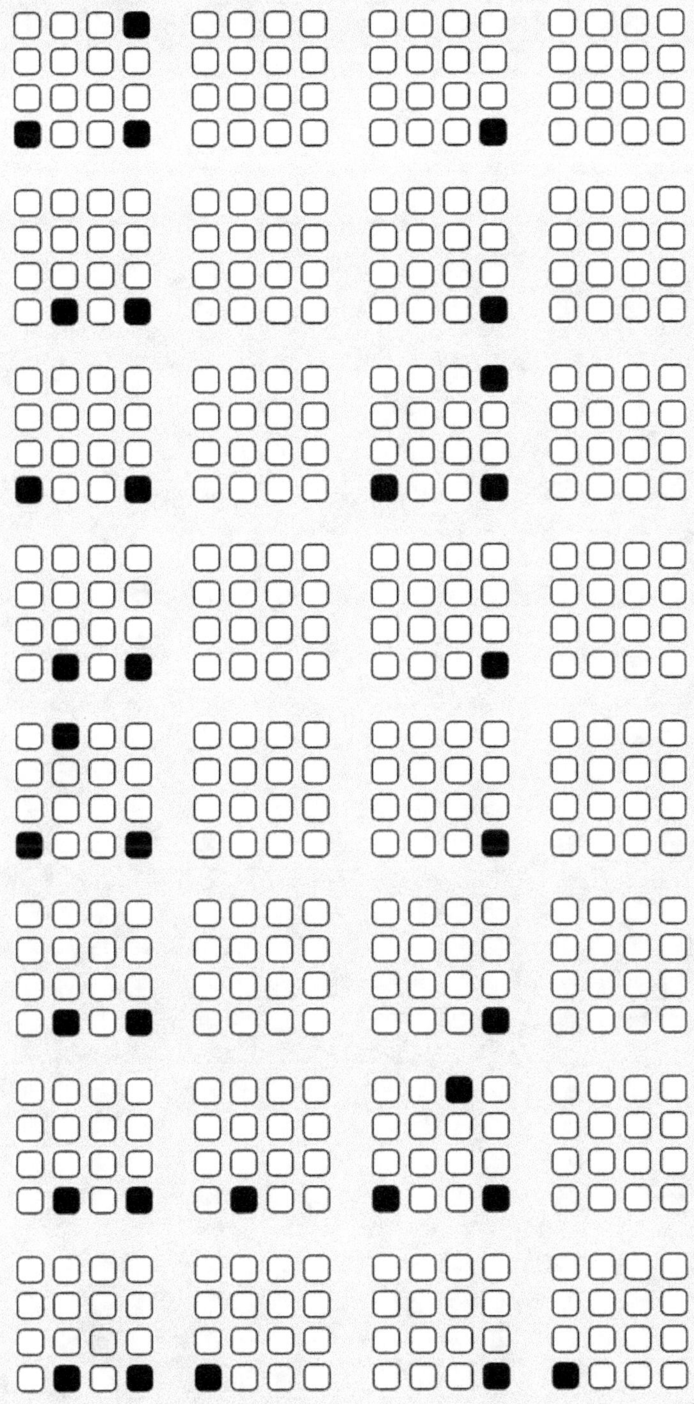

MP

85BPM

MUSIC CHOPS

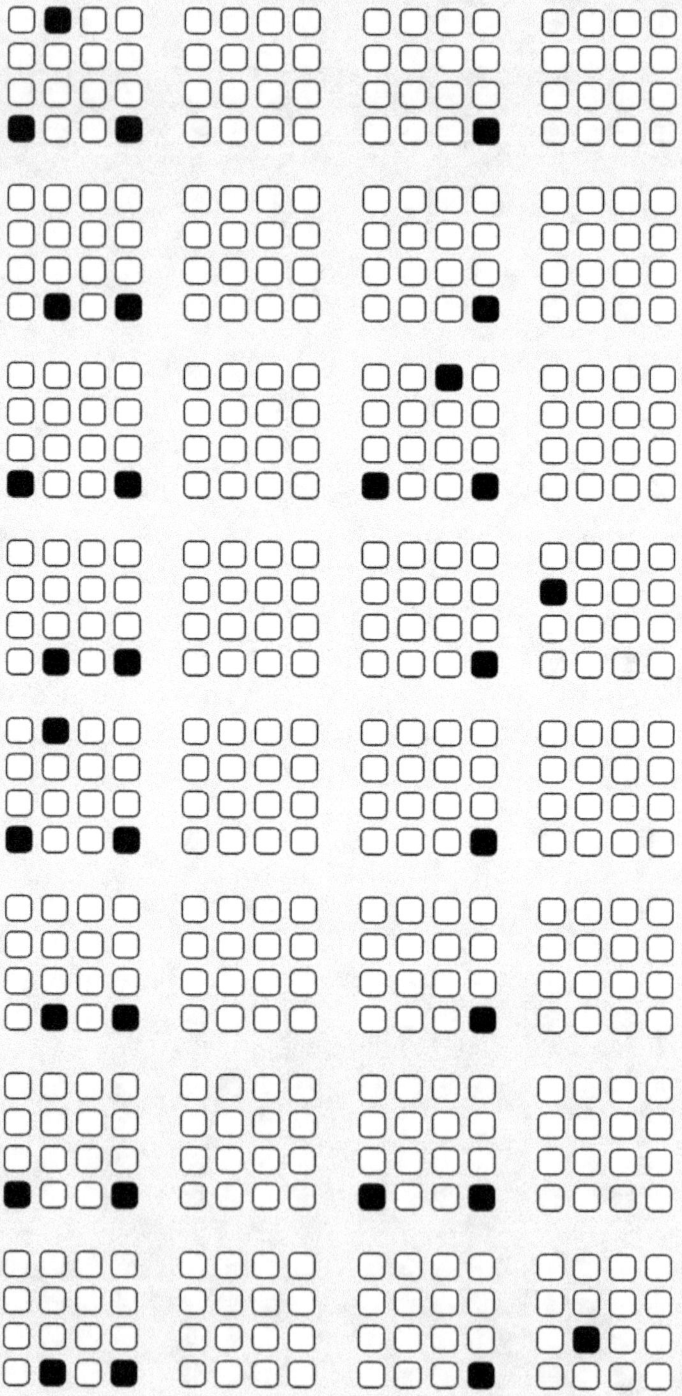

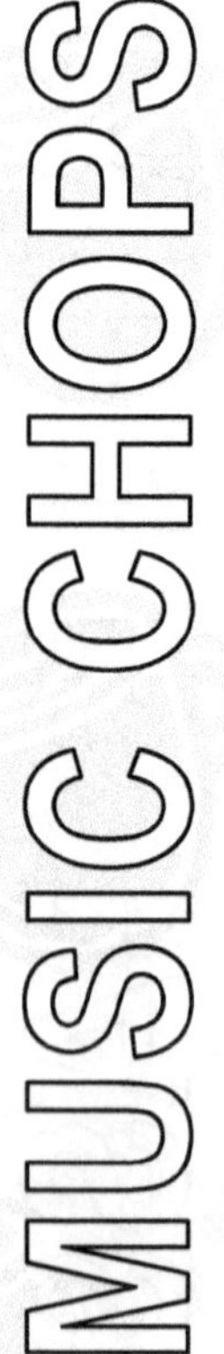
MUSIC CHOPS

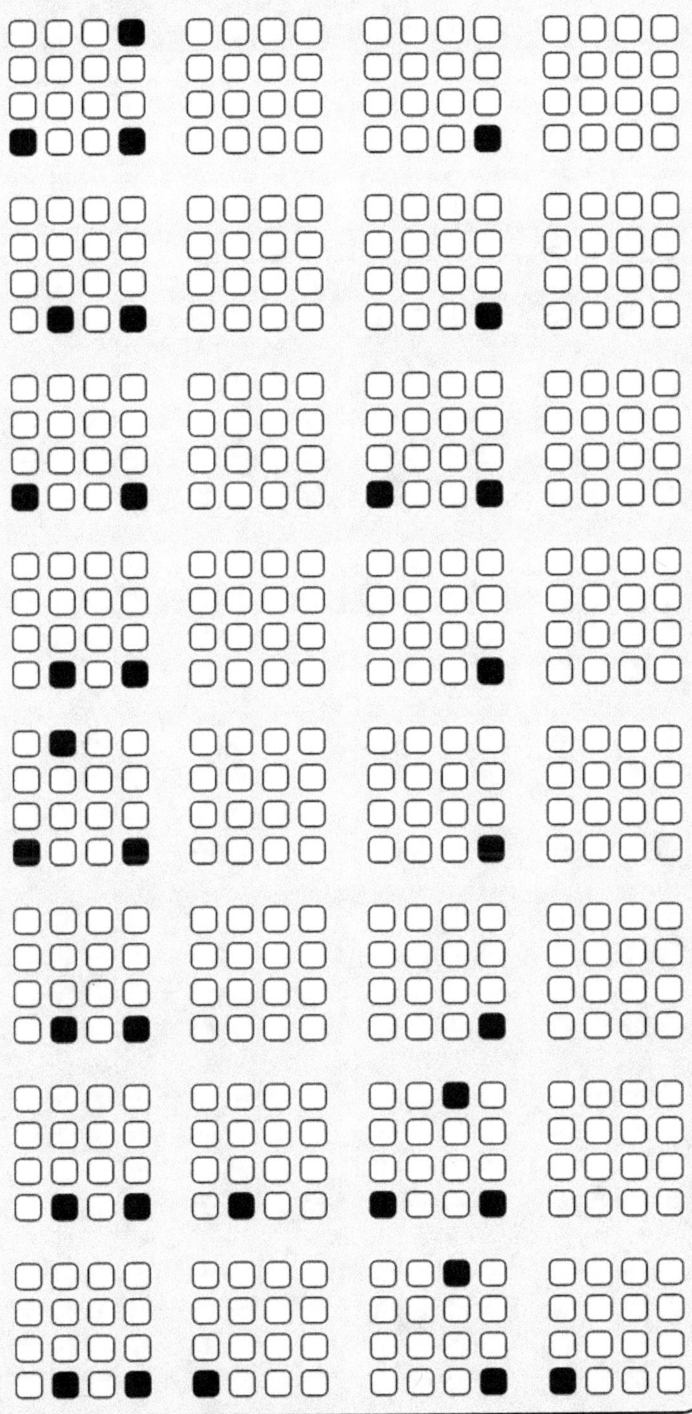

MOMENTS PASS 6/8
MOMENTS PASS

MP

85BPM

MUSIC CHOPS

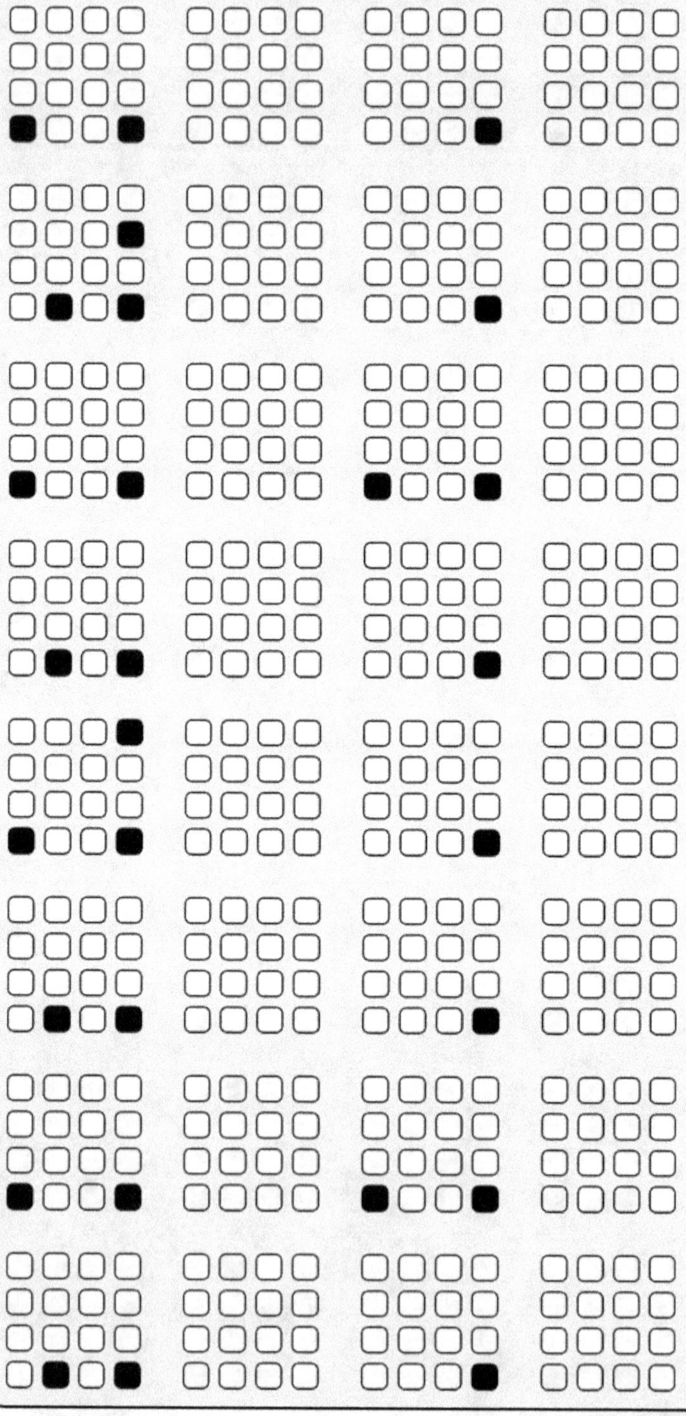

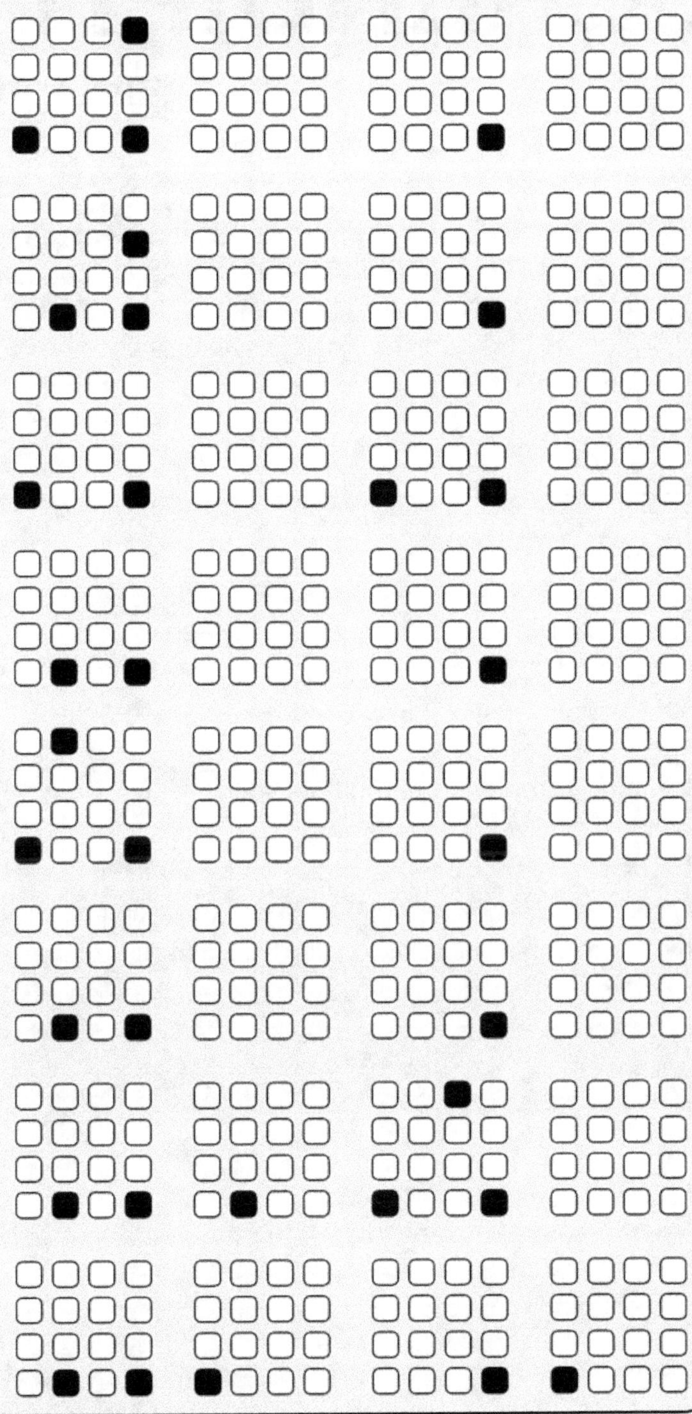

SERENDIPITY

This straightforward sample chop configuration features a laid-back, chill-hop vibe with lounge brass stabs, stand-up bass, and vocal chops. The samples in this example are not manipulated; instead, they are primarily rearranged in a fun and bouncy hip-hop pattern. This setup highlights how simple chops and rearrangement can create an engaging musical experience.

> **IDEAS:**
>
> **Keep it simple -** Sometimes there's no need to do anything fancy. Tastefully select ideal cue points in your sample and jam with it until you've found a new sequence you love!
>
> **Combine samples from multiple songs -** Try combining samples from two or more songs in different genres, such as a bass from one song and piano from another. If the multiple songs are in a similar musical key, you'll have a much easier time combining samples. If you don't know the key of the songs you are sampling, just do a quick search online as most songs have been analyzed and the key listed.

SERENDIPITY

CHOP 4	CHOP 3	CHOP 2	CHOP 1
CHOP 8	CHOP 7	CHOP 6	CHOP 5
BASS	SNARE 2	HAT CLOSED	HAT OPEN
KICK	CLAP	SNARE 1	RIDE

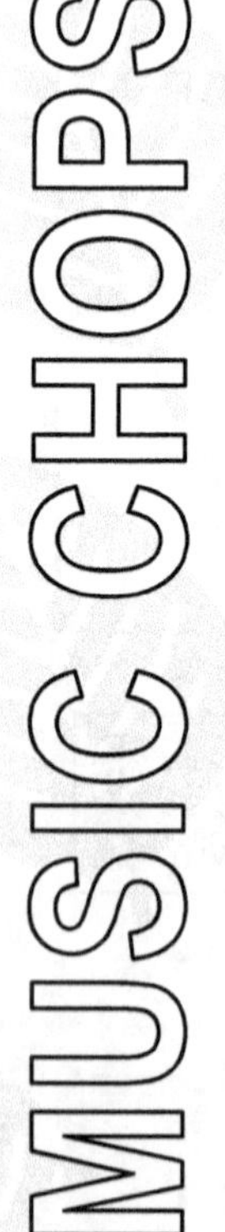
MUSIC CHOPS
90BPM
S
16

90BPM

MUSIC CHOPS

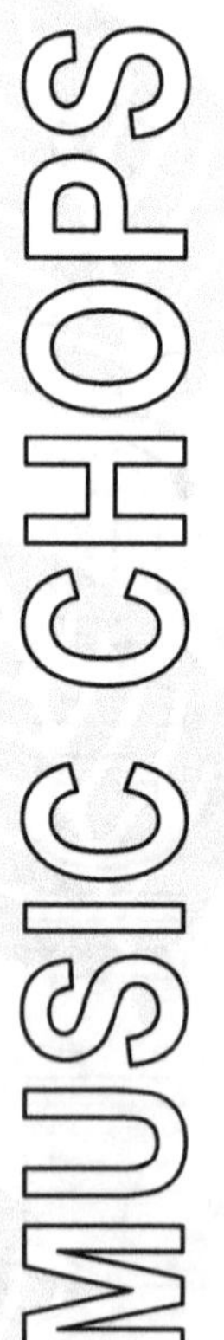

SERENDIPITY 5/8

MUSIC CHOPS

90BPM (S)

LAZY
AFTERNOON

This layout demonstrates how pitch control can transform a sample into something completely new. Nearly all of the sample chops have been transposed up and down, creating a modern and laid-back vibe. Depending on the sample contents, you can rearrange the pitch of several chops in a sequence to create new melodies. This example also uses the reverse function, adding to the dreamy, laid-back pattern. Additionally, time-stretching is applied to several samples. This setup has a chill-hop vibe.

IDEAS:

Pitch control - Transpose sample chops up and down to create new textures.

Rearrange pitch in sequences - Create new melodies by rearranging the pitch of chops in a sequence.

Reverse function - Use the reverse function to add a dreamy effect.

Time-stretching - Apply time-stretching to alter the feel of the samples.

LAZY AFTERNOON

CHOP 4 13	CHOP 3 14	CHOP 2 15	CHOP 1 16
CHOP 8 9	CHOP 7 10	CHOP 6 11	CHOP 5 12
CRASH 5	SNARE ROLL 6	HAT CLOSED 7	WOOD PERC 8
KICK 1	SNARE 1 2	SNARE 2 3	RIDE 4

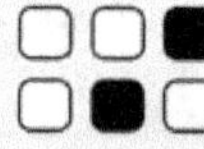
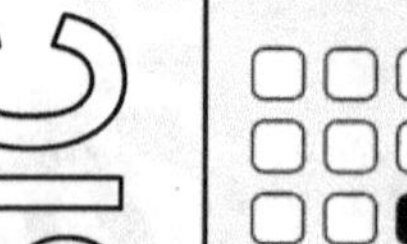
90BPM
LA
16

MUSIC CHOPS

LAZY AFTERNOON

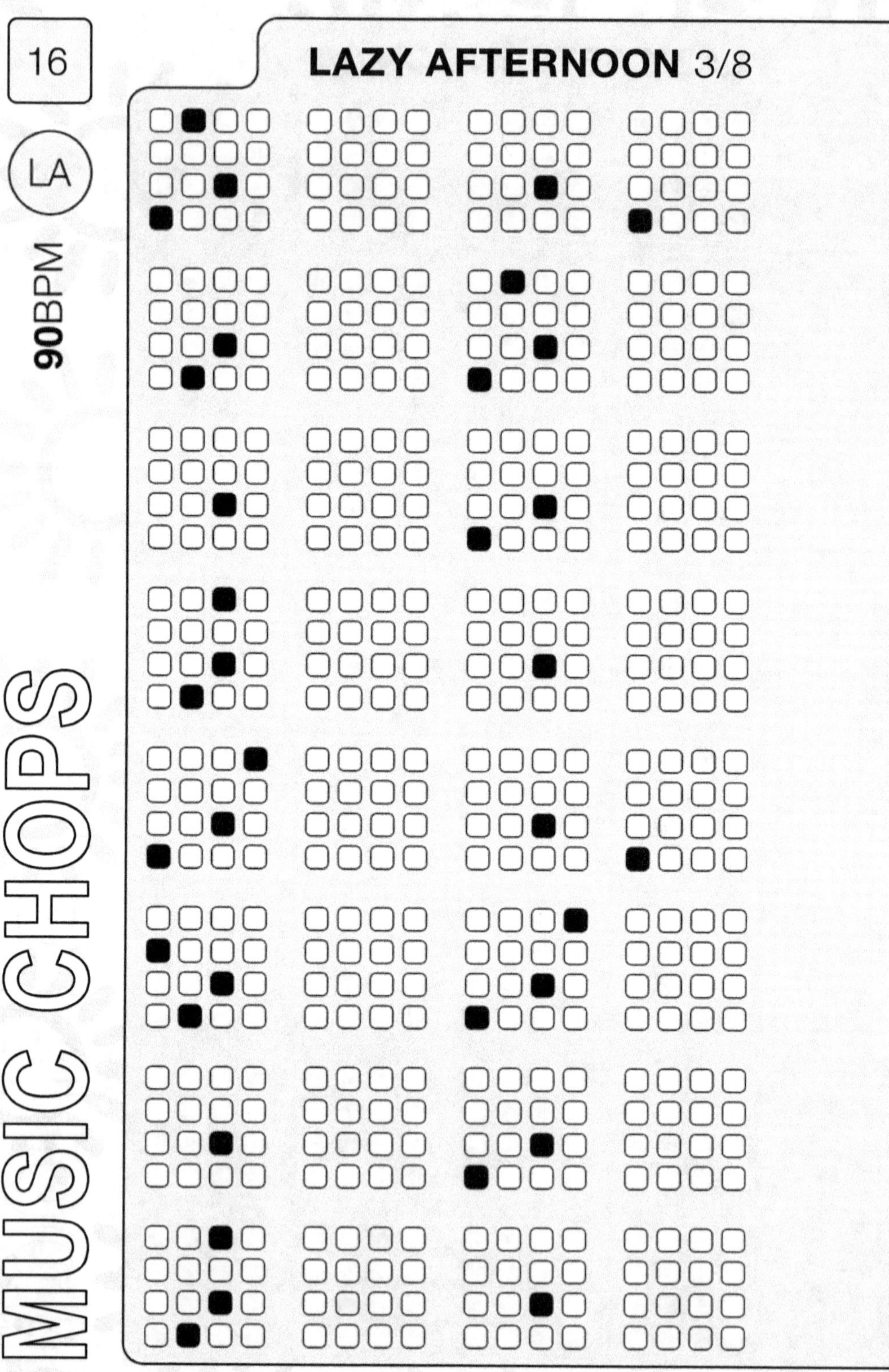
MUSIC CHOPS
16
90BPM
LA
LAZY AFTERNOON 3/8
Page 191

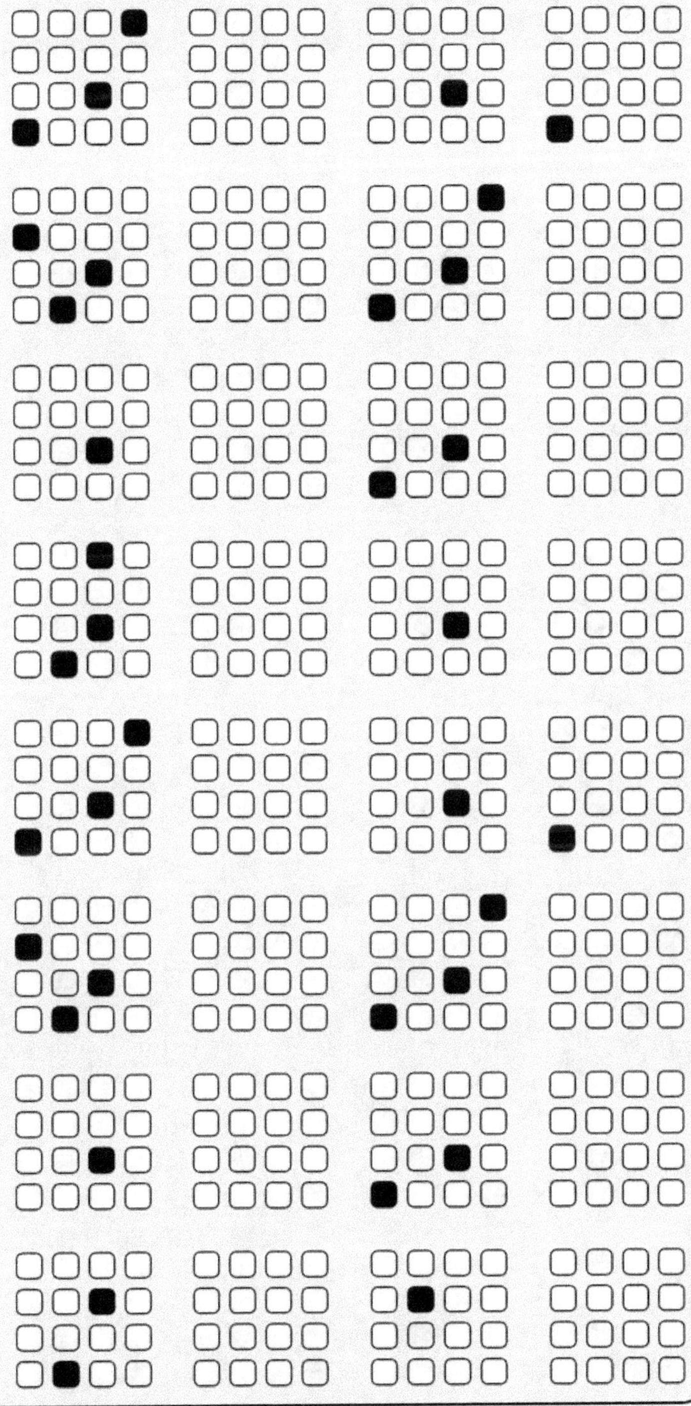

90BPM

LA

MUSIC CHOPS

LAZY AFTERNOON 5/8

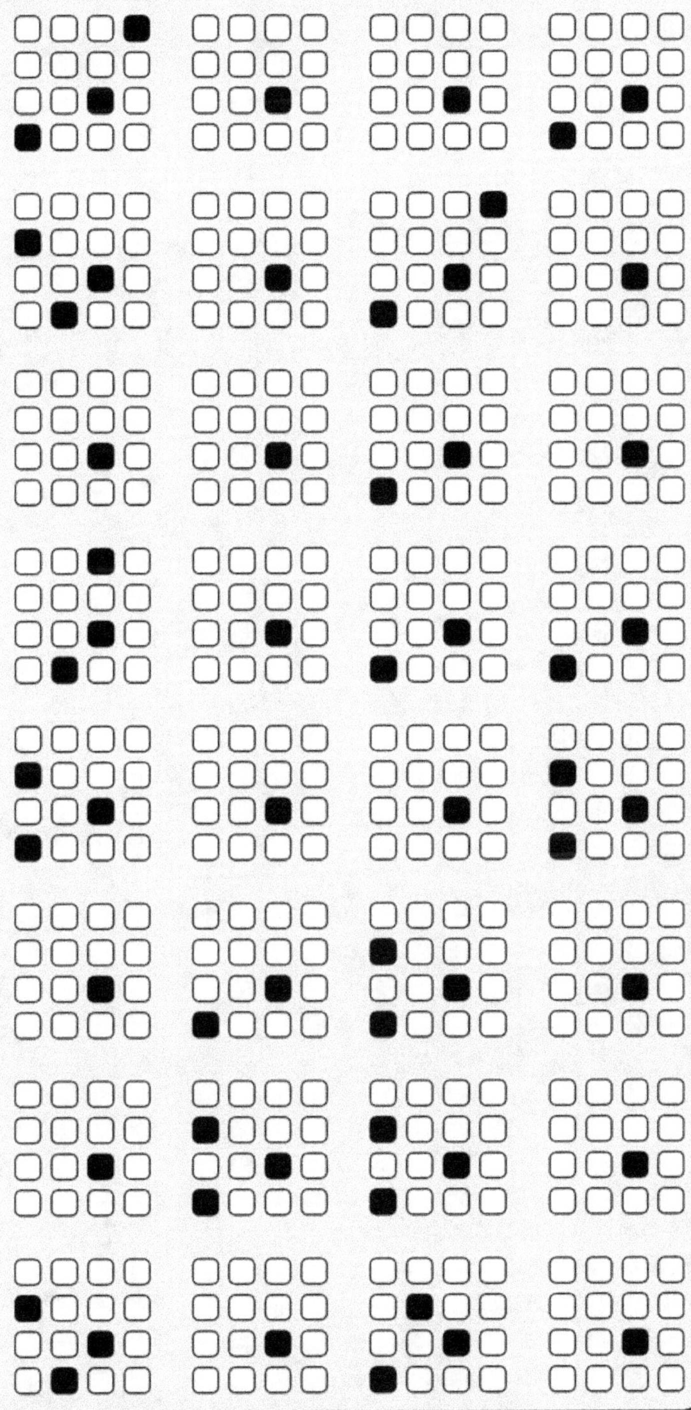

90BPM (LA)

MUSIC CHOPS

LAZY AFTERNOON 7/8

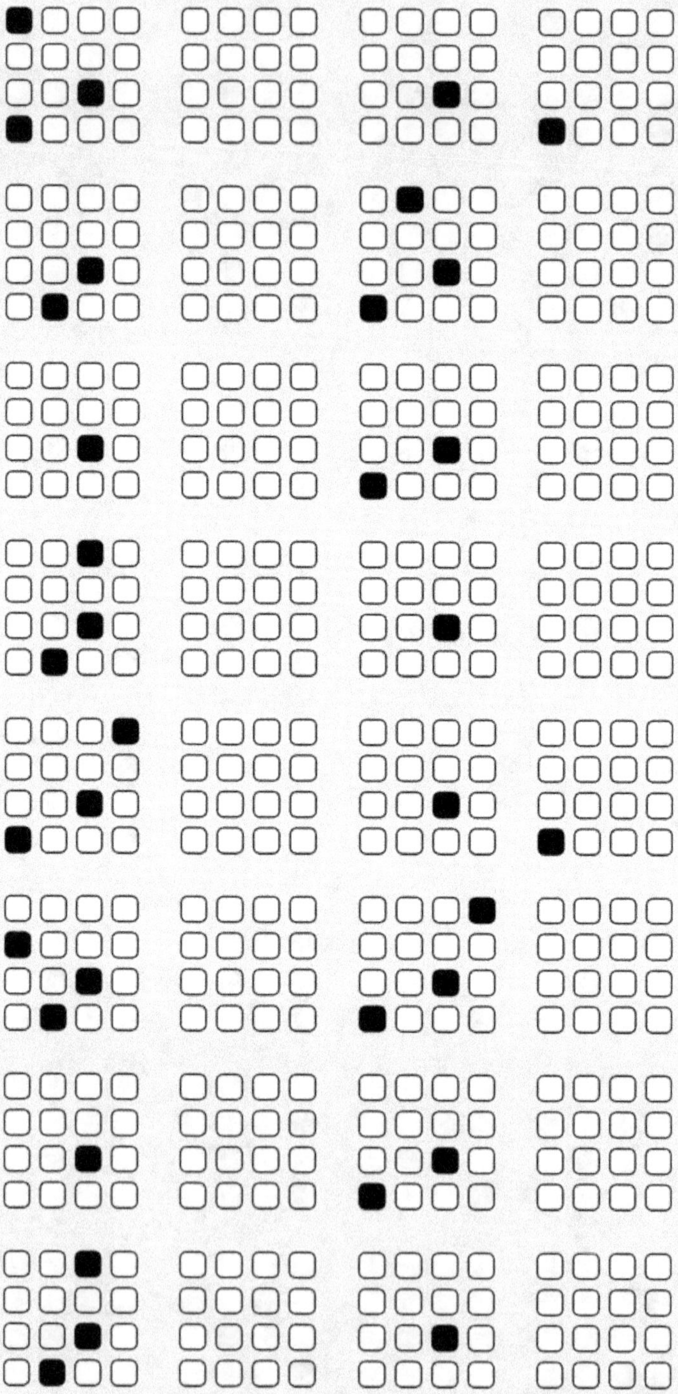

LAZY AFTERNOON

LATELY

This example utilizes two notable techniques to create a dynamic and ethereal performance. The first technique involves using multiple bass samples per pad, each an octave apart. With the cycle/random/alt feature enabled, this setup produces different but musically relevant pitch changes upon repeated pad triggers. Additionally, vocal chops, saturated with echo and reverb, are layered with long ethereal synth pads. These pads are grouped using the same choke/mute group to prevent unwanted muddiness and dissonance. This setup delivers a liquid drum and bass vibe.

IDEAS:

Multiple bass samples per pad - Assign multiple bass samples per pad, each an octave apart, with the cycle/random/alt feature enabled for varied pitch changes on repeated pad triggers..

Echo and reverb on vocal chops - Saturate vocal chops with echo and reverb for an ethereal effect.

Layered synth pads - Layer long ethereal synth pads with vocal chops.

Choke/mute groups - Use choke/mute groups to prevent muddiness and dissonance.

MUSIC CHOPS

LATELY

VOXPAD 1 13	VOXPAD 2 14	VOXPAD 3 15	VOXPAD 4 16
BASS 1 9	BASS 2 10	BASS 3 11	BASS 4 12
SIDESTICK 5	SNARE ROLL 6	HAT 1 7	HAT 2 8
KICK 1	SNARE 1 2	SNARE 2 3	RIDE 4

DOWNLOAD ALL KITS: 

MUSIC CHOPS

145BPM

L

16

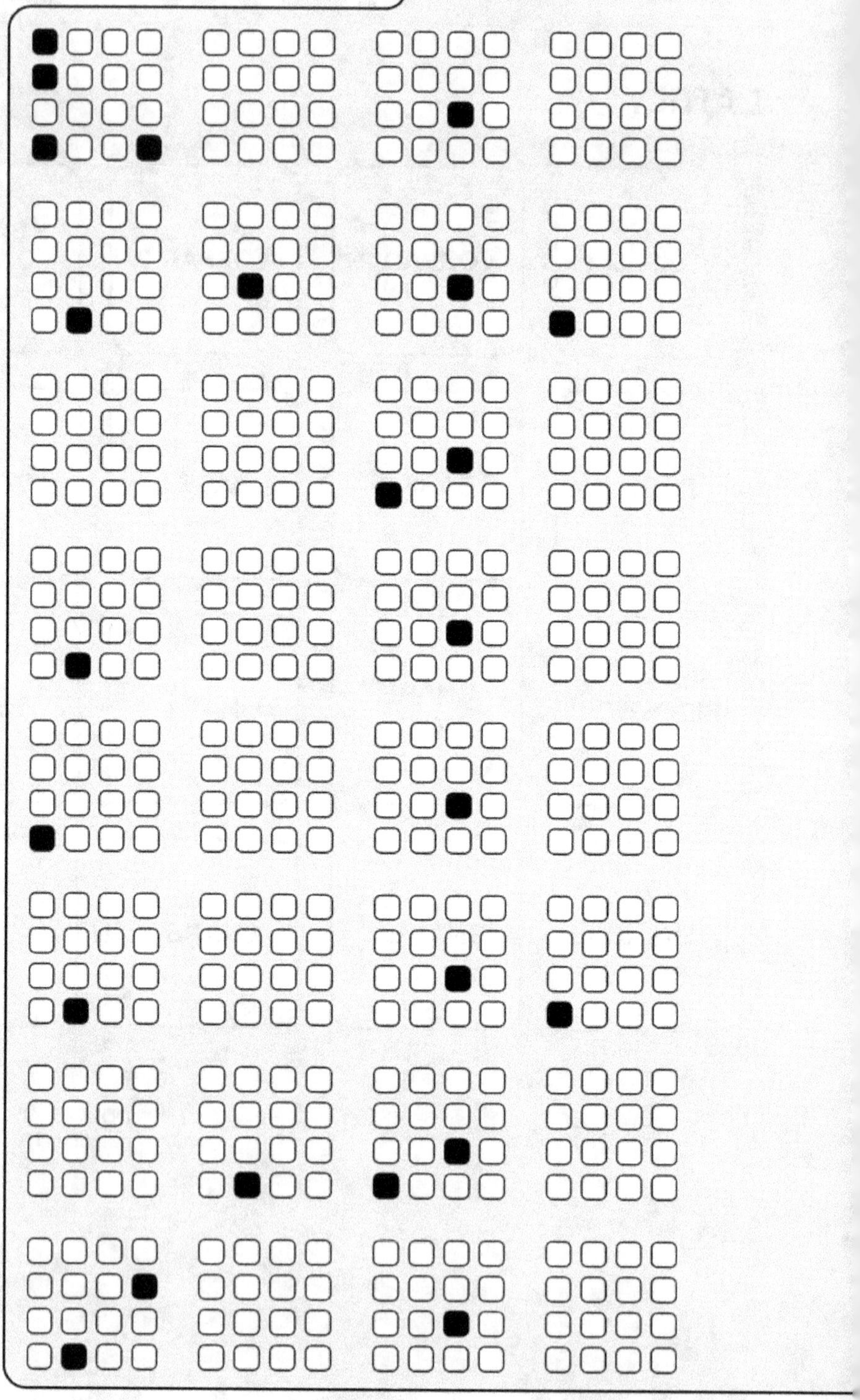

145BPM

L

MUSIC CHOPS

LATELY 5/8

145BPM

MUSIC CHOPS

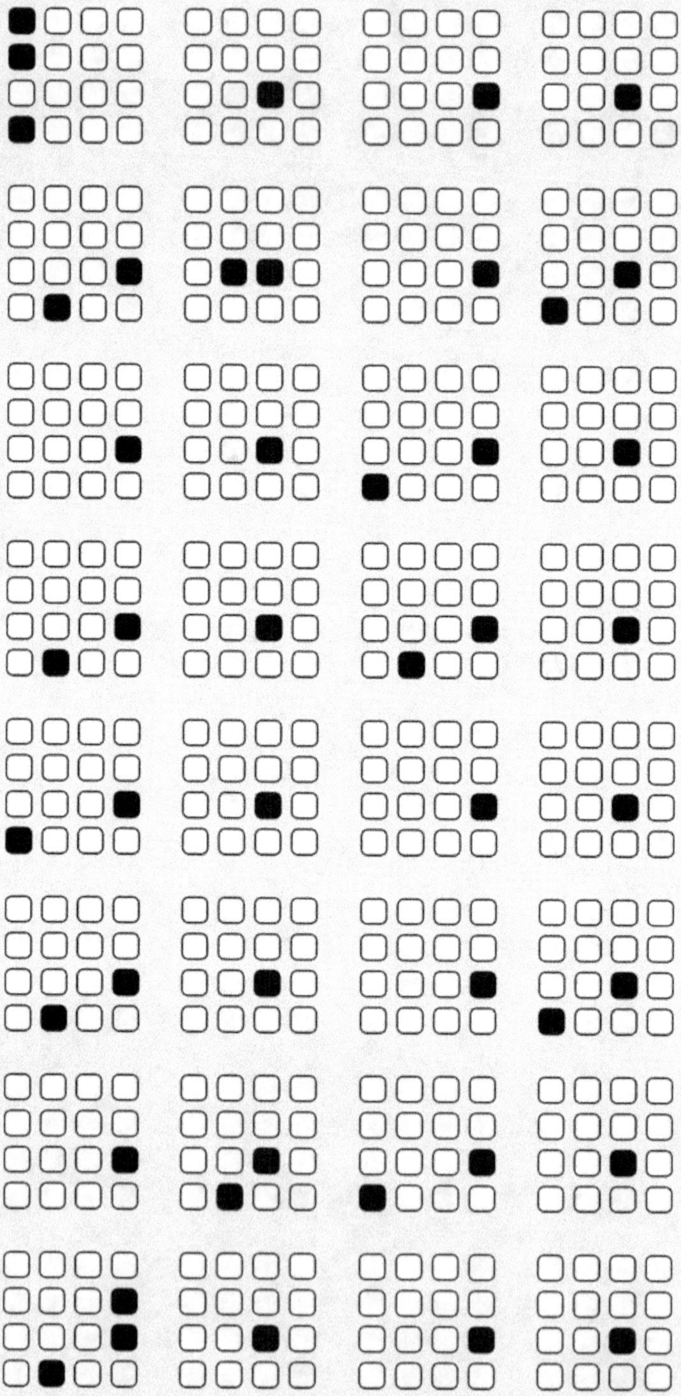

L

145BPM

MUSIC CHOPS

LATELY 7/8

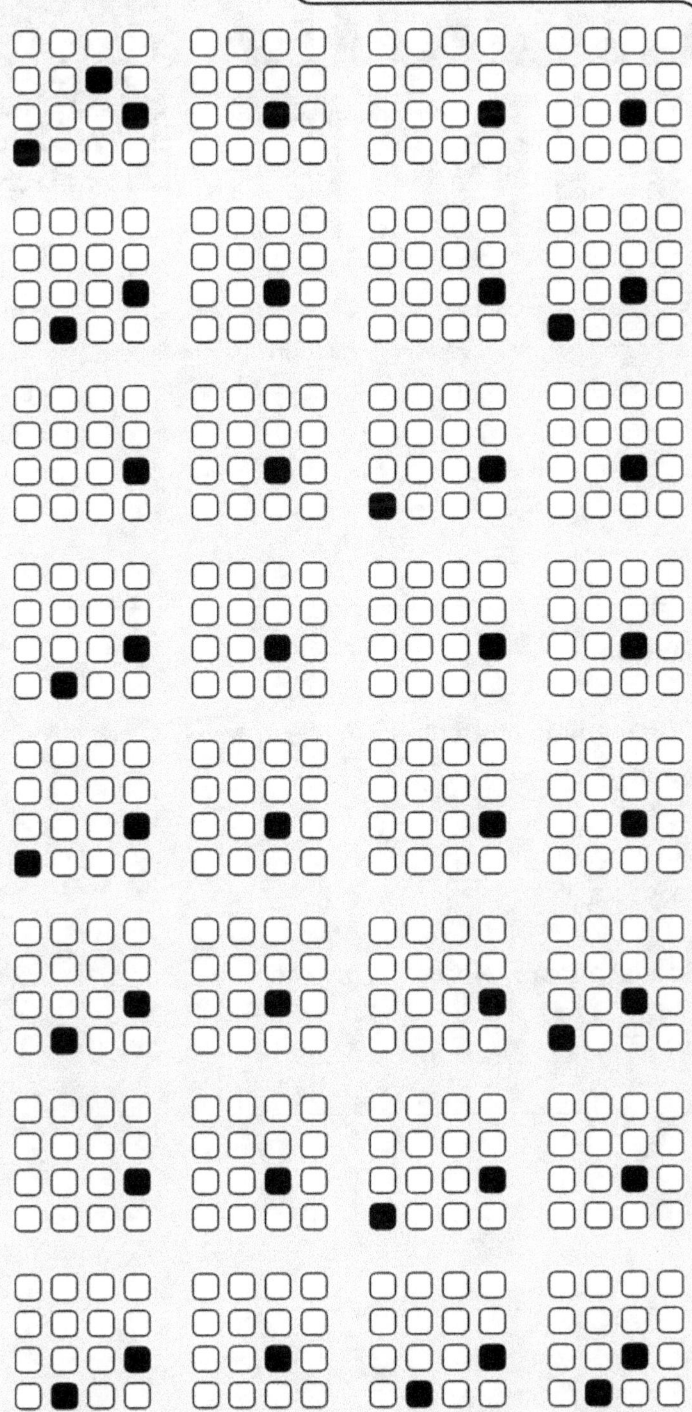

LATELY

LIQUID TIME

This example showcases the creative possibilities of using extreme time stretching and reverse effects combined with spatial effects such as reverb and echo. The piano takes on a unique texture due to the time-stretching modes. This setup features syncopated rhythmic sequences paired with lo-fi jazz piano, creating a captivating and textured soundscape.

IDEAS:

Extreme time stretching - Apply extreme time stretching to transform the texture of samples.

Reverse effects - Use reverse effects to create interesting sound variations.

Spatial effects - Add reverb and echo to enhance the spatial dimension of the sound and to smooth out abrupt releases due to the sample chopping process.

LIQUID TIME

CHOP 1 13	CHOP 2 14	CHOP 3 15	CHOP 4 16
CHOP 5 9	CHOP 6 10	CHOP 7 11	CHOP 8 12
HAT OPEN 5	SNARE ROLL 6	HAT 7	SNARE 3 8
KICK 1	SNARE 1 2	SNARE 2 3	RIDE 4

DOWNLOAD ALL KITS:

16

LT

160BPM

MUSIC CHOPS

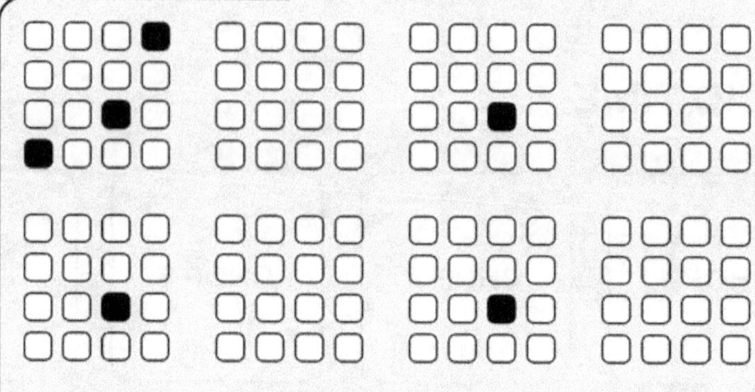

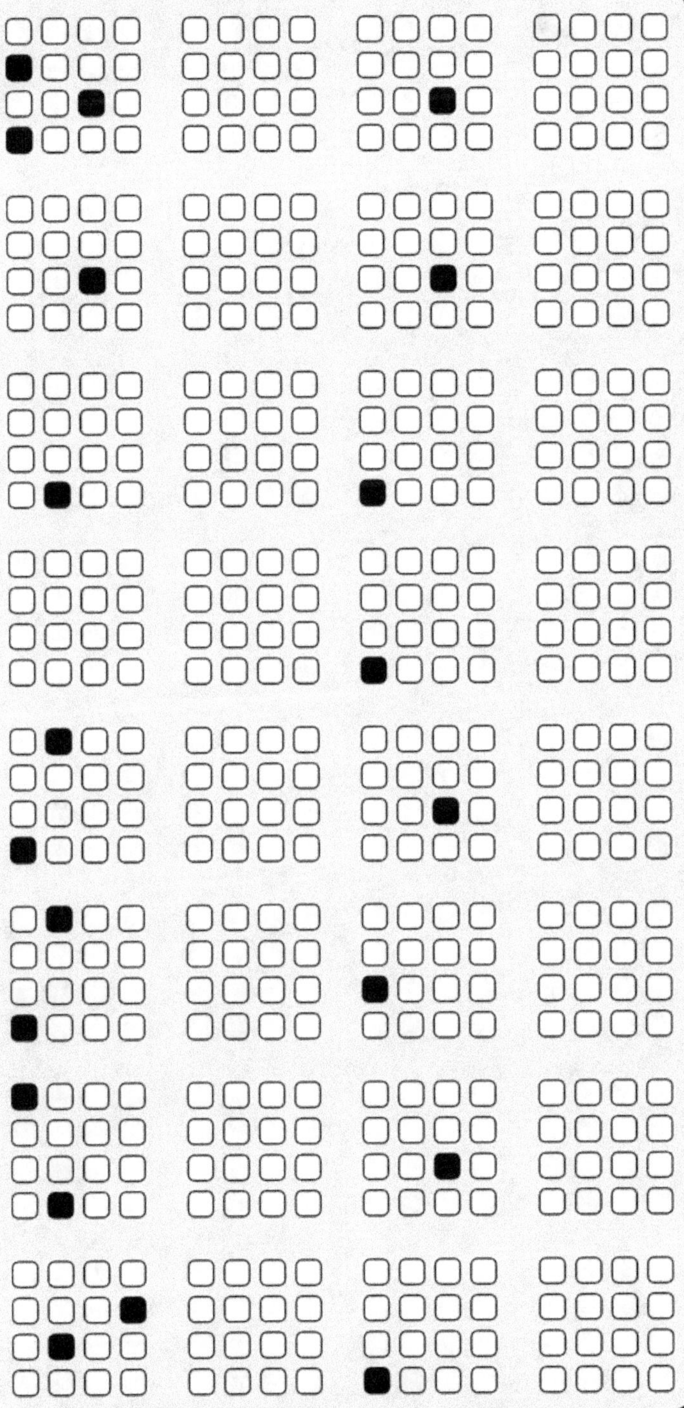

LT

160BPM

MUSIC CHOPS

LIQUID TIME 3/8

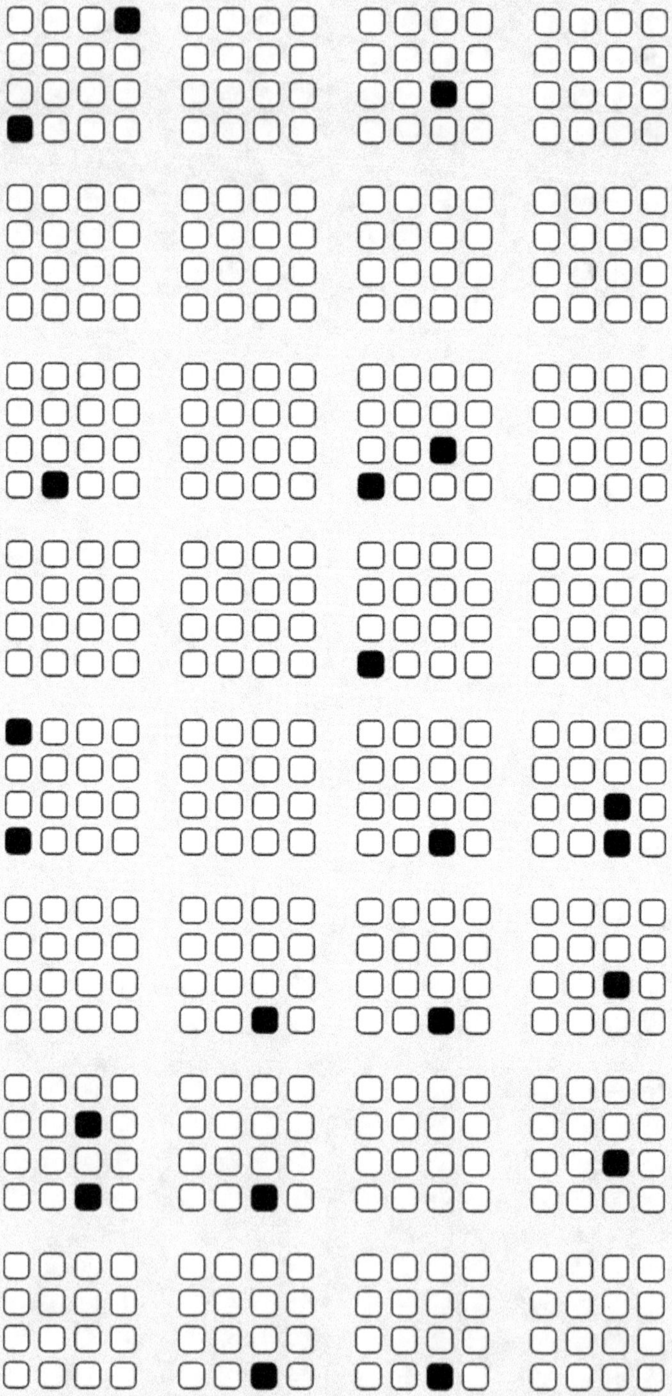

LT

160BPM

MUSIC CHOPS

LIQUID TIME 5/8

160BPM LT

MUSIC CHOPS

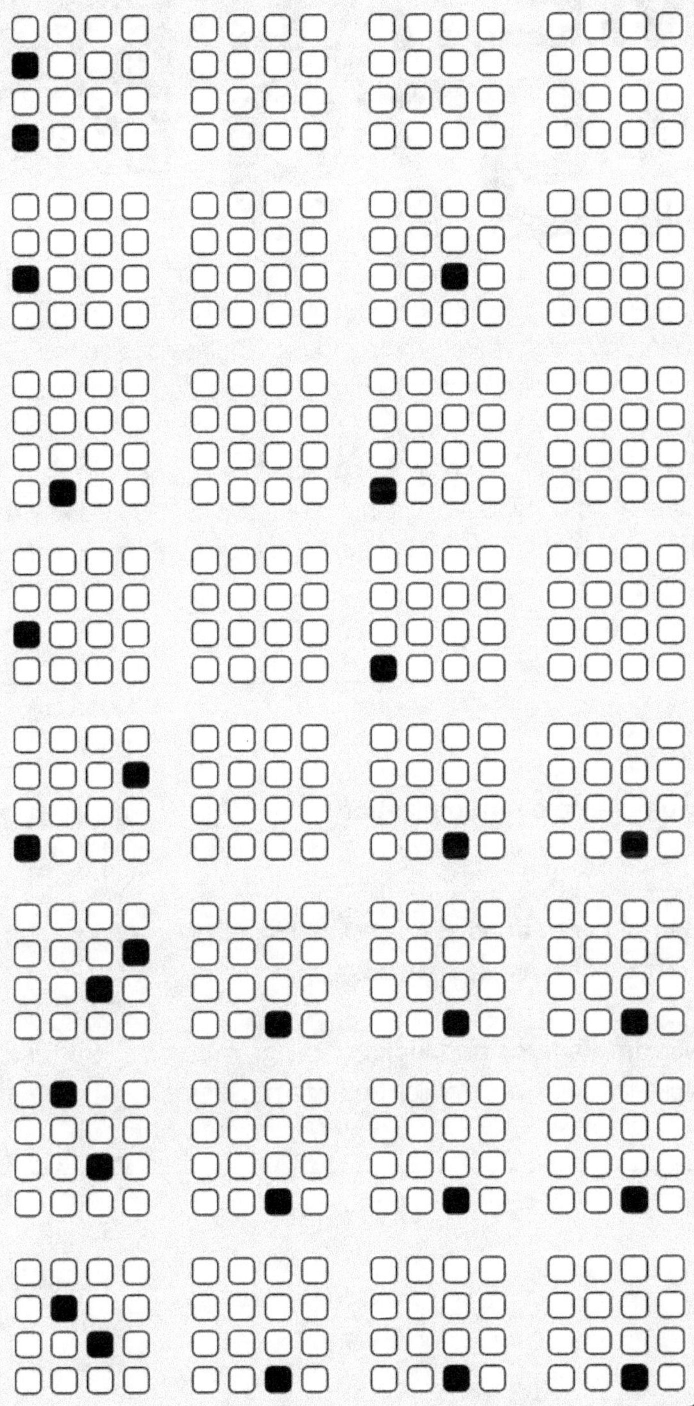
LIQUID TIME

METAL 1979

Nearly every sample in this layout utilizes multi-sample randomization to create a more organic and realistic sound. The snare drums, kicks, and bass one-shots are each sampled four times, with slight tonal variations to mimic the natural human imperfections of a drummer or bassist. In addition to the multi-sample configuration, this layout features mirrored snares and kicks, facilitating quick double kick and snare patterns common in metal and rock music.

> **IDEAS:**
>
> **Multi-sample randomization** - Use multiple samples of each sound to create a more organic and realistic texture.
>
> **Sample variations** - Include slight tonal variations for each instance of snare, kick, and bass one-shots.
>
> **Mirrored snares and kicks** - Arrange mirrored snares and kicks for quick double kick and snare patterns.

METAL 1979

A2 DISTORTED BASS 13	B2 DISTORTED BASS 14	F#3 DISTORTED BASS 15	C#4 DISTORTED BASS 16
F# DISTORTED BASS 9	G DISTORTED BASS 10	A DISTORTED BASS 11	E DISTORTED BASS 12
HAT CLOSED LEFT 5	SNARE LEFT 6	SNARE RIGHT 7	HAT OPEN RIGHT 8
LOW TOM LEFT 1	KICK LEFT 2	KICK RIGHT 3	CRASH RIGHT 4

MUSIC CHOPS
157BPM
M9
16
METAL 1979 1/8

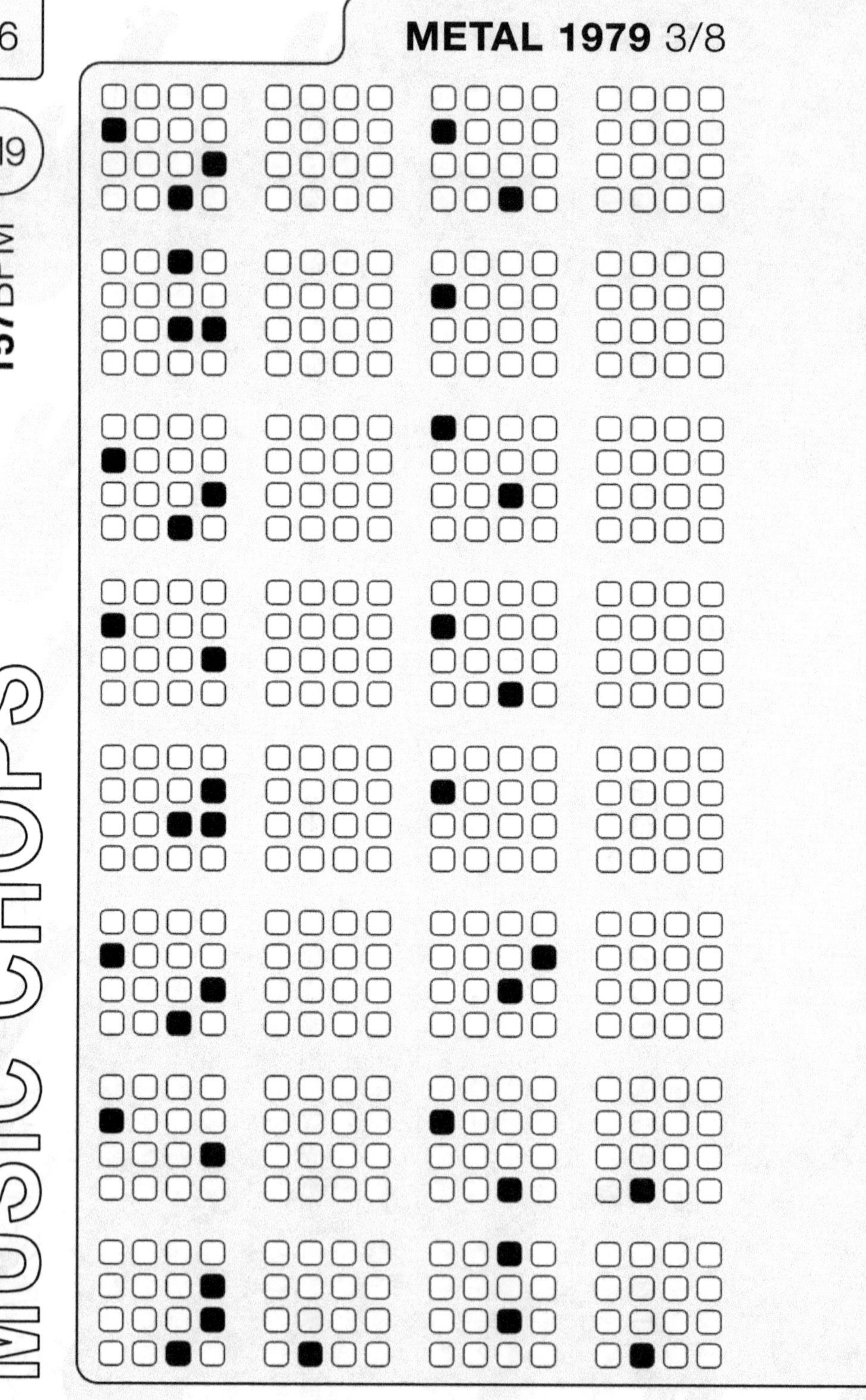

MUSIC CHOPS

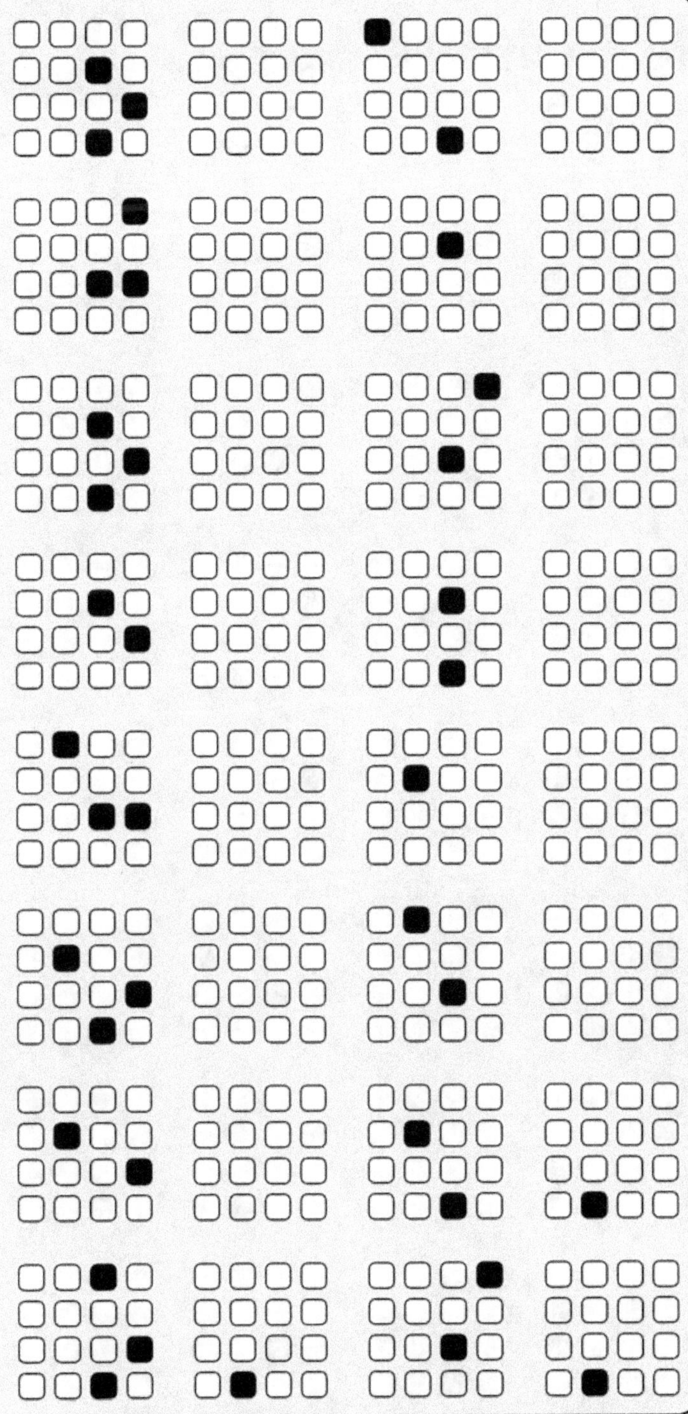

157BPM

M9

MUSIC CHOPS

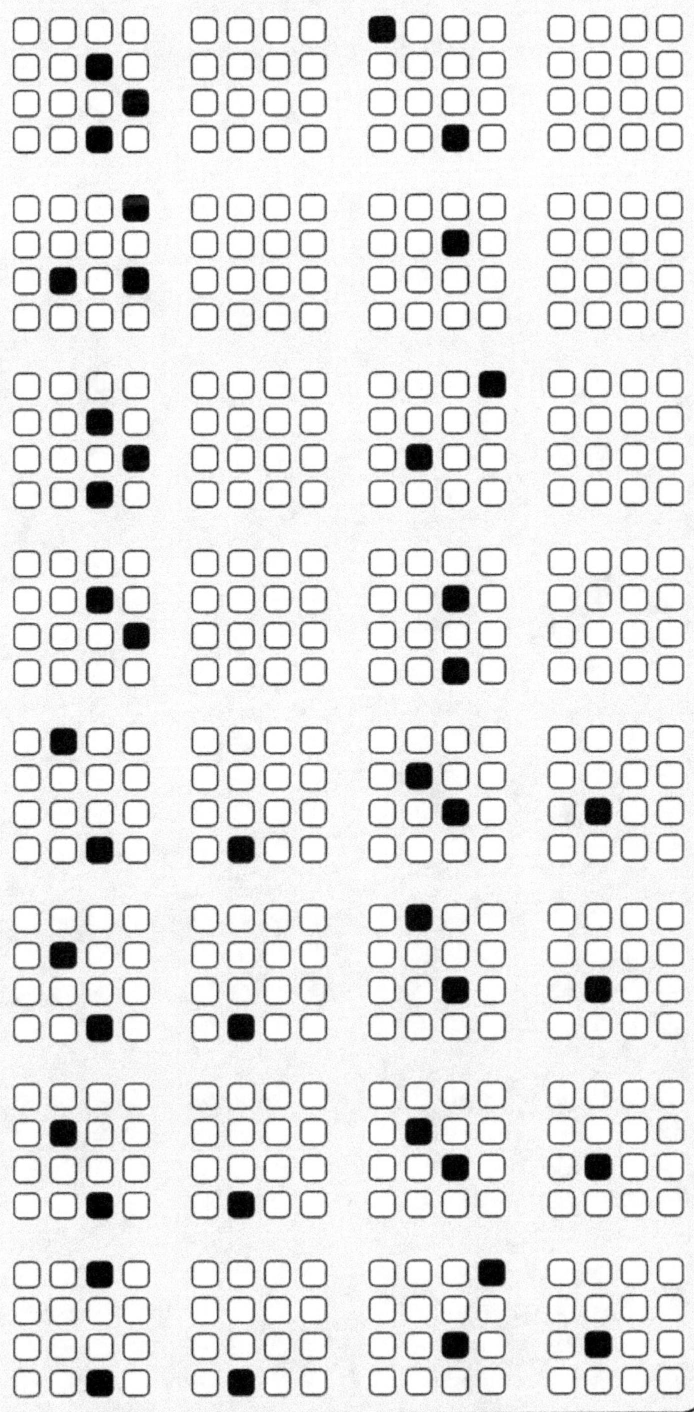

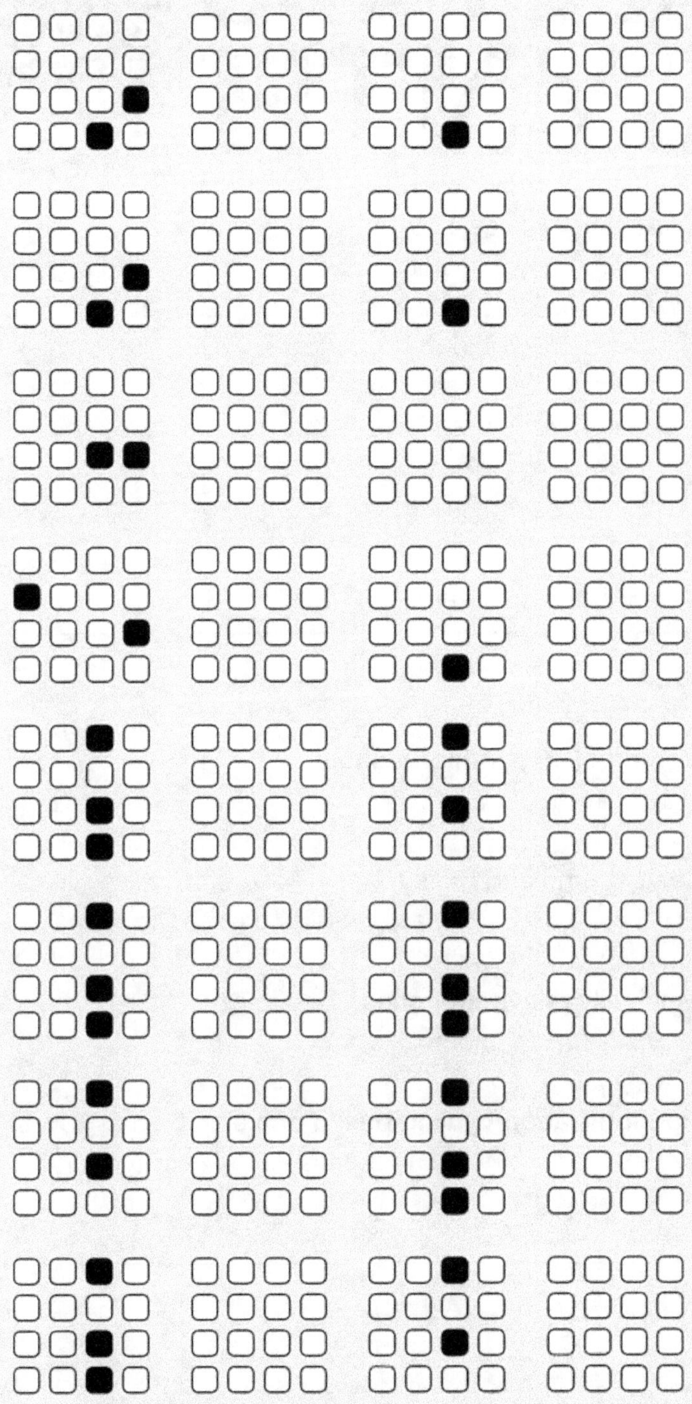

METAL 1979

ALL PADS SYNTH

This example features a spread of 16 synth one-shots within the same musical key. The bottom two rows contain lead synths, while the top two rows are dedicated to bass tones. This technique not only looks impressive during a performance but also ensures that only musically relevant pitches are included, making it perfect for improvisation. Additionally, this method becomes even more powerful when multiple samples are randomized or cycled based on velocity changes. This setup creates a trance-style electronic sequence.

IDEAS:

Spread of 16 synth one-shots - Arrange 16 synth one-shots in the same musical key.

Lead synths and bass tones - Place lead synths on the bottom two rows and bass tones on the top two rows.

Musically relevant pitches - Ensure all pitches are musically relevant for easy improvisation.

Randomization/cycling based on velocity - Randomize or cycle through multiple samples based on velocity changes.

ALL SYNTH

D **BASS** 13	**A** **BASS** 14	**G** **BASS** 15	**D** **BASS** 16
G **BASS** 9	**F** **BASS** 10	**A#** **BASS** 11	**A** **BASS** 12
D **LEAD** 5	**D** **LEAD** 6	**A** **LEAD** 7	**A#** **LEAD** 8
A# **LEAD** 1	**F** **LEAD** 2	**G** **LEAD** 3	**C** **LEAD** 4

DOWNLOAD
ALL KITS:

MUSIC CHOPS

95BPM

SY

16

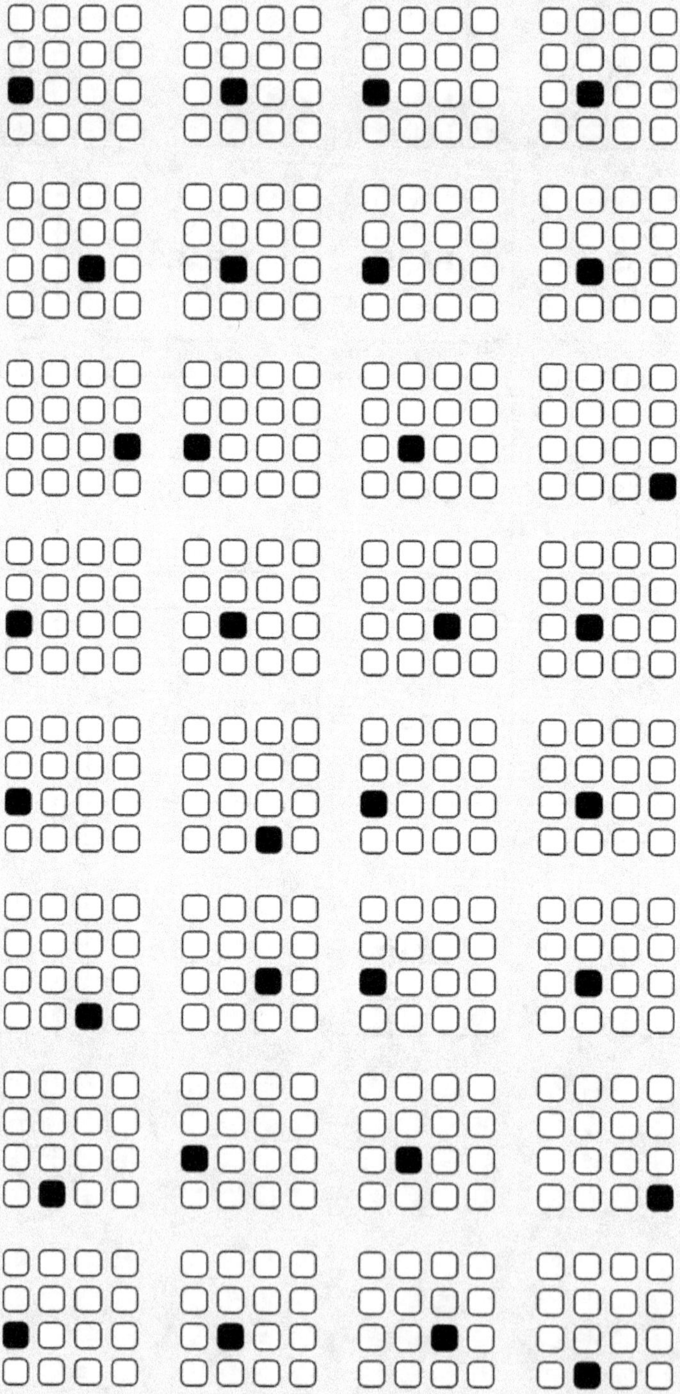

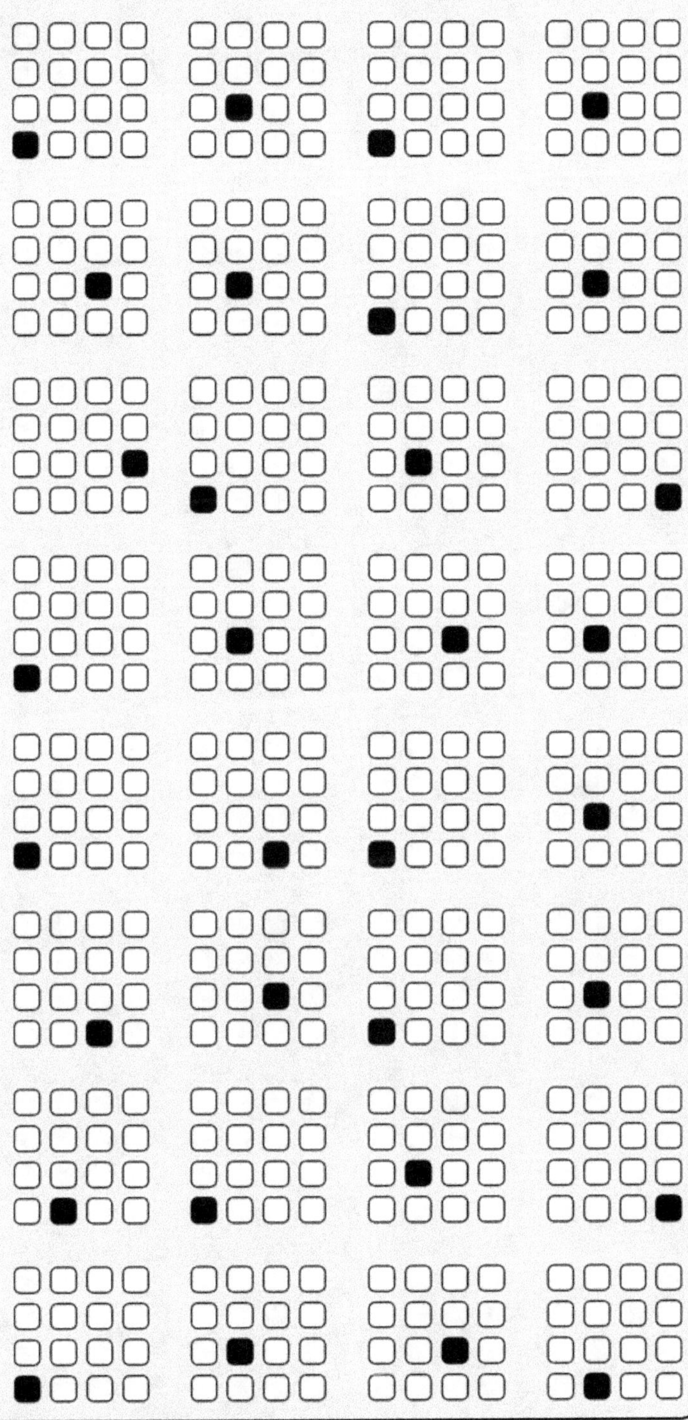

ALL SYNTH

MUSIC CHOPS

MUSIC CHOPS

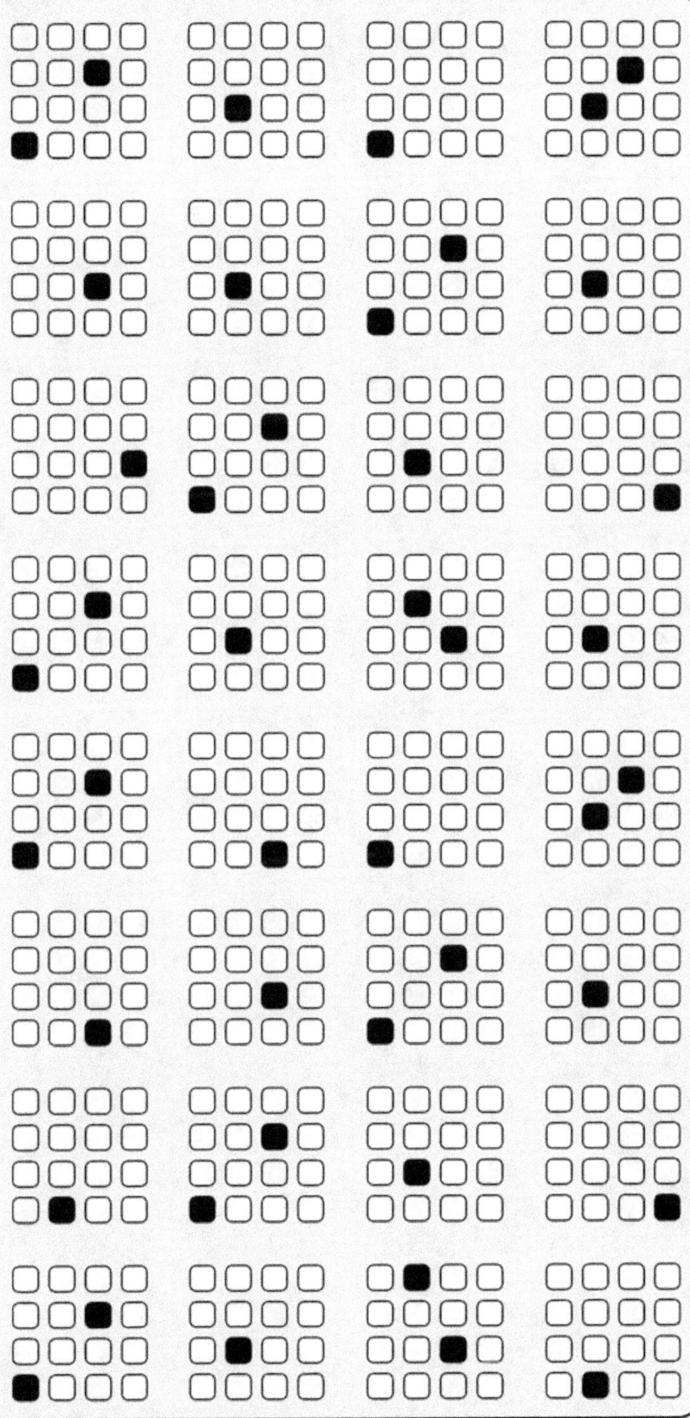

MUSIC CHOPS

95BPM

16

SY

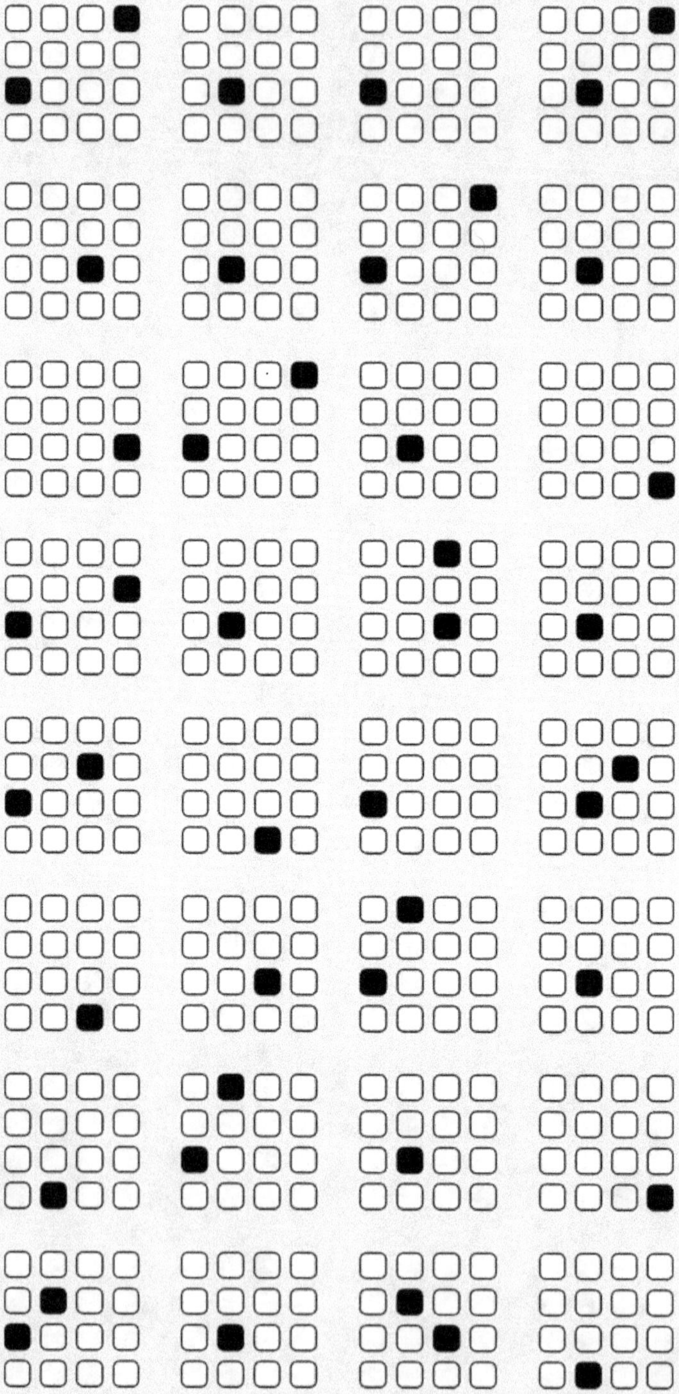

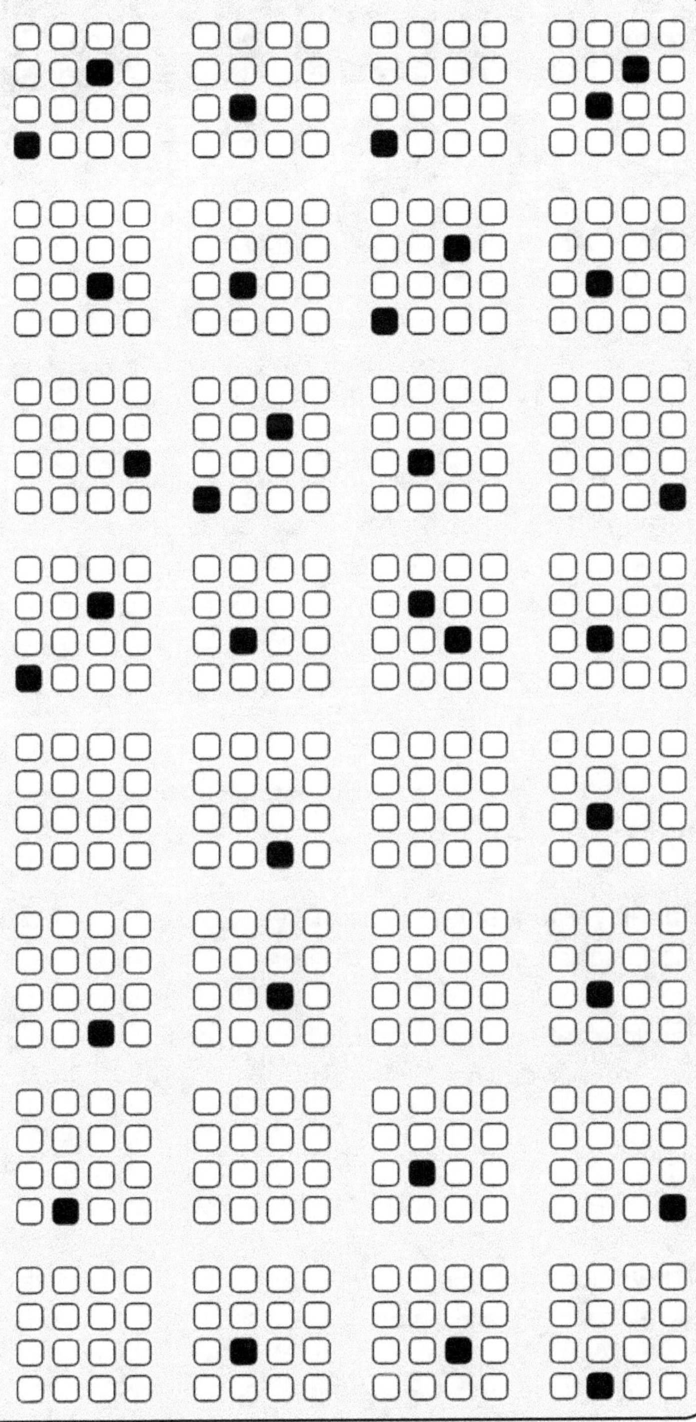

ALIEN BASS

This example leverages multi-layer triggering to create captivating bass and drum sequences. This approach involves triggering different slices of a modulated bass sample simultaneously with each pad loaded with drum sounds. By activating randomization on the bass slices, a unique but cohesive wobble bass effect is achieved with every pad hit. To maintain clarity between the bass and drum one-shots, a slow attack is set on the amp envelope of the bass slices, creating a short, silent space that accommodates the drum attacks. Additionally, a mute/choke group is applied to all bass and hi-hat one-shots to prevent overlapping and resonant build-ups.

IDEAS:

Multi-layer triggering - Assign different slices of a modulated bass sample to trigger simultaneously with drum pads.

Randomization - Activate randomization on bass slices for unique wobble effects with each pad hit.

Slow attack on amp envelope - Set a slow attack on the bass amp envelope to create space for drum attacks.

Mute/Choke groups - Apply mute/choke groups to bass and hi-hat one-shots to avoid overlapping and resonant build-ups.

ALIEN BASS

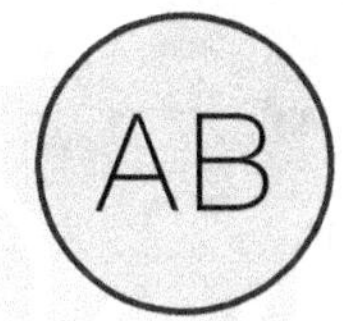

LOW TOM 13	MID TOM 14	HIGH TOM 15	CRASH 16
HAT OPEN 9	SIDESTICK 10	HAT LID 11	SHAKER 12
FLOOR TOM 5	SNARE ROLL 6	HAT CLOSED 7	HAT ROLL 8
KICK 1	SNARE 1 2	SNARE 2 3	RIDE 4

DOWNLOAD ALL KITS: 

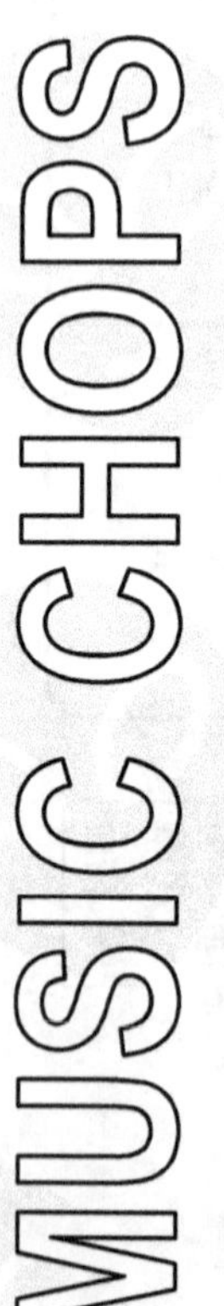

8

AB

90BPM

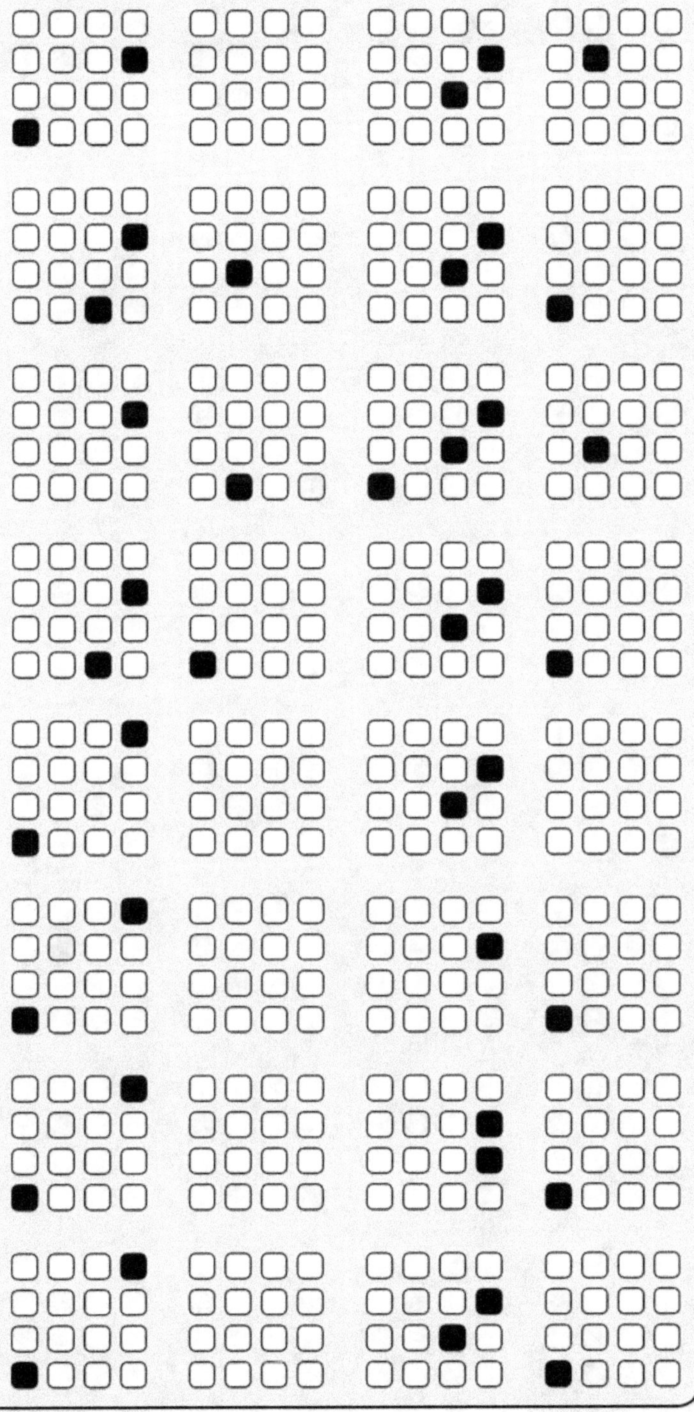

ALIEN BASS

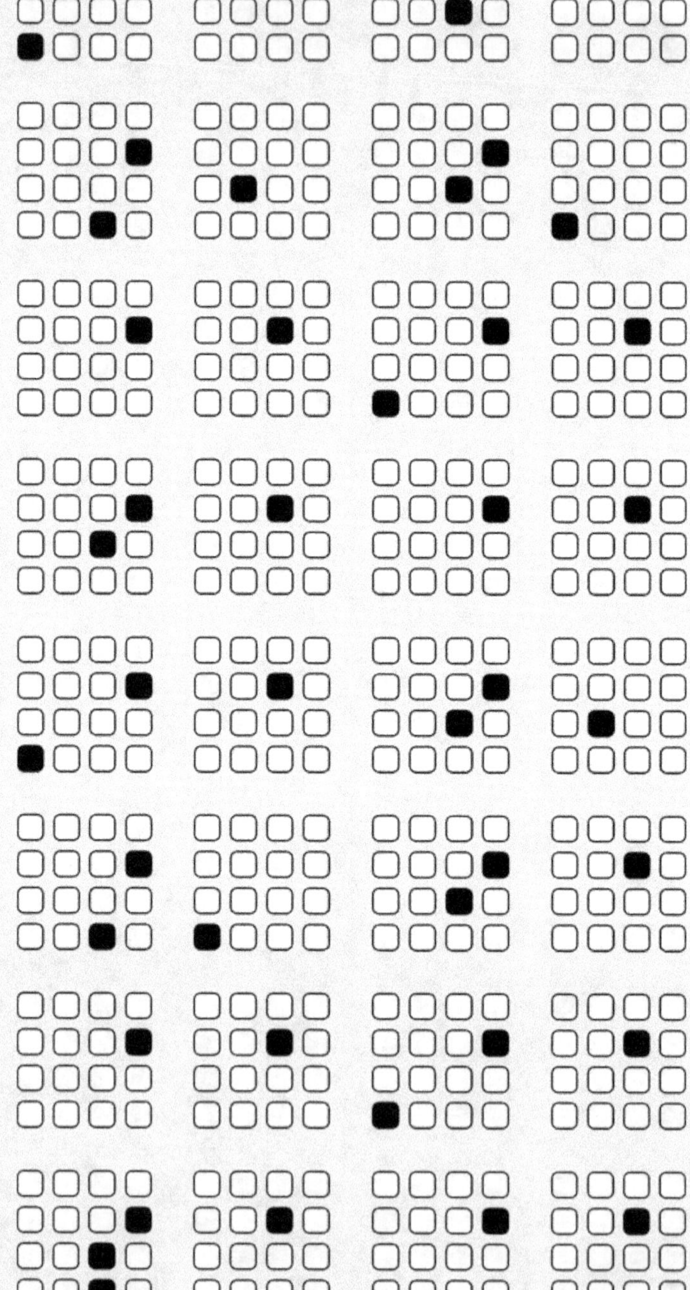

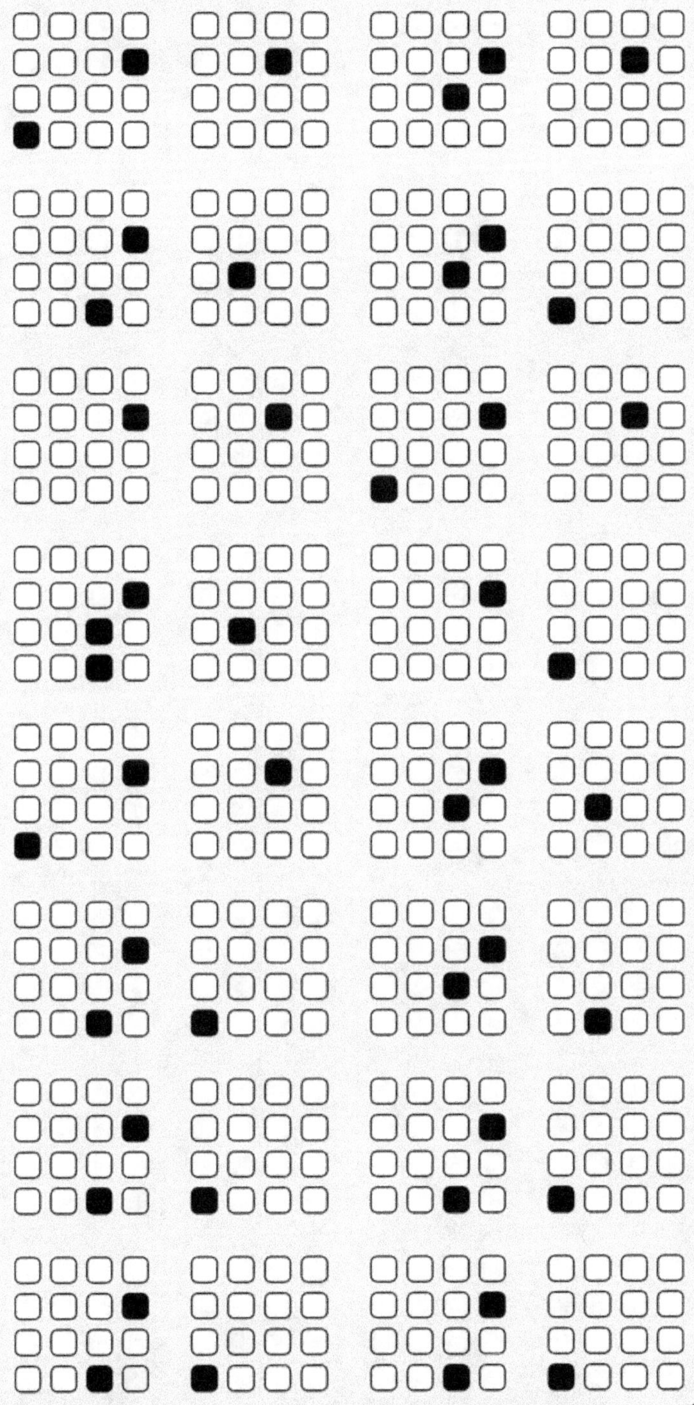
ALIEN BASS

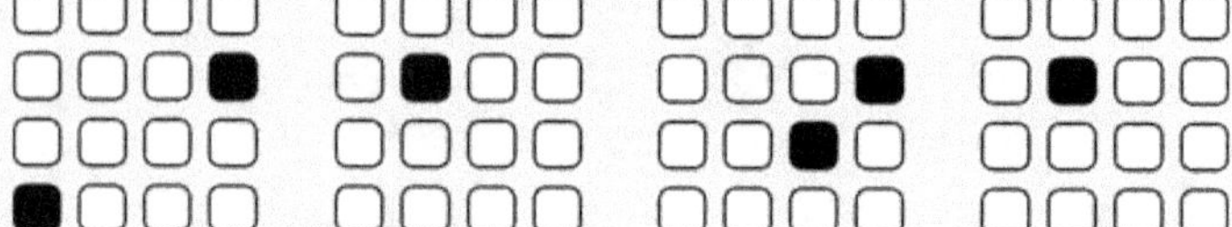

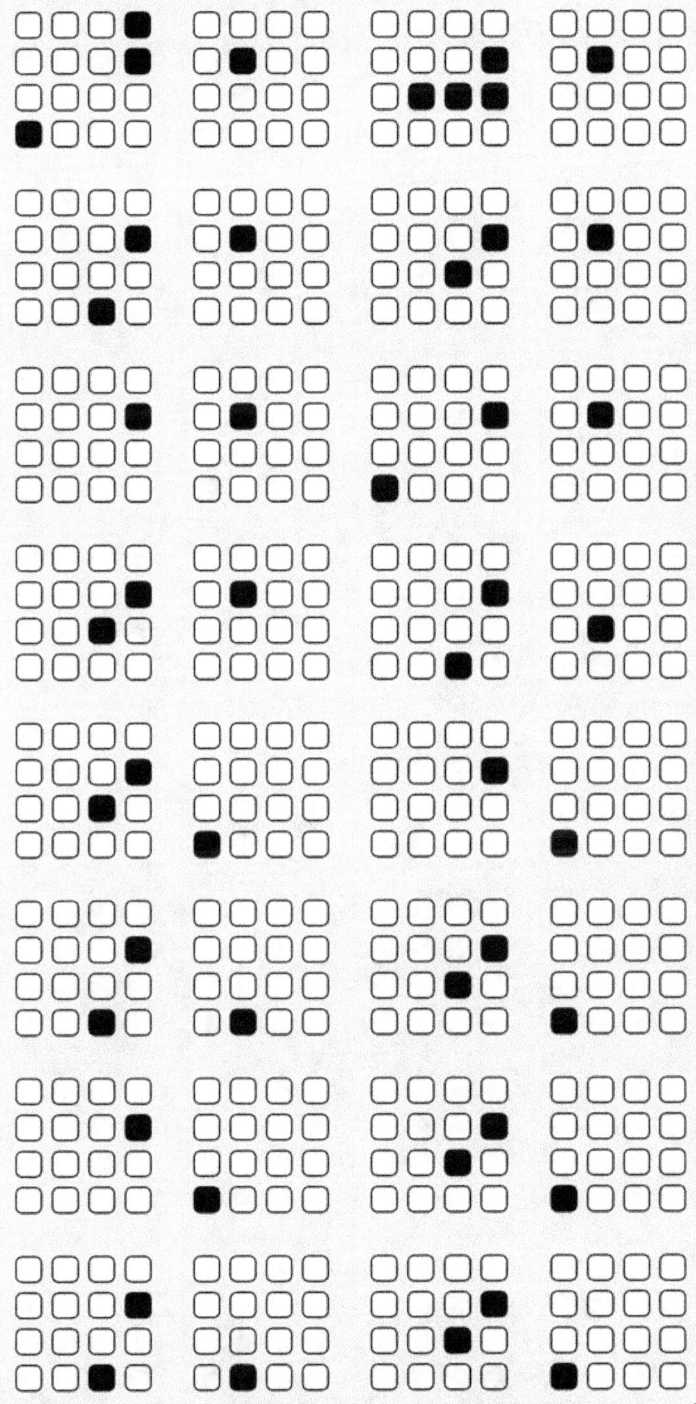

8
AB
90BPM
MUSIC CHOPS

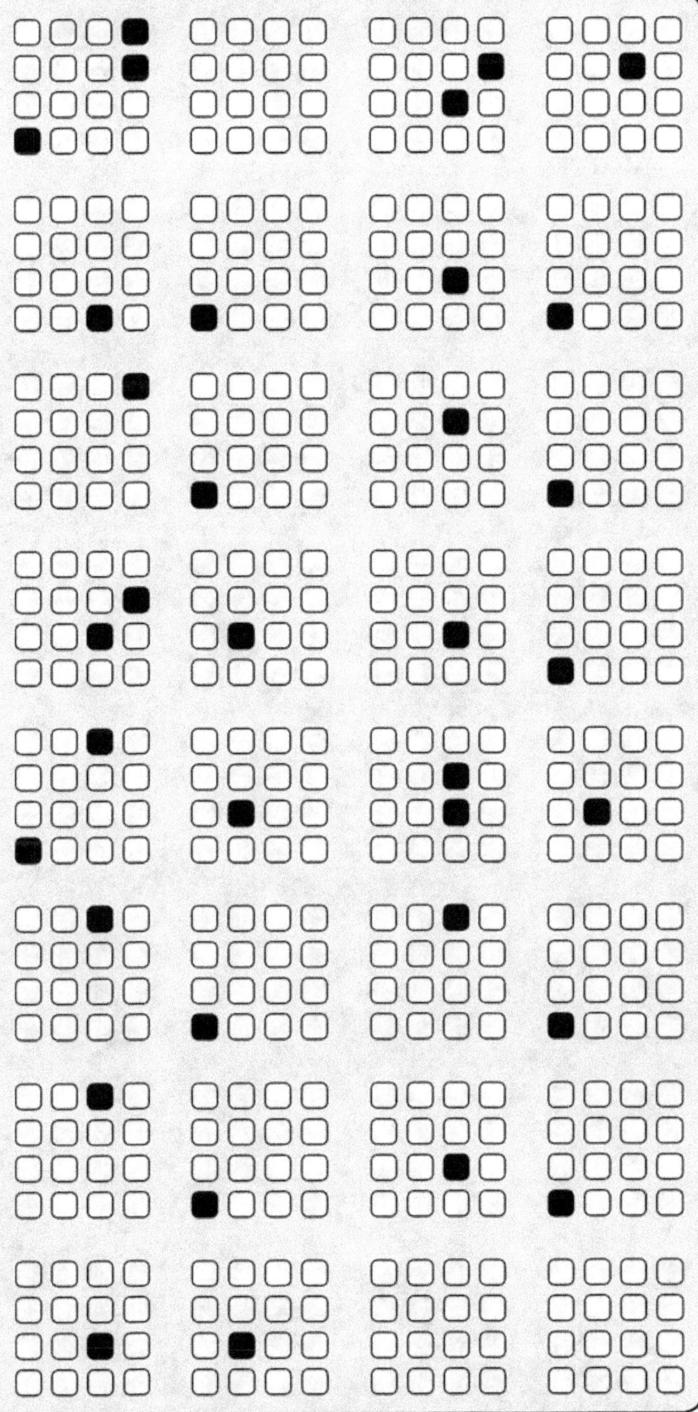

ALIEN BASS

FAVORITES
FAVORITES
FAVORITES
FAVORITES
FAVORITES
FAVORITES
FAVORITES
FAVORITES
FAVORITES

16

SPL

90BPM

FAVORITES

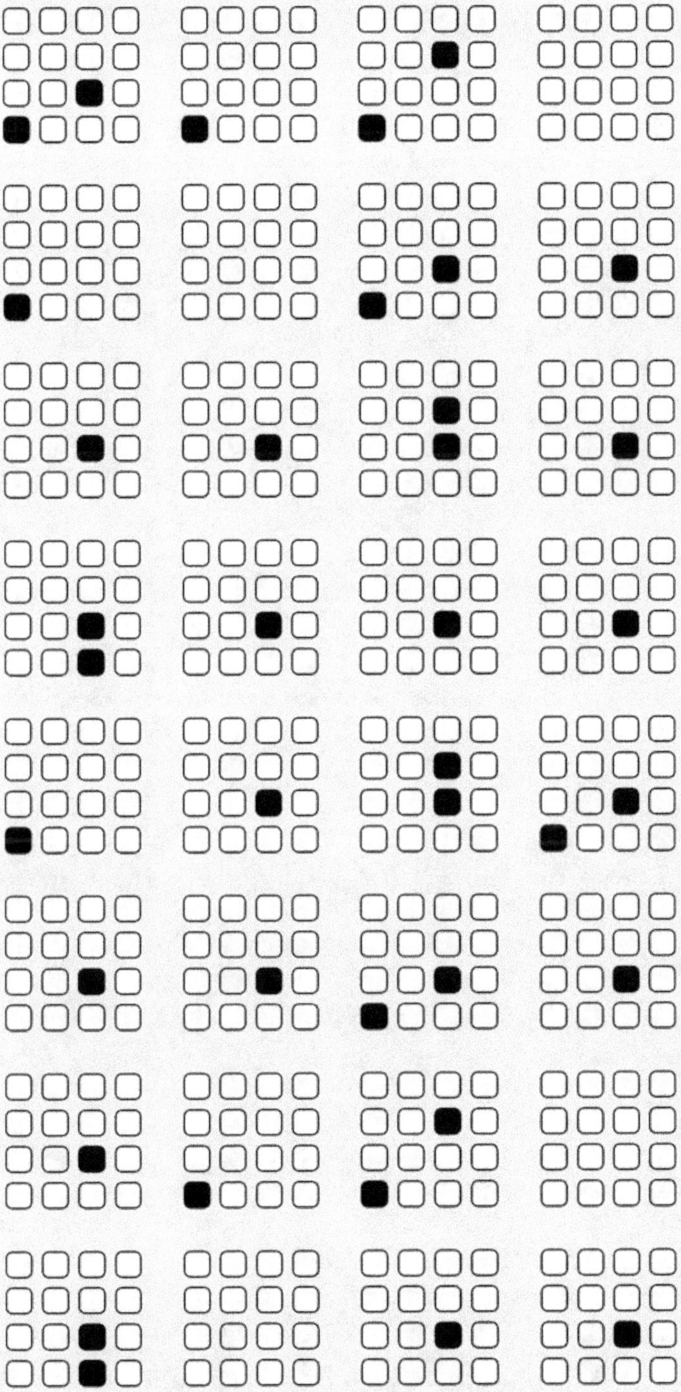

AXIOM

FAVORITES

16

SPL

80BPM

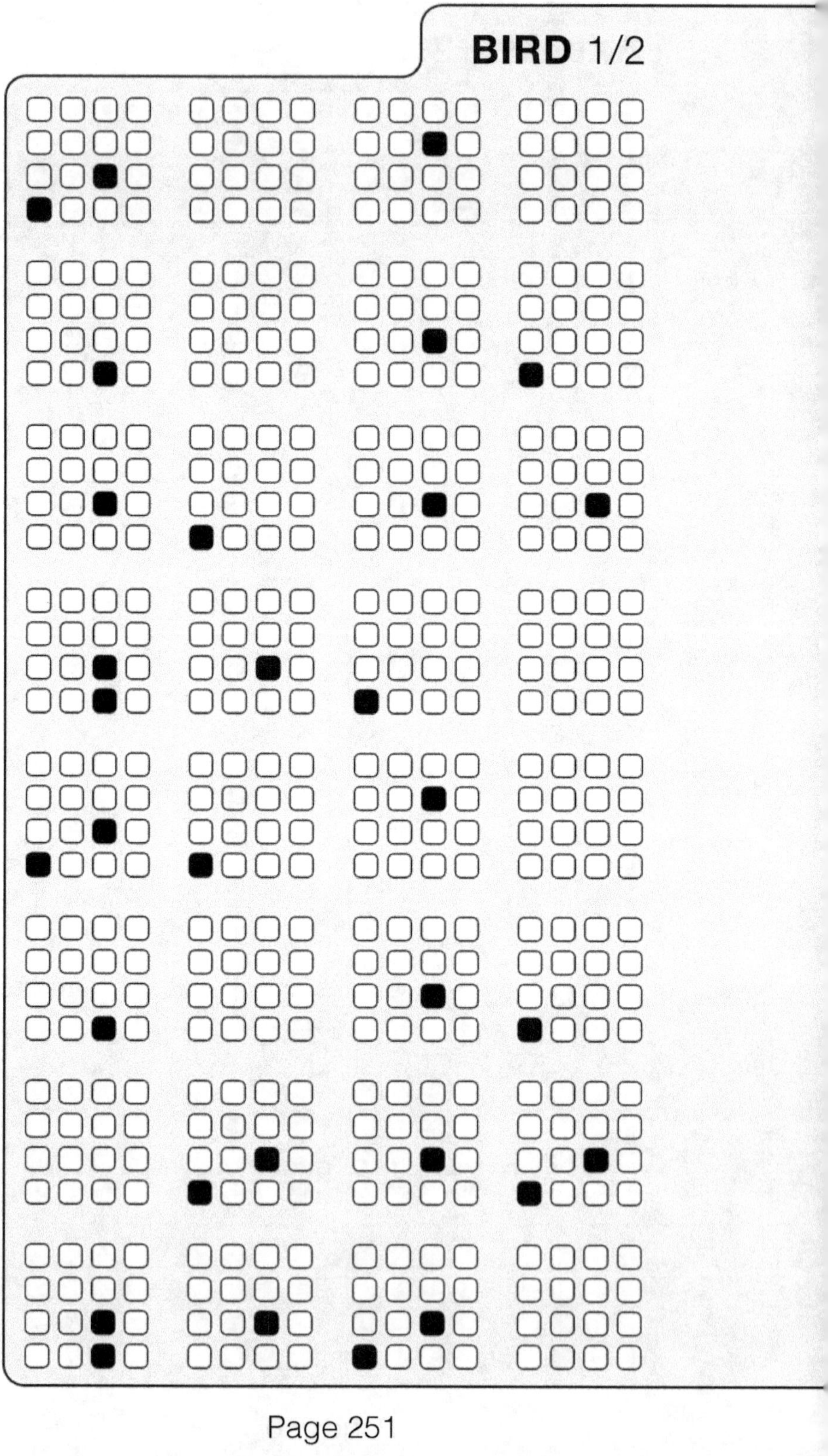

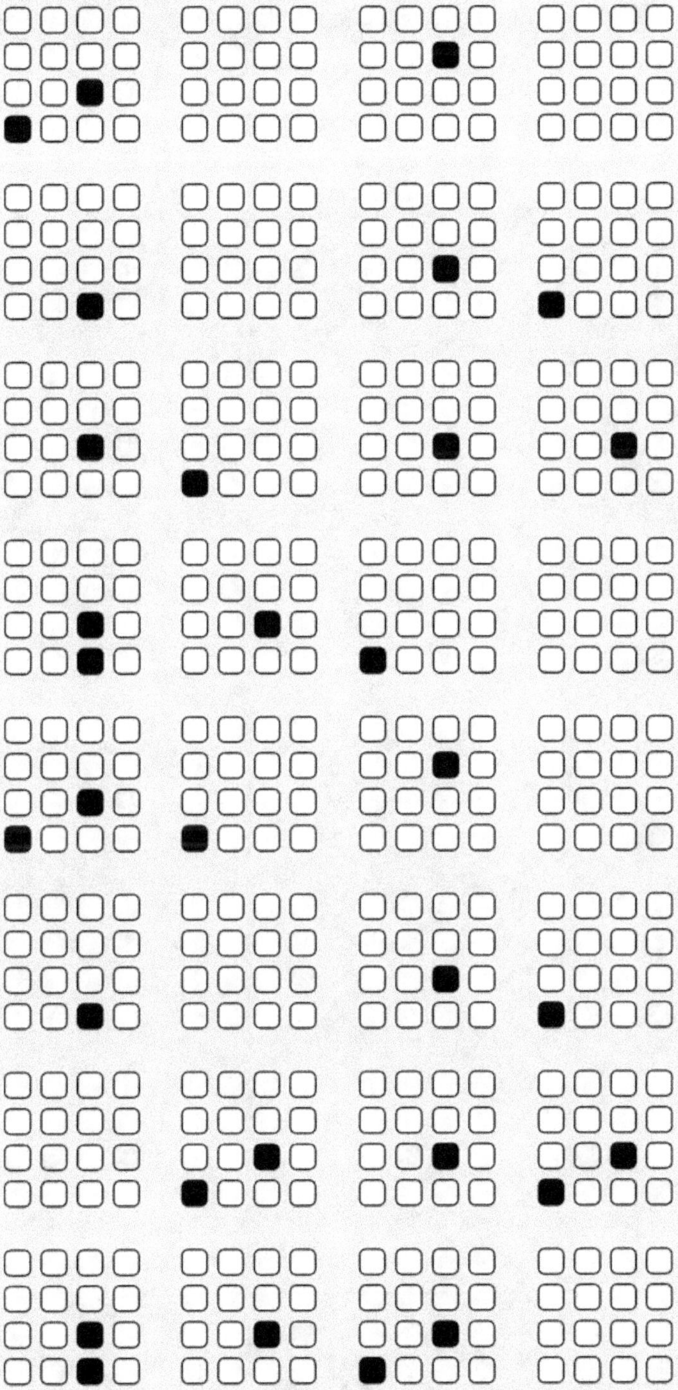

16

SPL

100BPM

FAVORITES

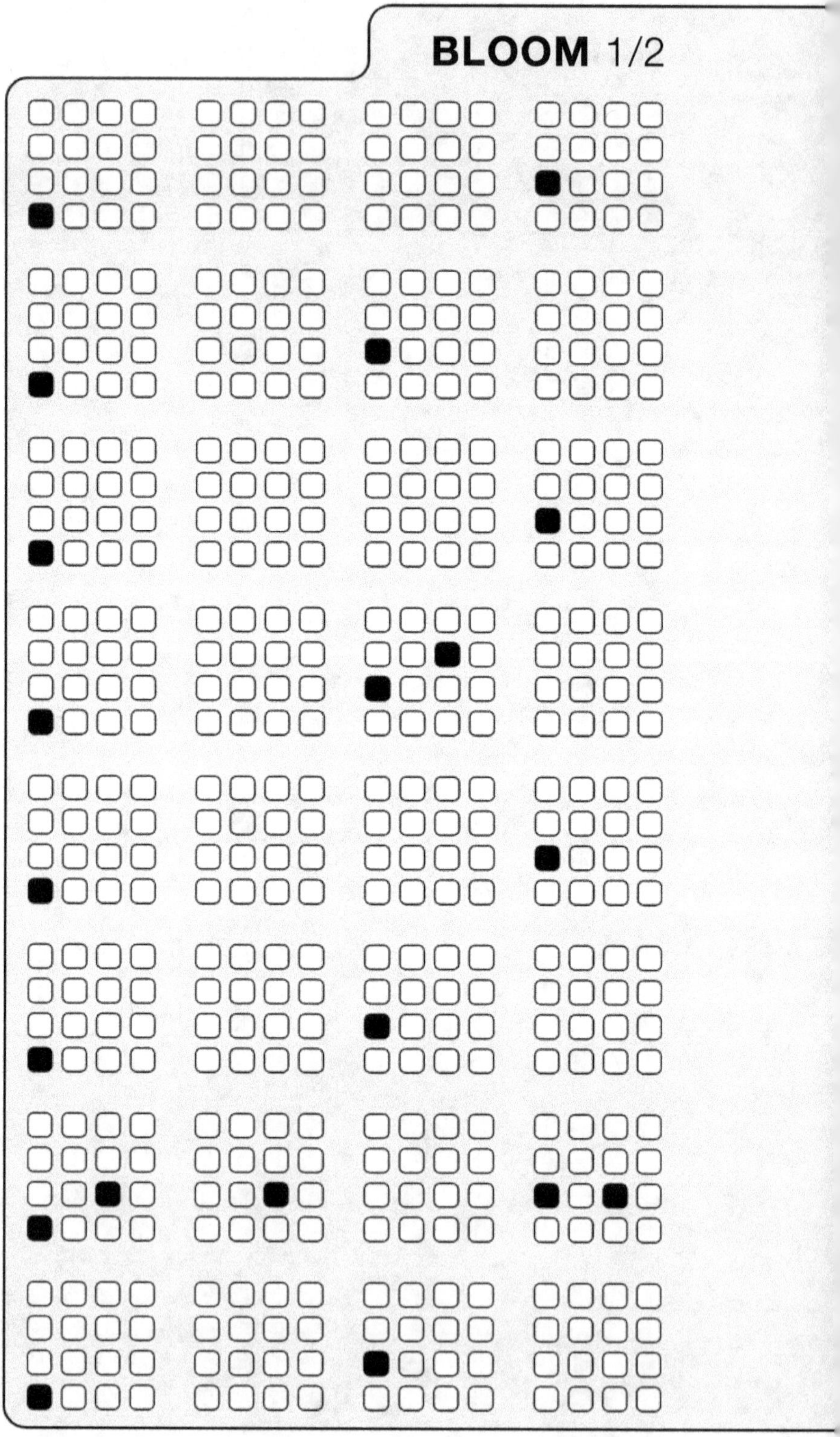

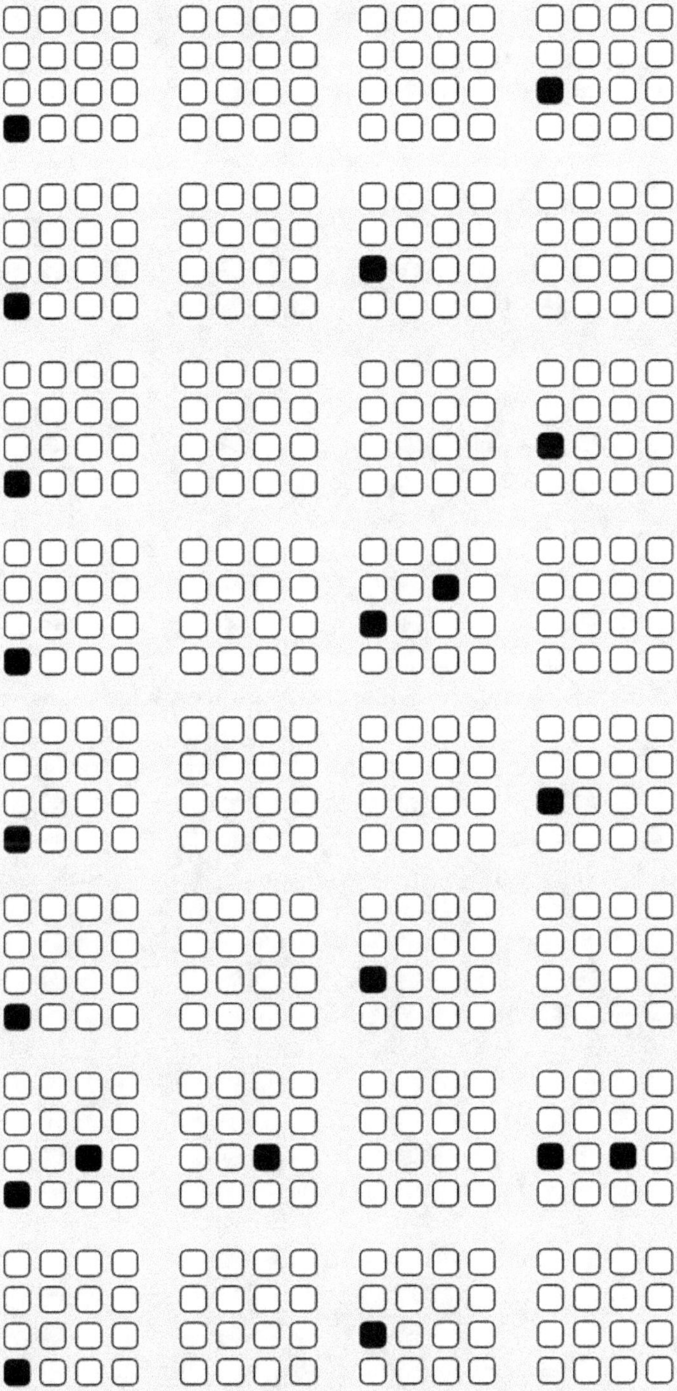

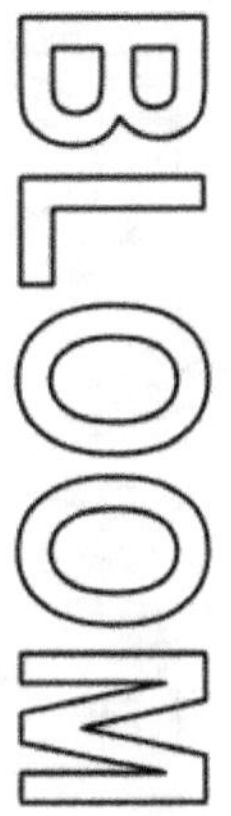
BLOOM

16

SPL

90BPM

BUTTER 1/2

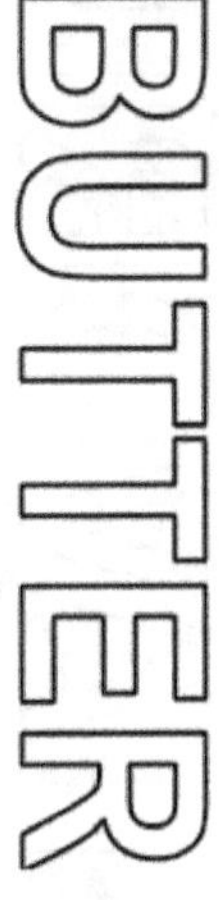
BUTTER

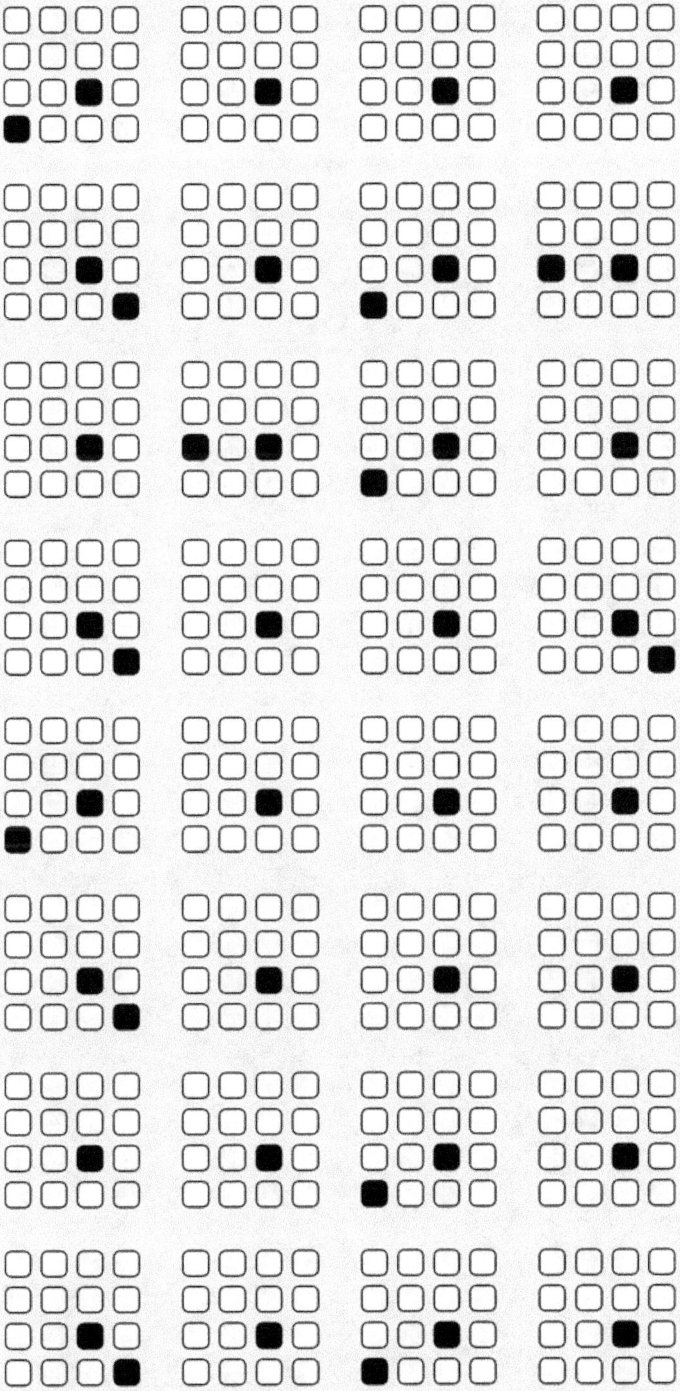

FAVORITES
16
SPL
90BPM

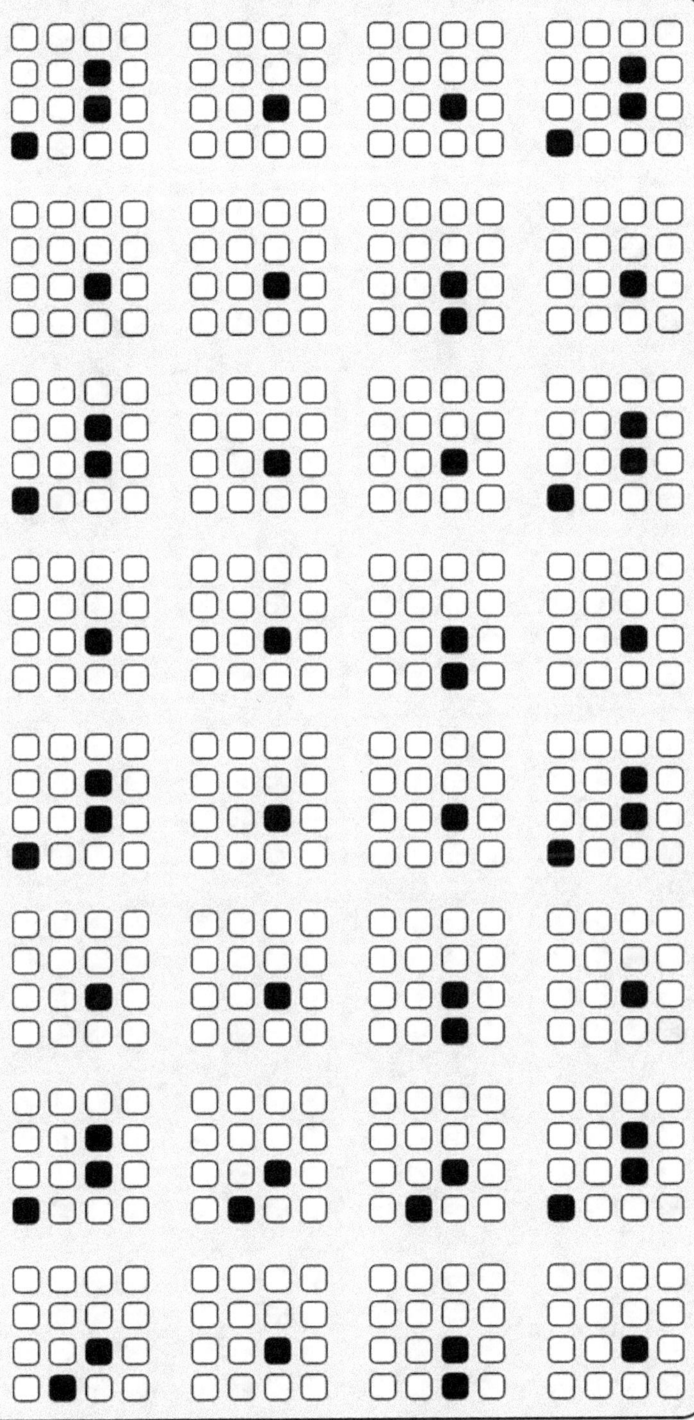

16

SPL

94BPM

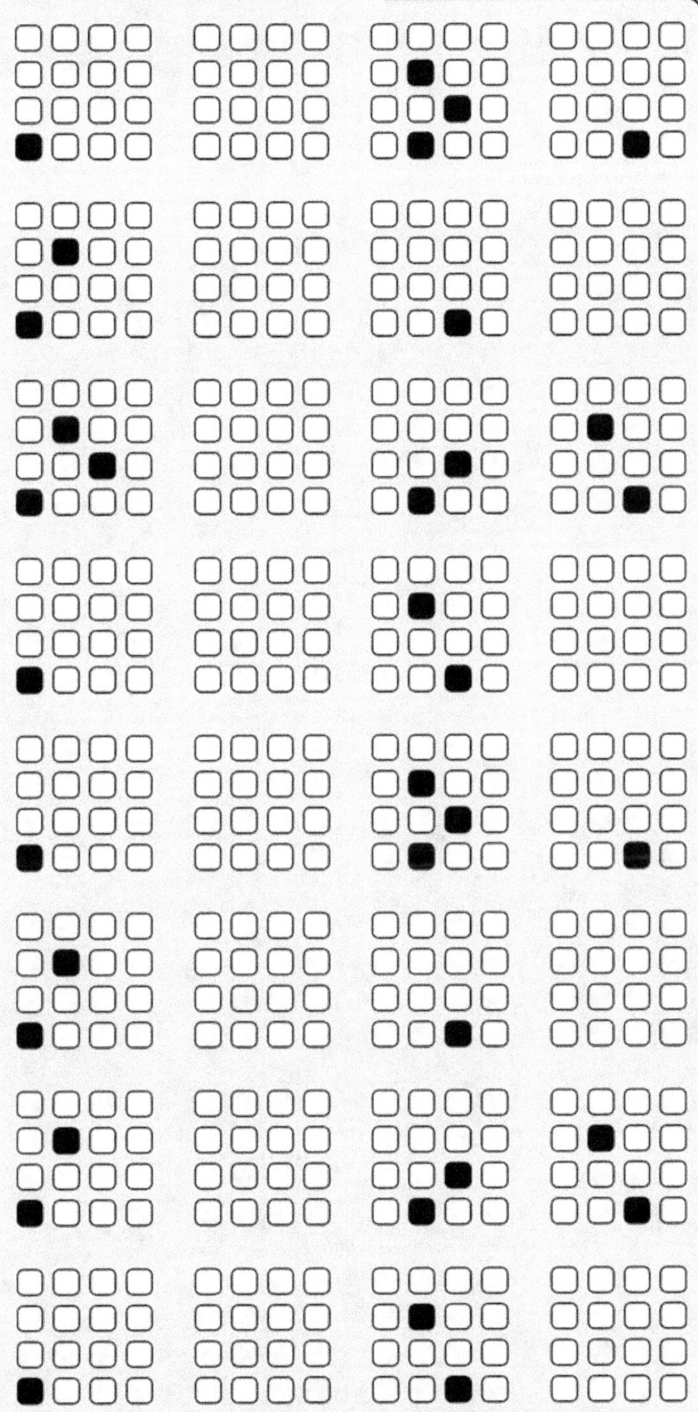

FAVORITES
16
SPL
120BPM
CHRONOS 1/2

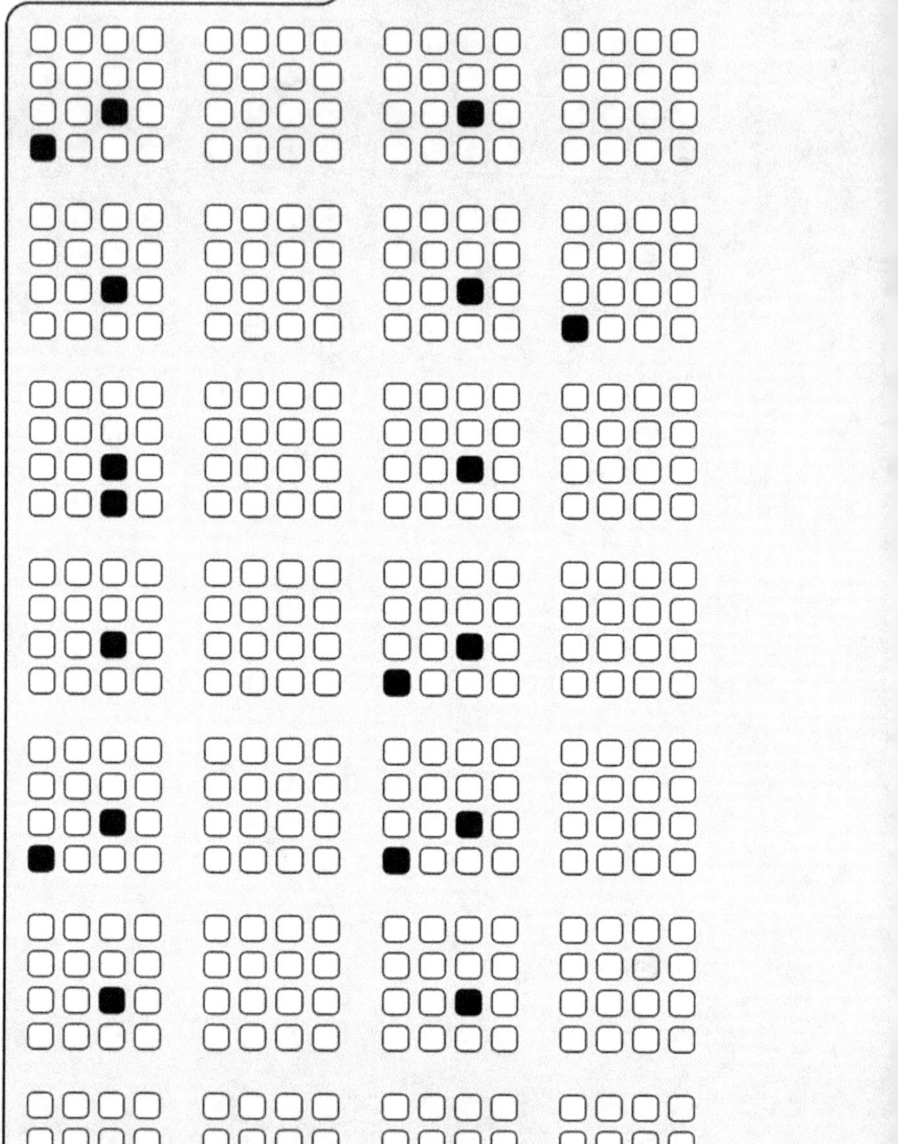

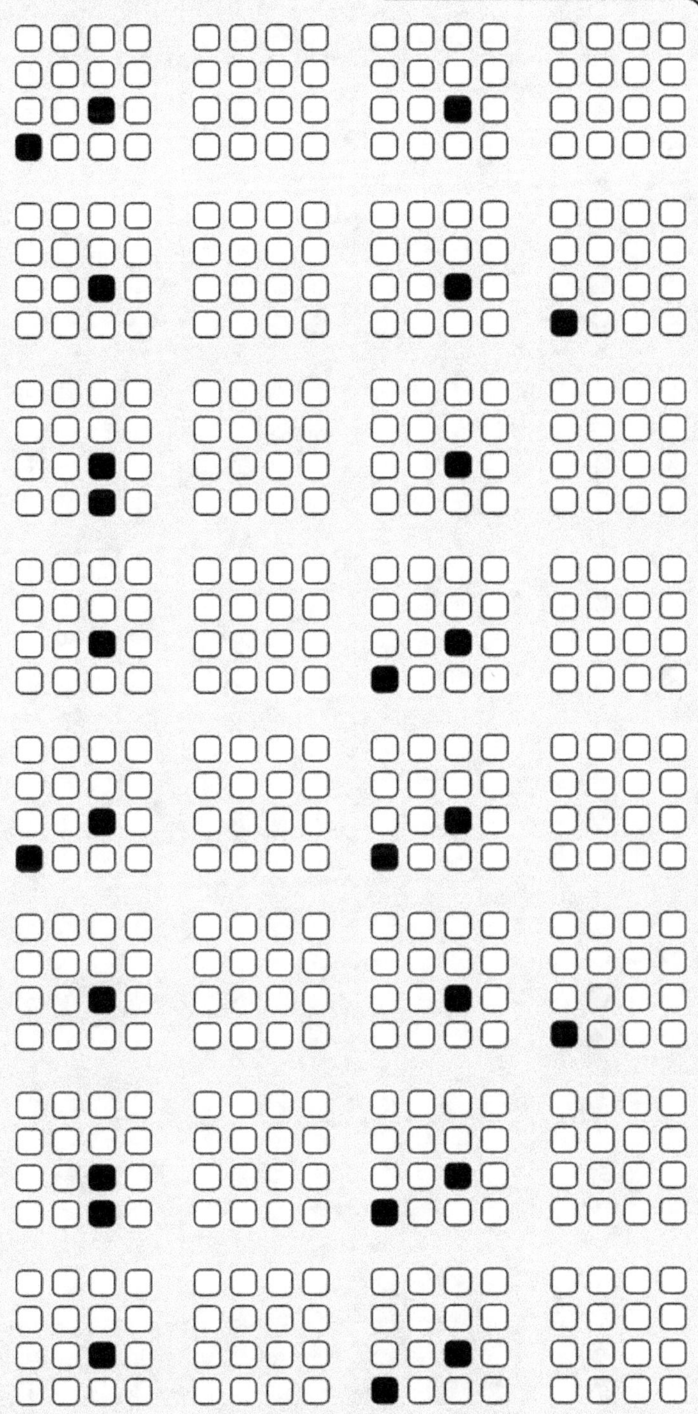

CHRONOS

16
SPL
110BPM

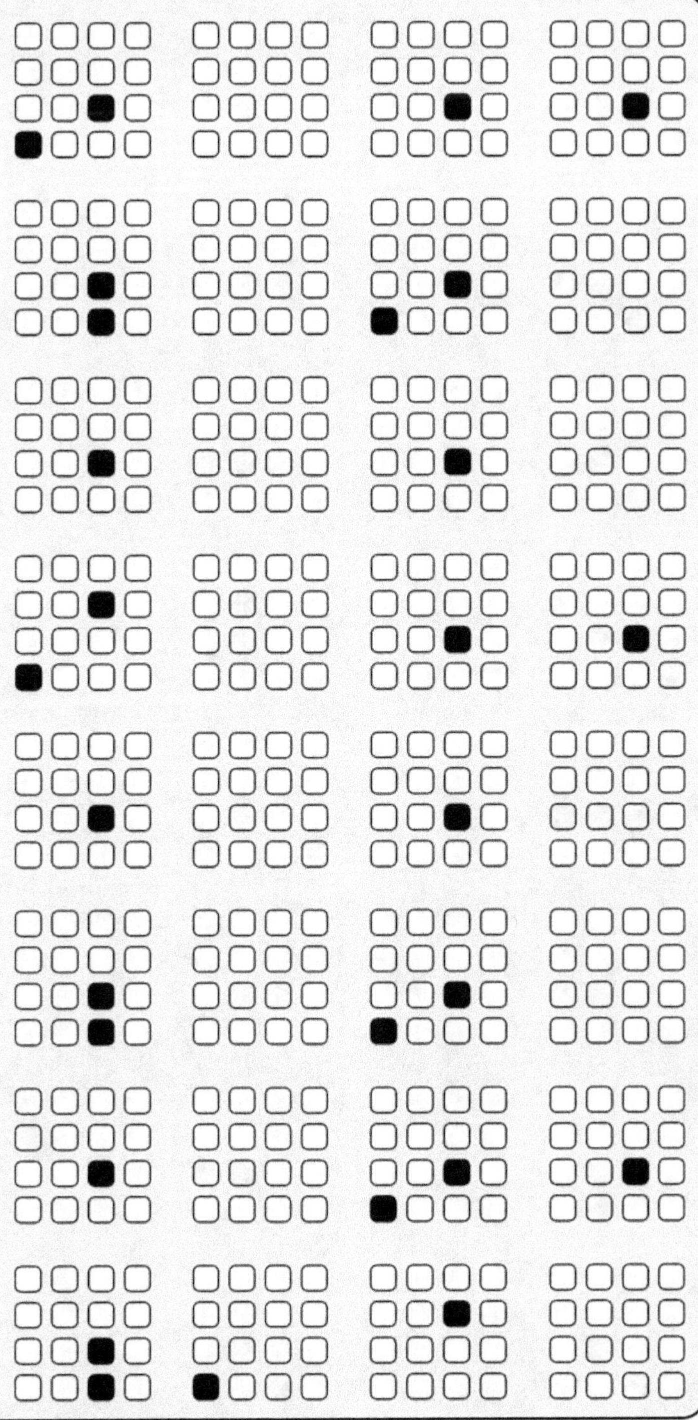

FAVORITES
16
SPL
176BPM

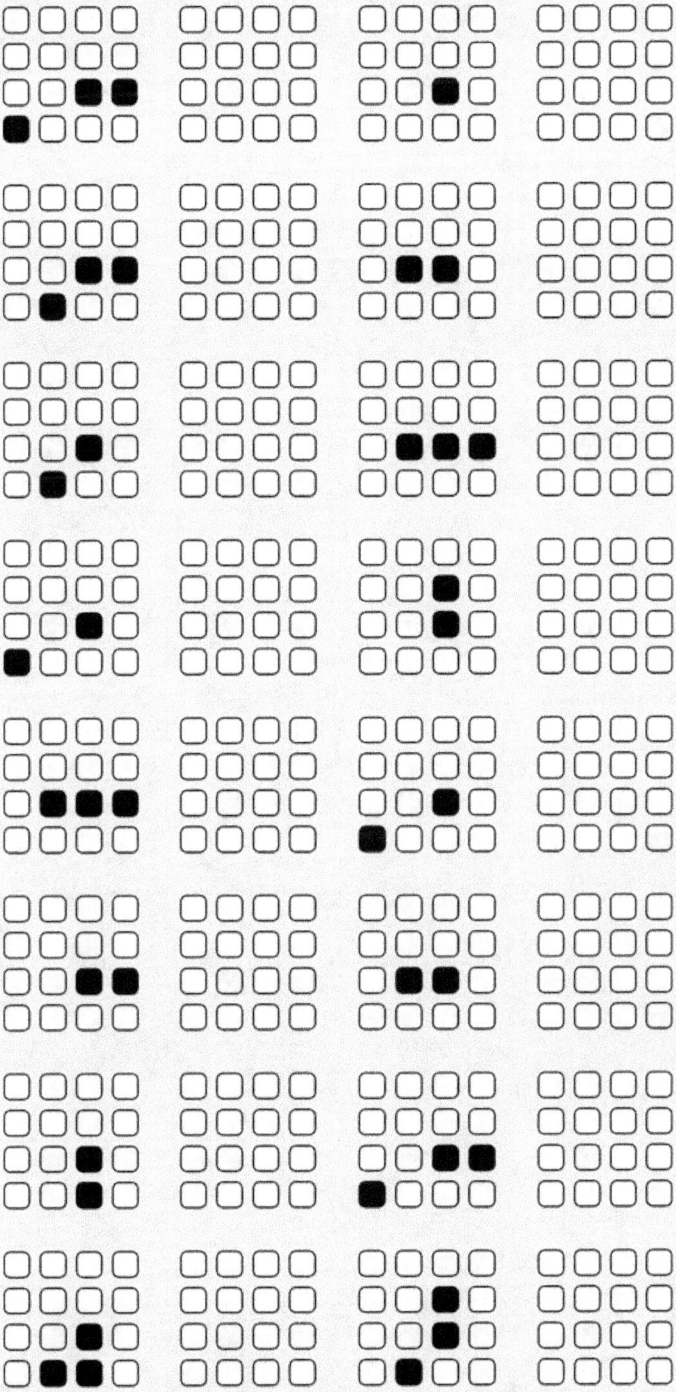

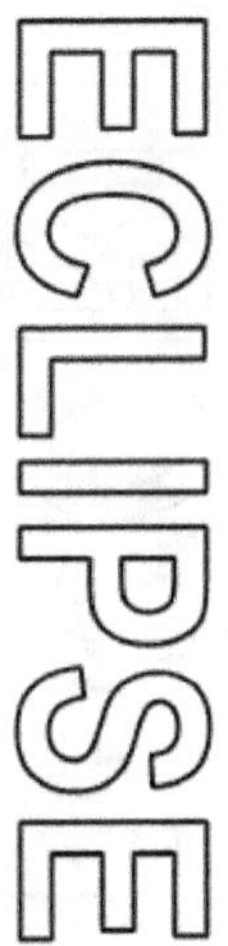

16

SPL

100BPM

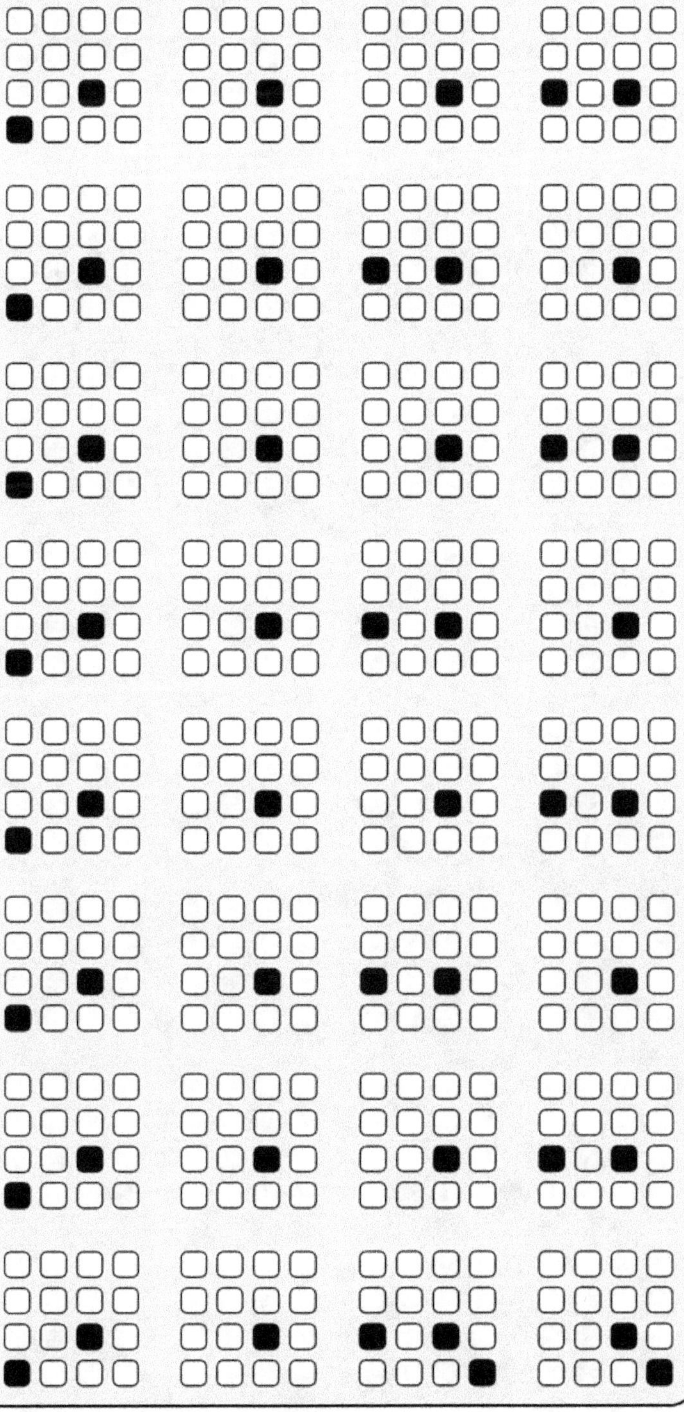

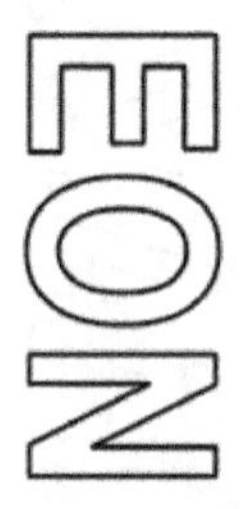

EPOCH 1/2
16
SPL
100BPM

FAVORITES

EPOCH 2/2

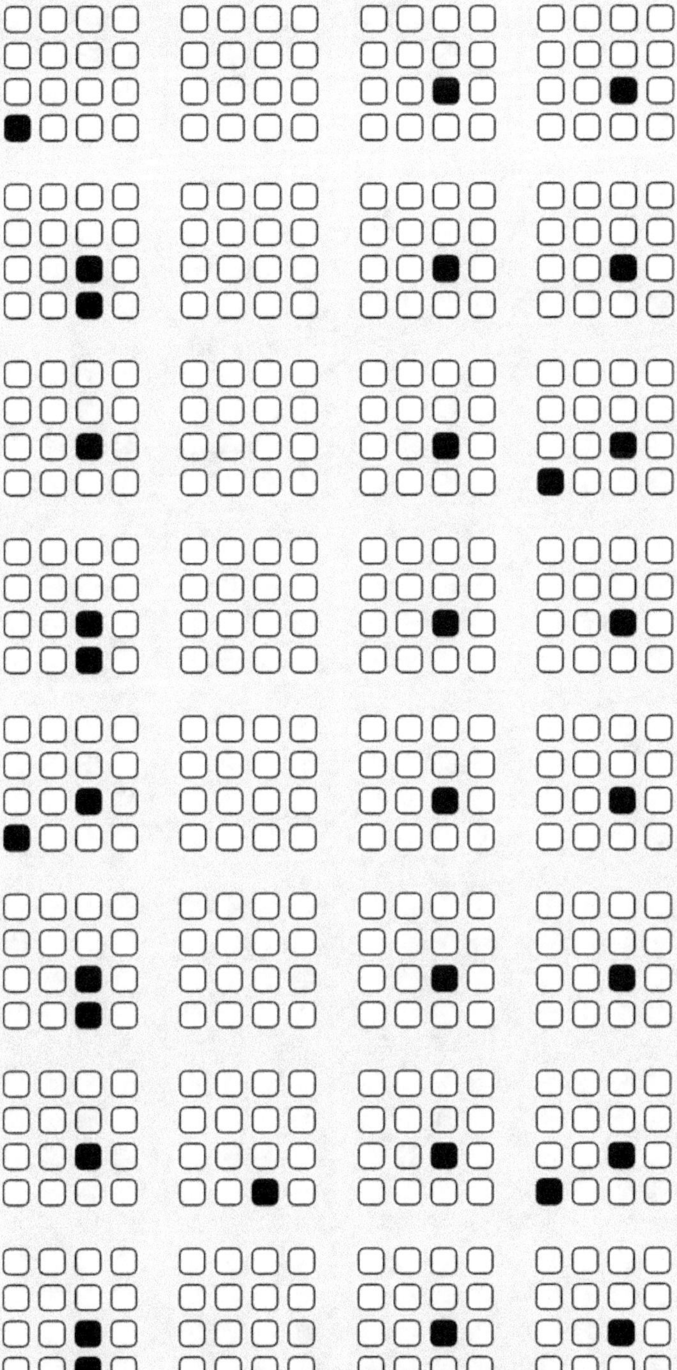

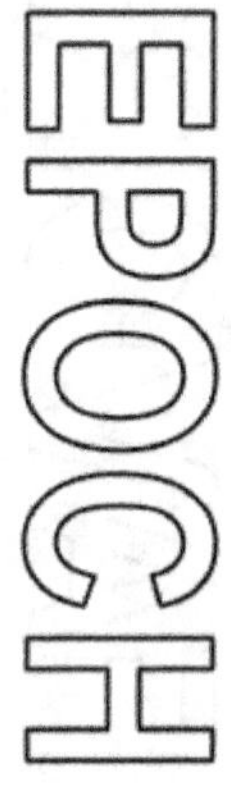

FAVORITES

100BPM

SPL

16

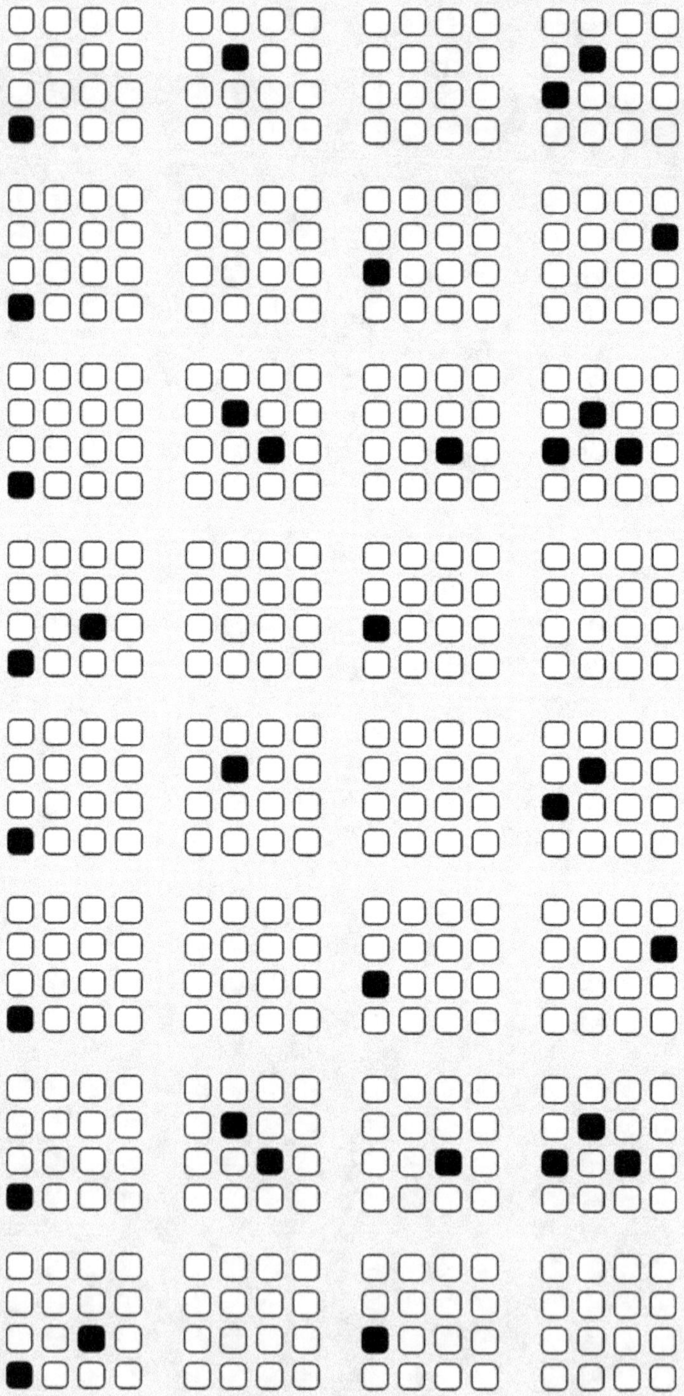

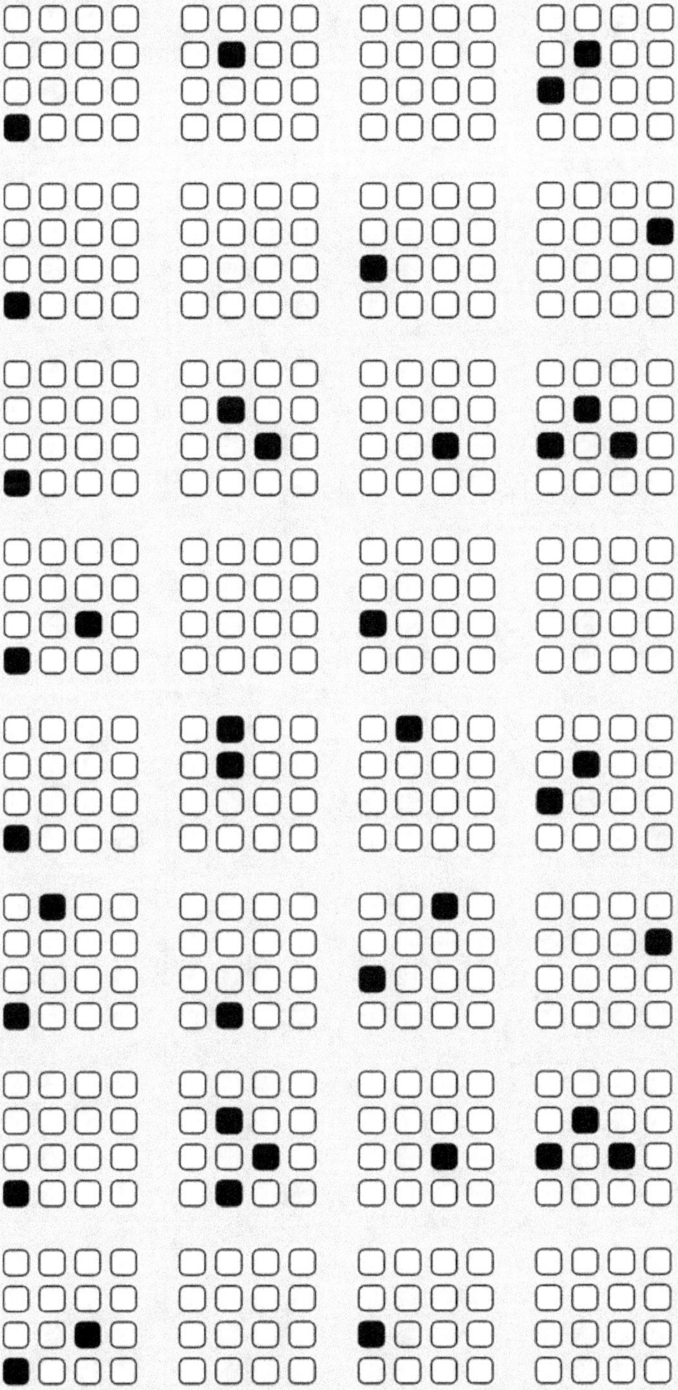

EVOLVE

16
SPL
95BPM

FAVORITES

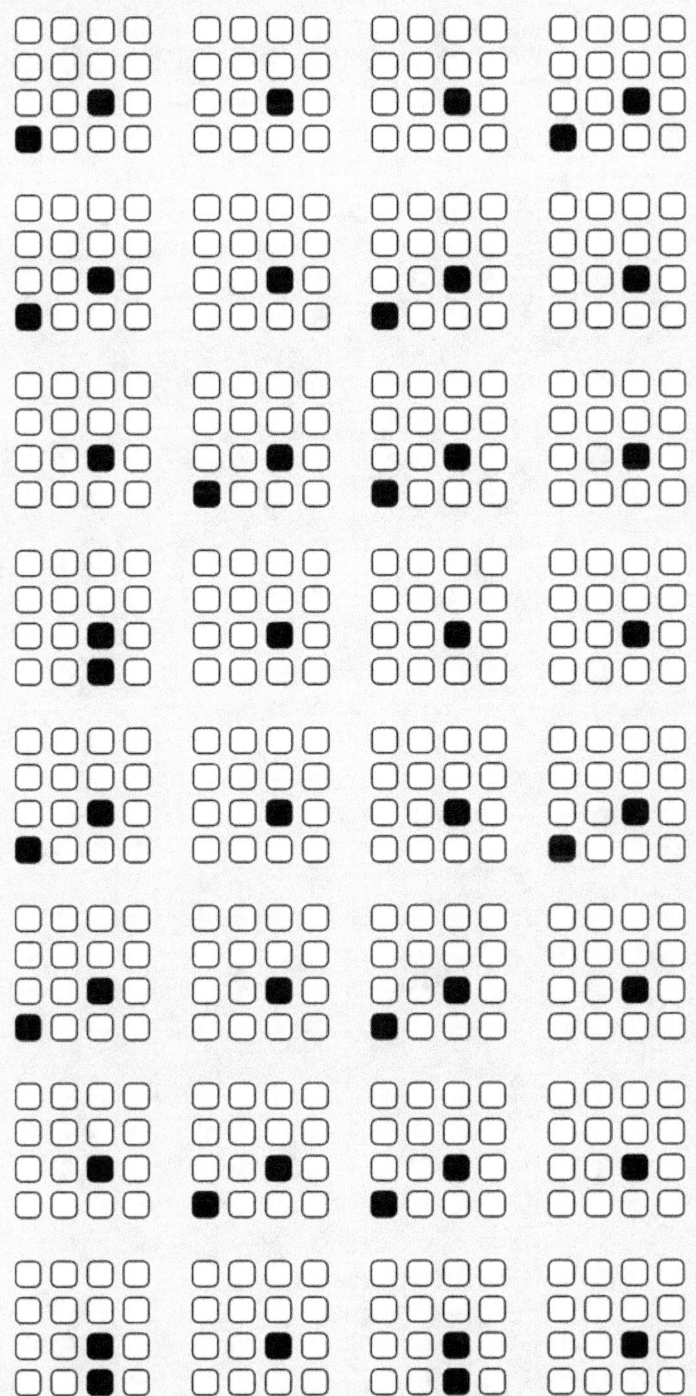

16
SPL
95BPM

FAVORITES

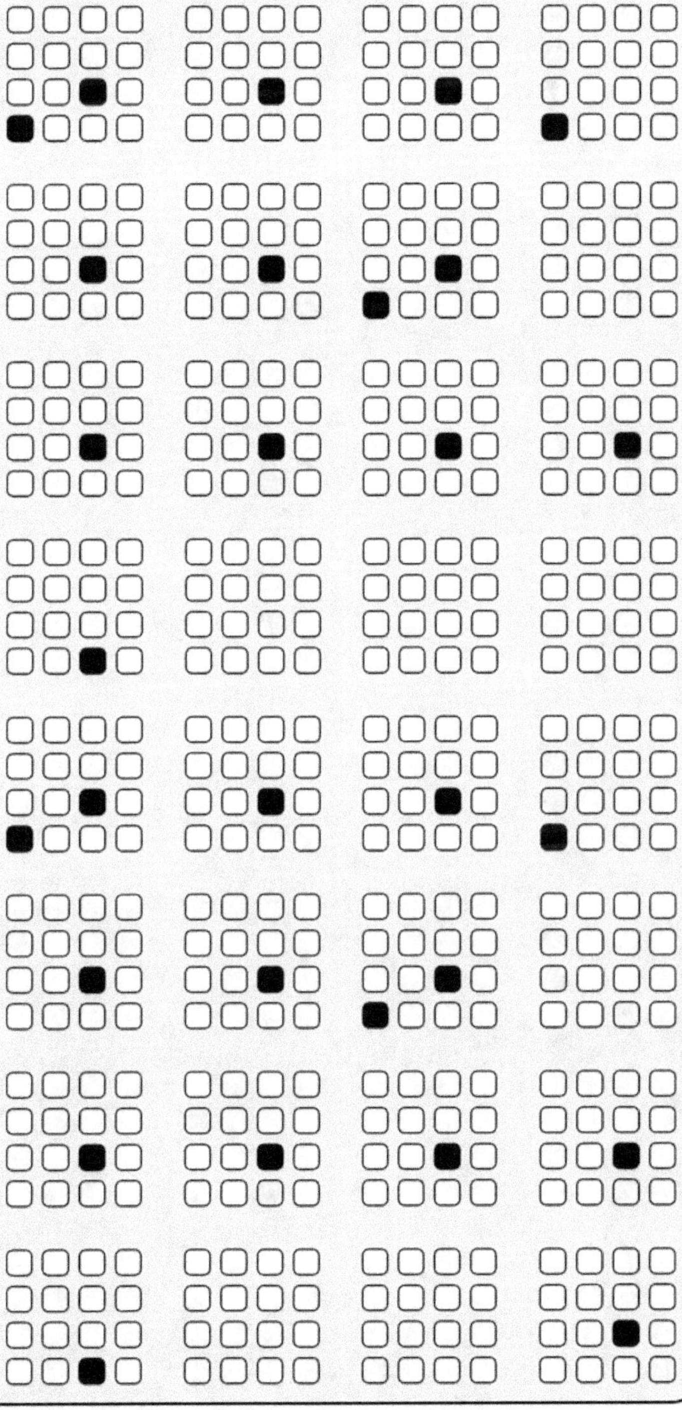

HYDRO

16

SPL

145BPM

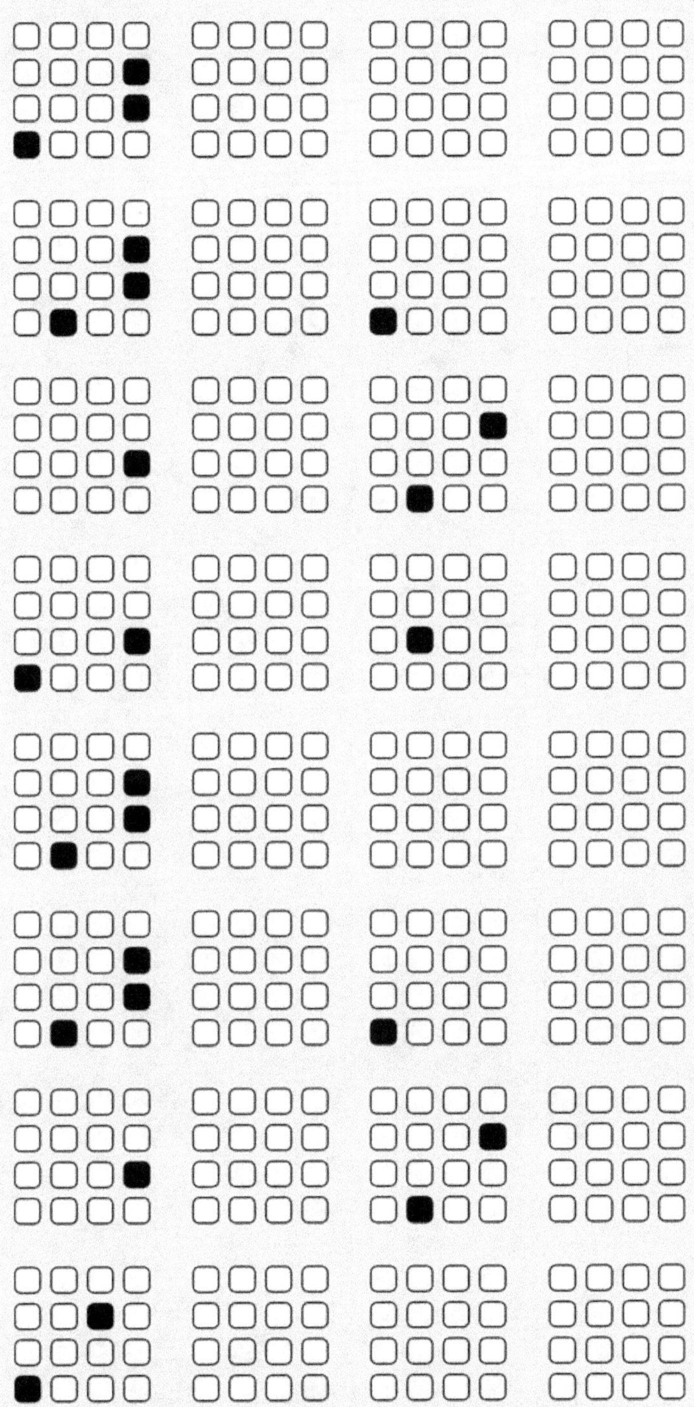

16

SPL

125BPM

FAVORITES

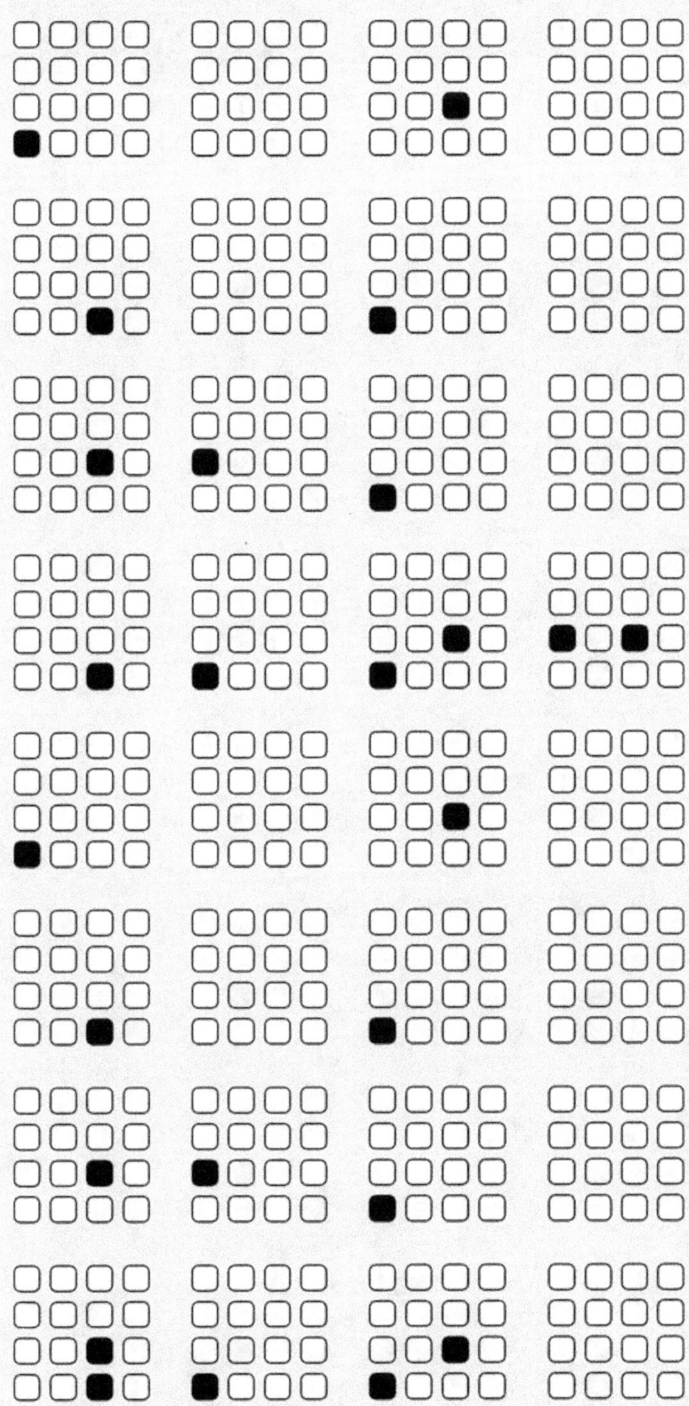

FAVORITES
16
SPL
110BPM

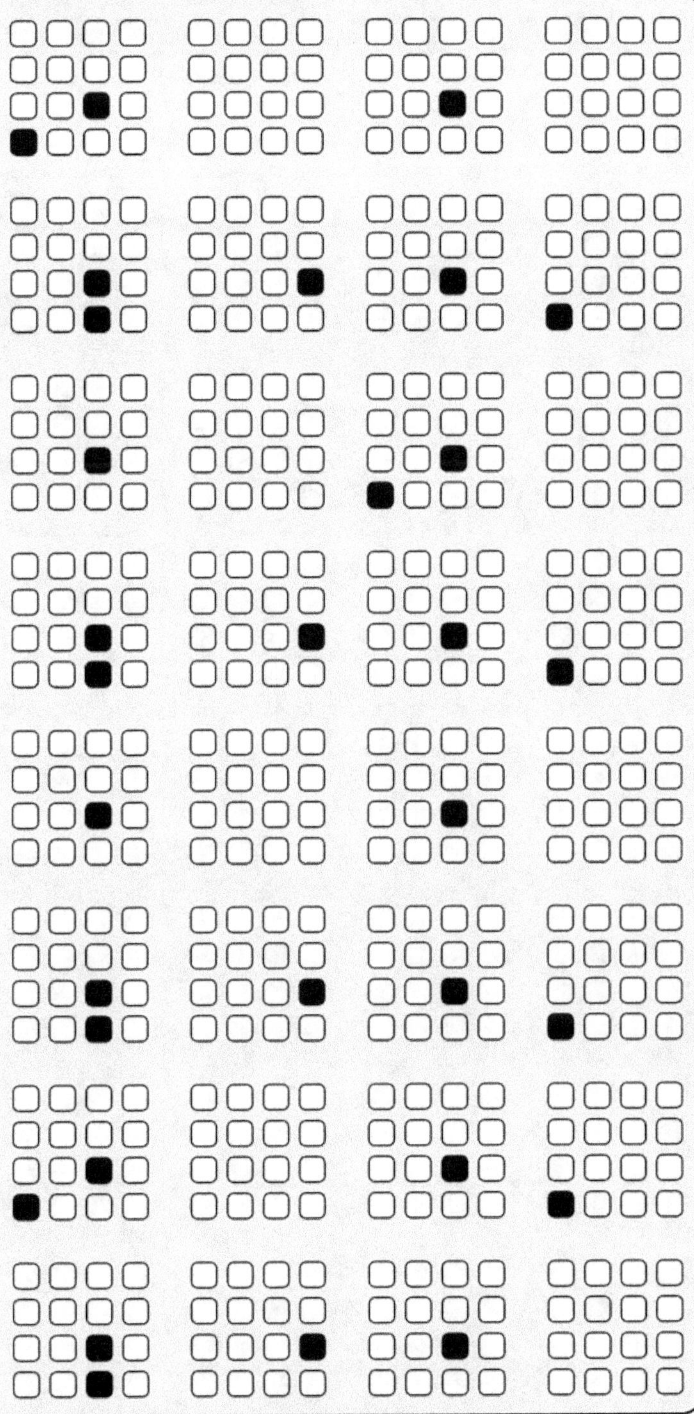

16

SPL

176BPM

FAVORITES

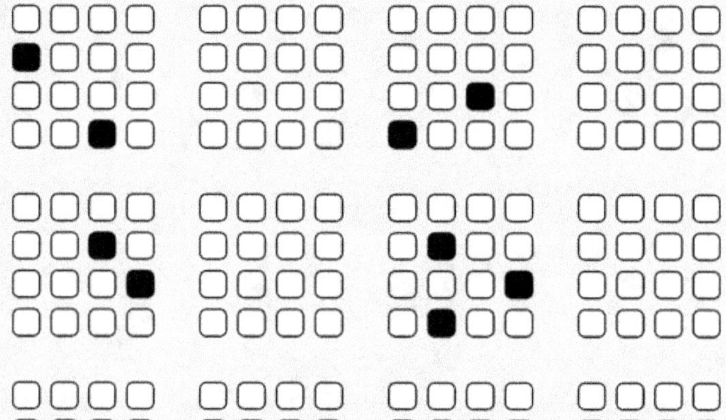

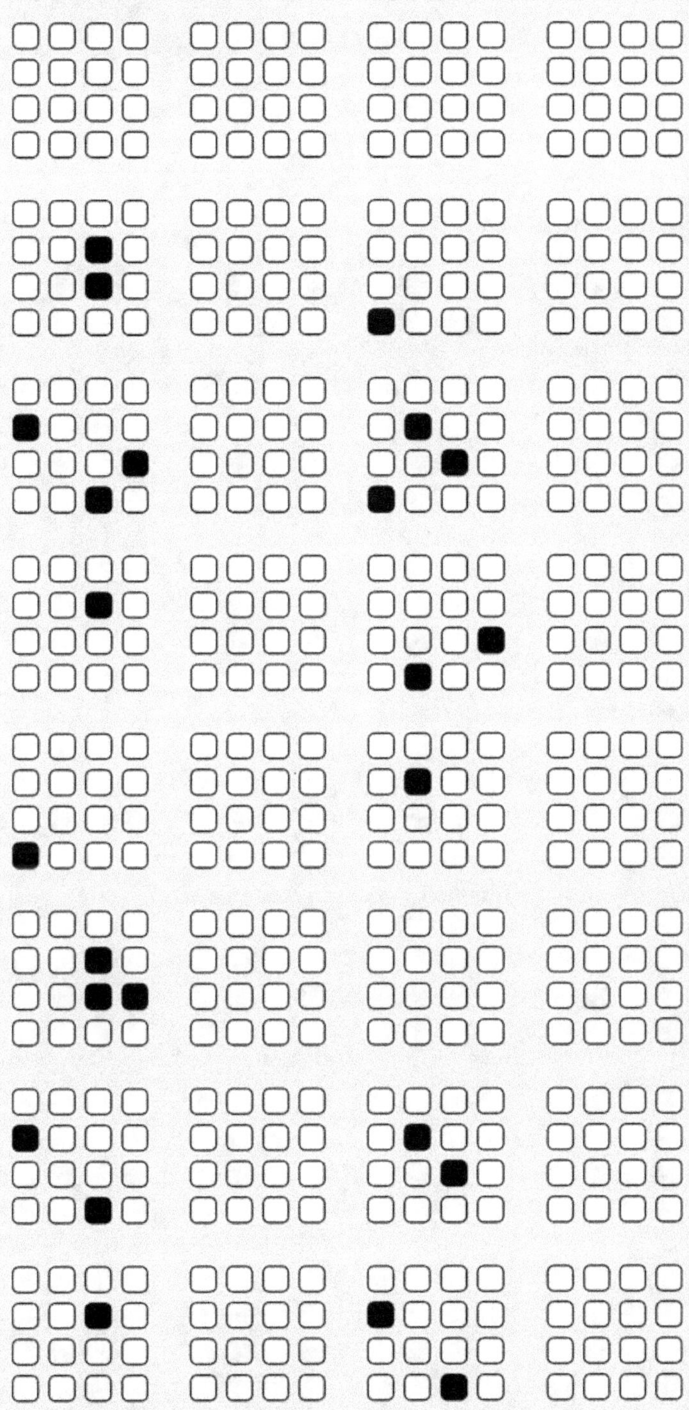

NEBULON

16

SPL

100BPM

FAVORITES

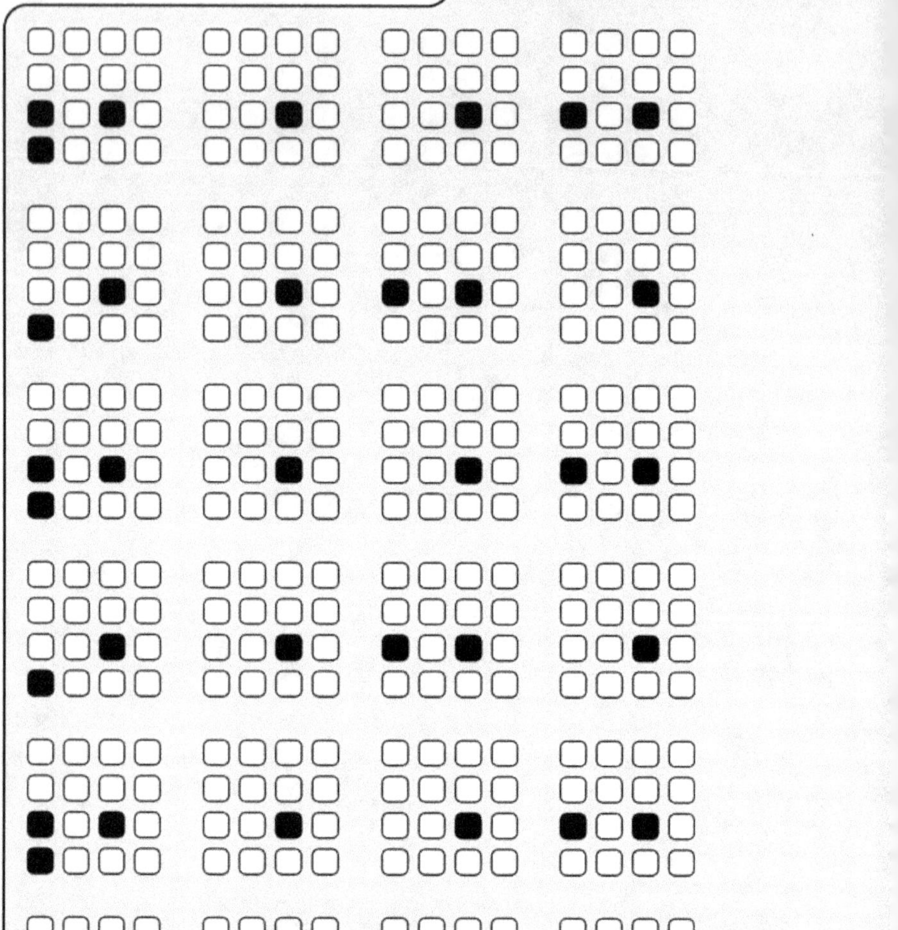

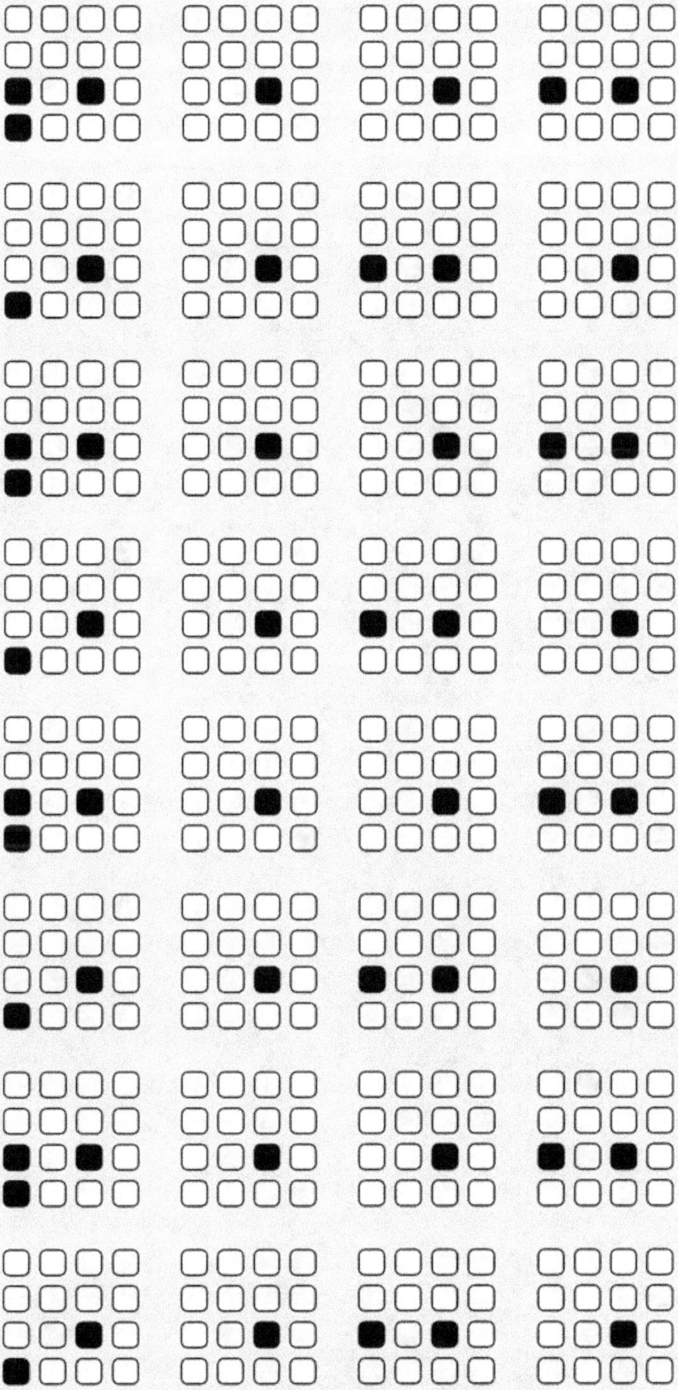

NOW

FAVORITES
90BPM
SPL
16

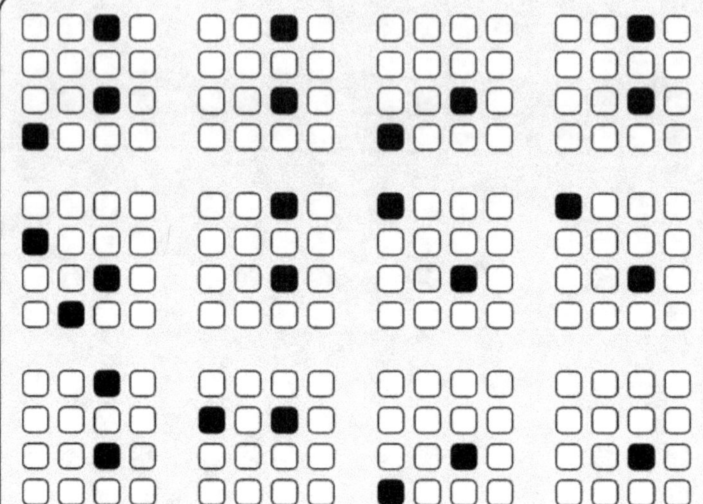

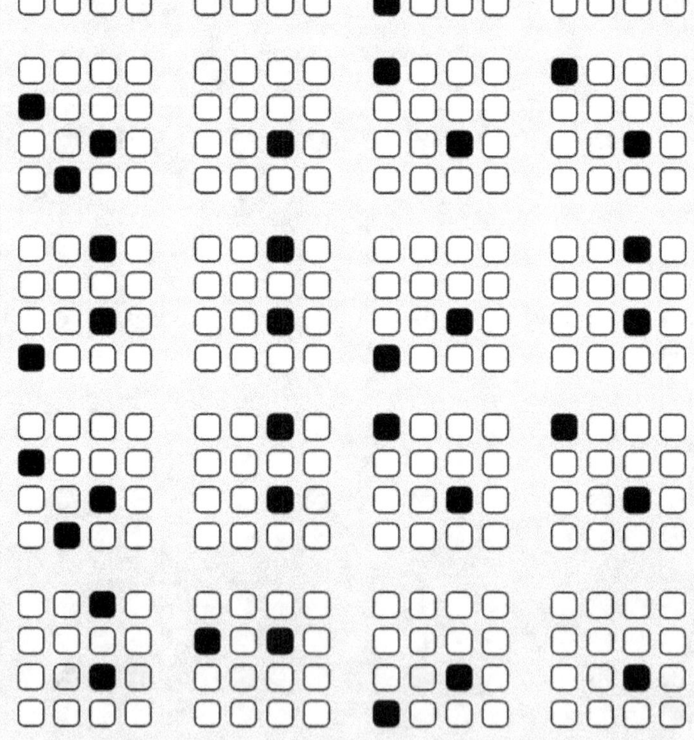

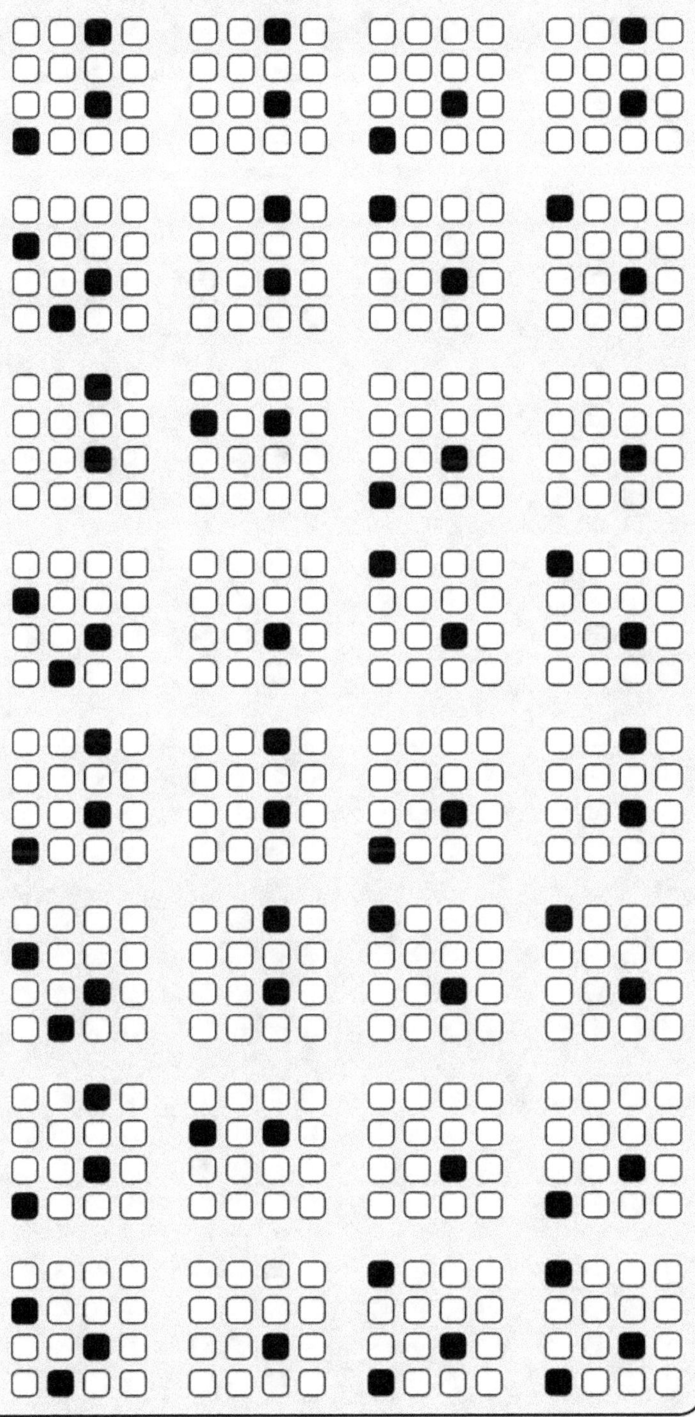

FAVORITES
16
SPL
176BPM

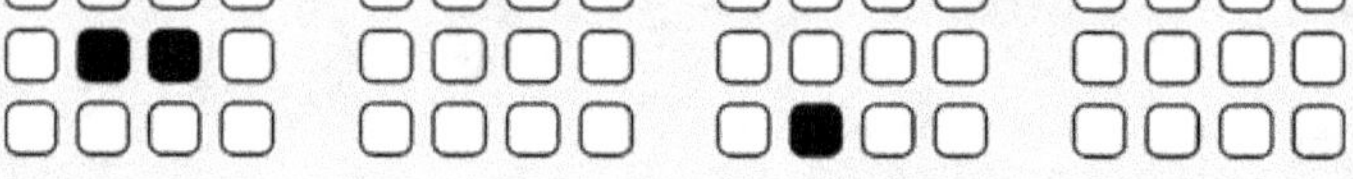
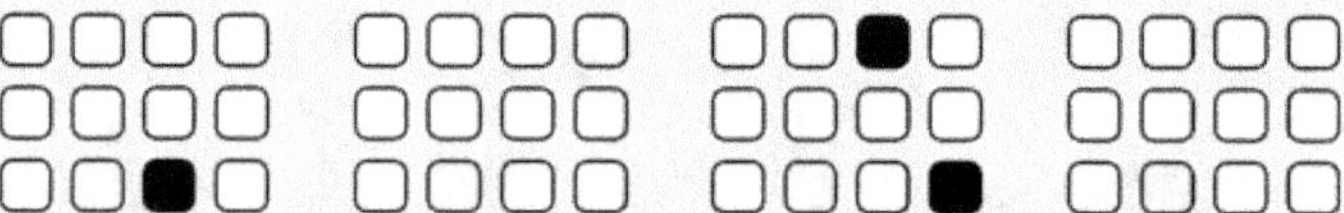

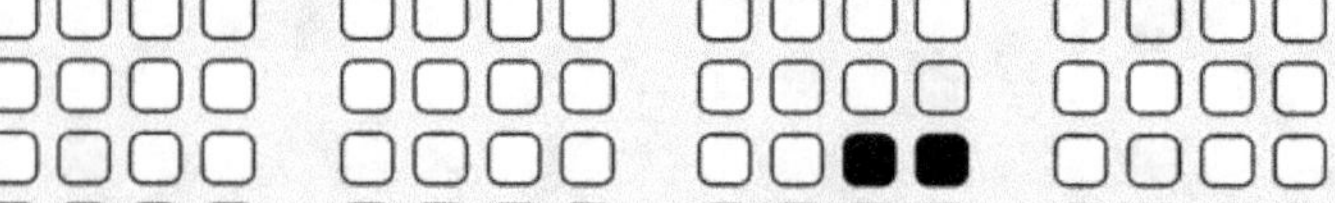
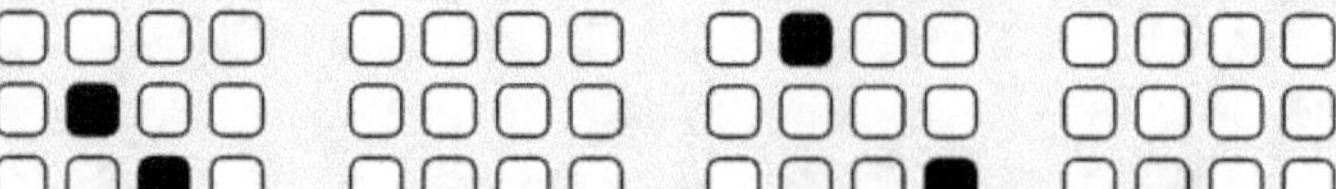

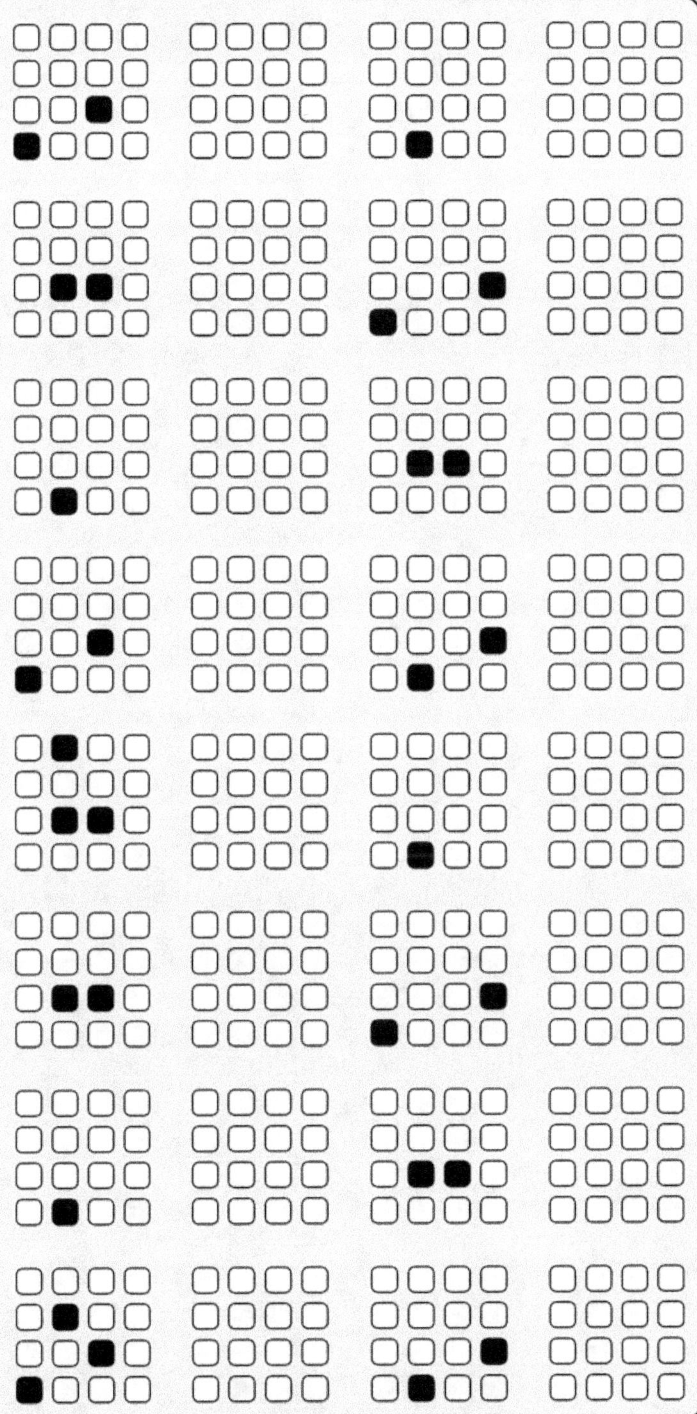

16

SPL

110BPM

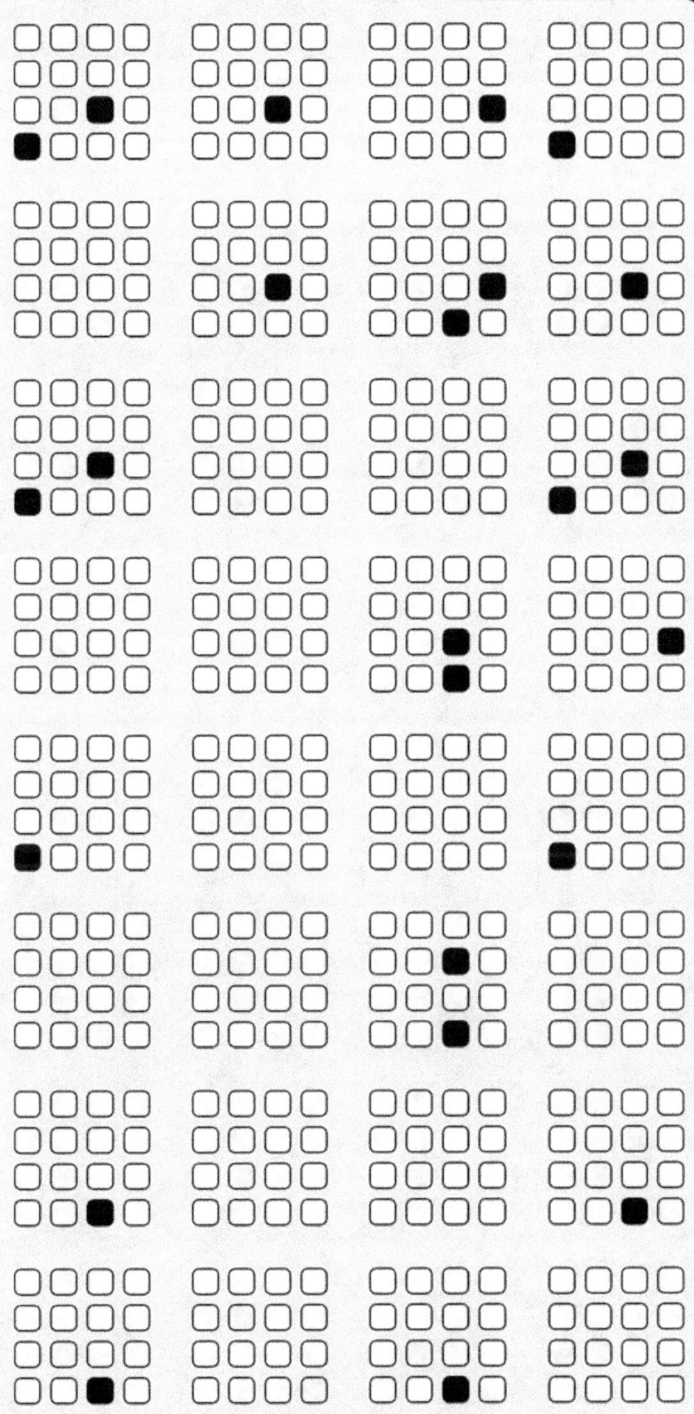
REGENERATE

FAVORITES
16
SPL
140BPM

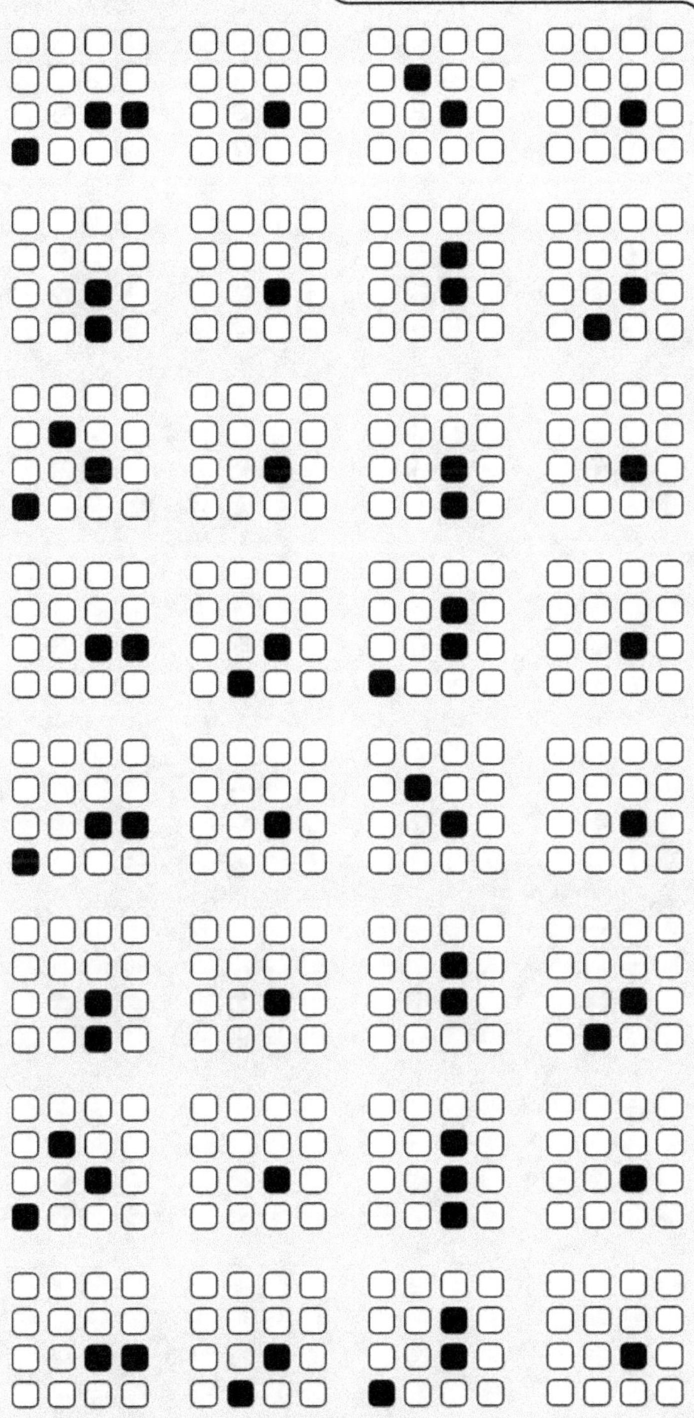

FAVORITES

16

SPL

90BPM

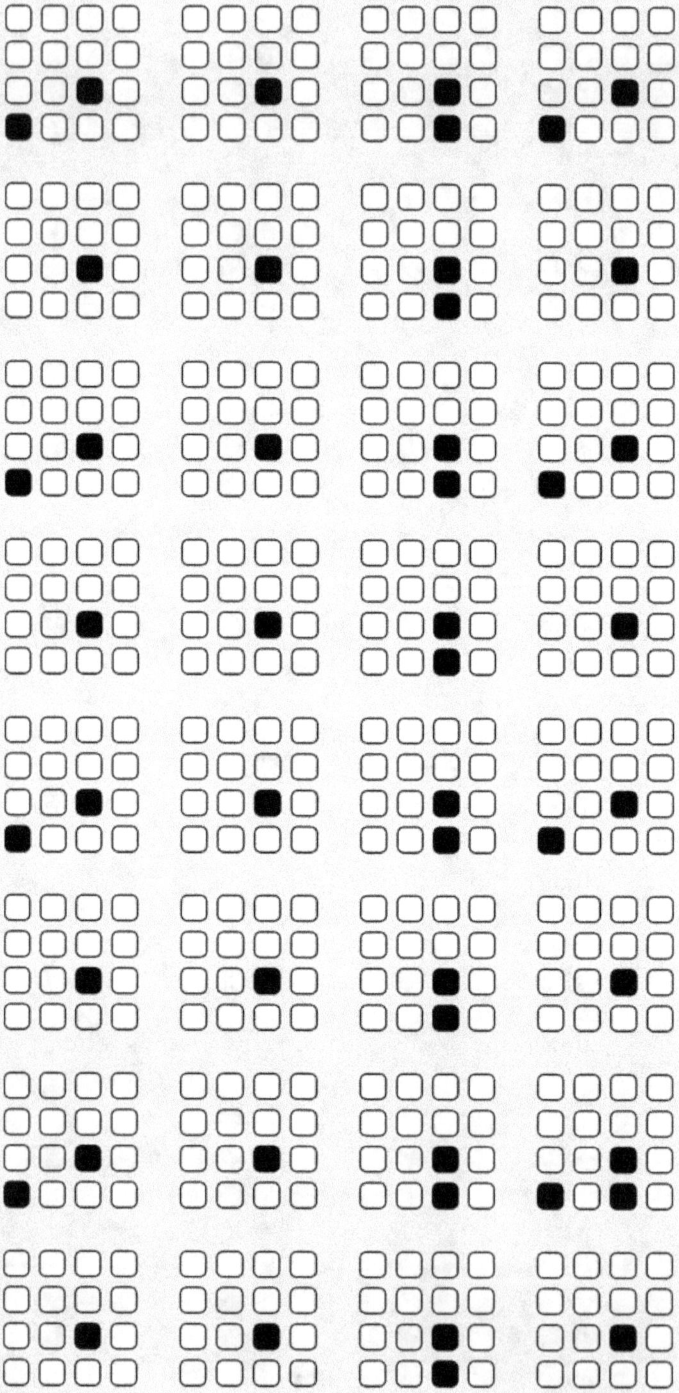

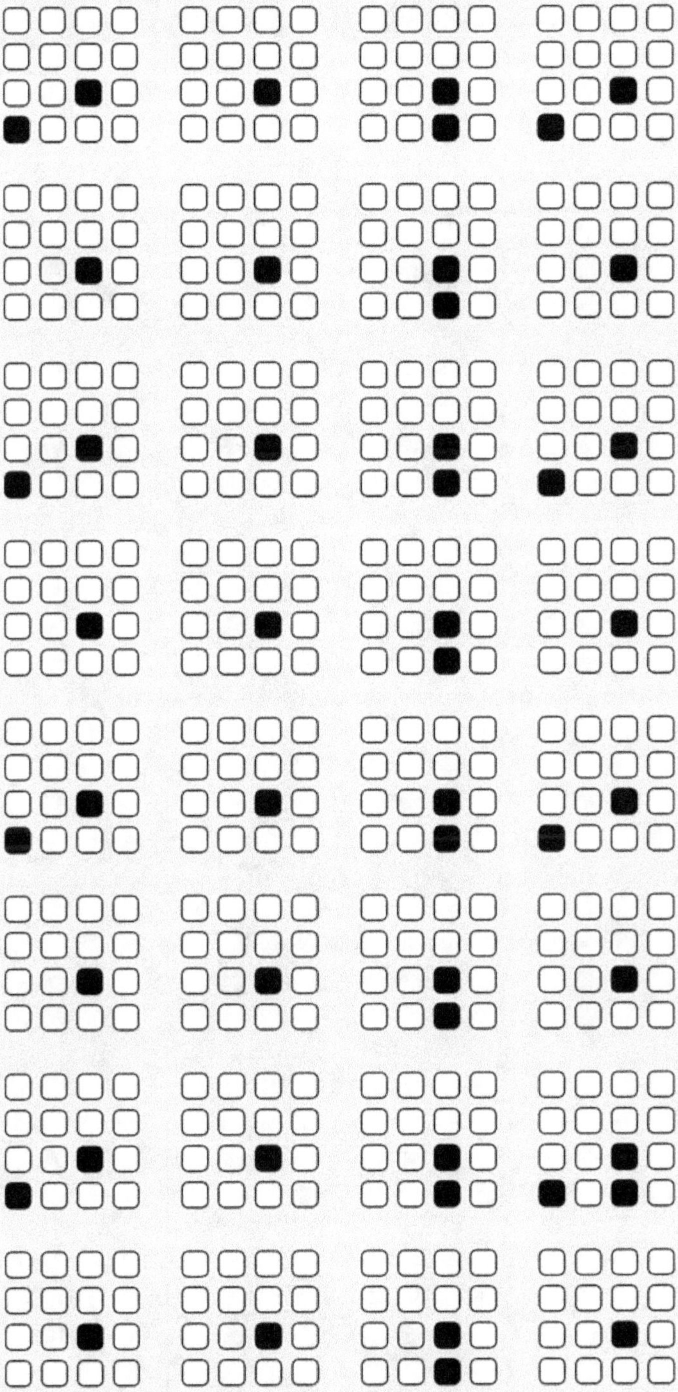

SUNJA

16
SPL
100BPM

FAVORITES

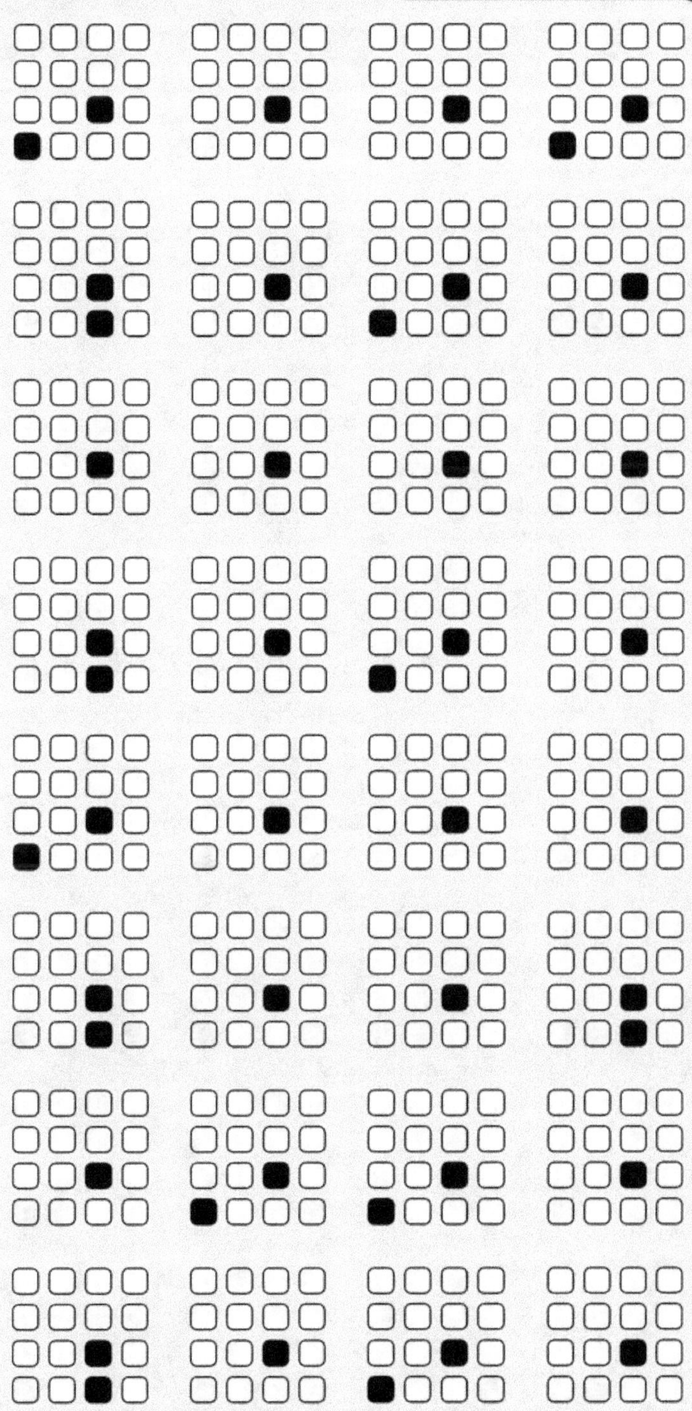

TEMPORAL

16

SPL

100BPM

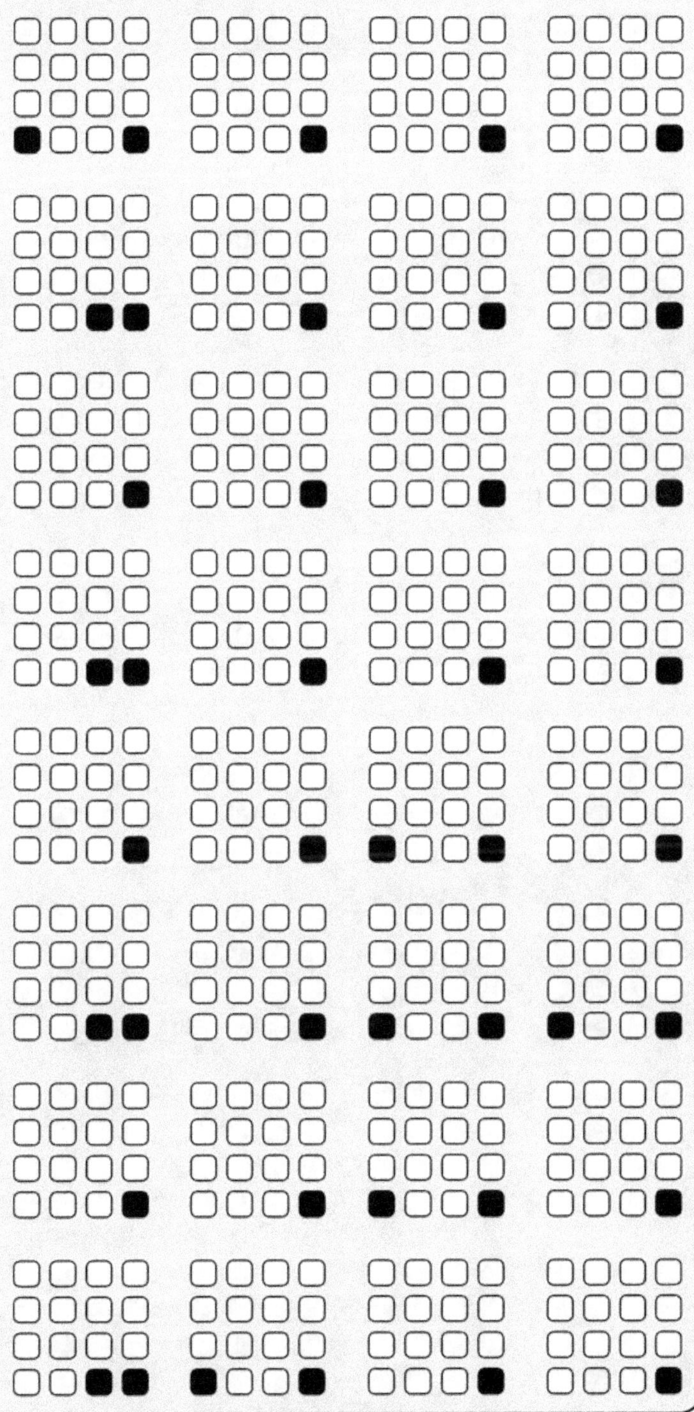

16

SPL

125BPM

FAVORITES

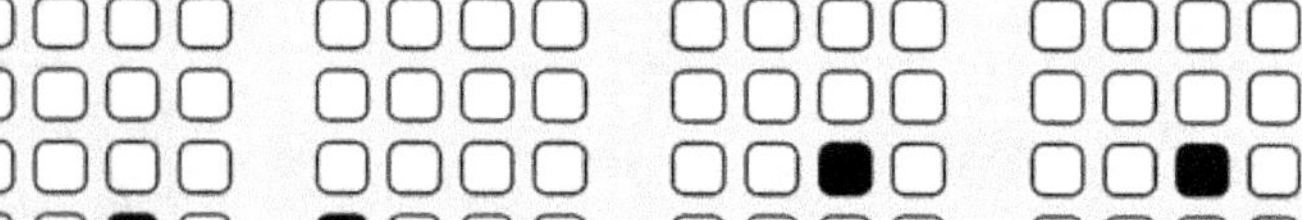

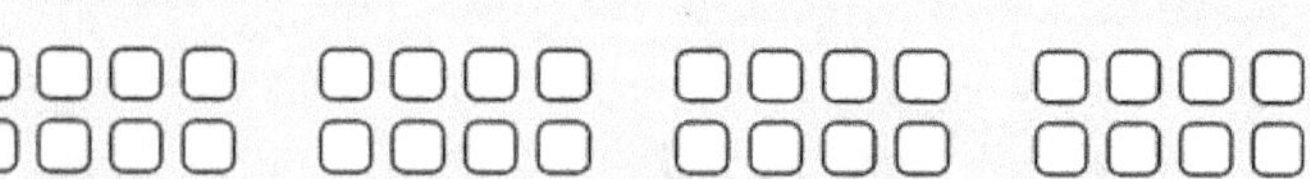
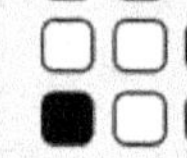
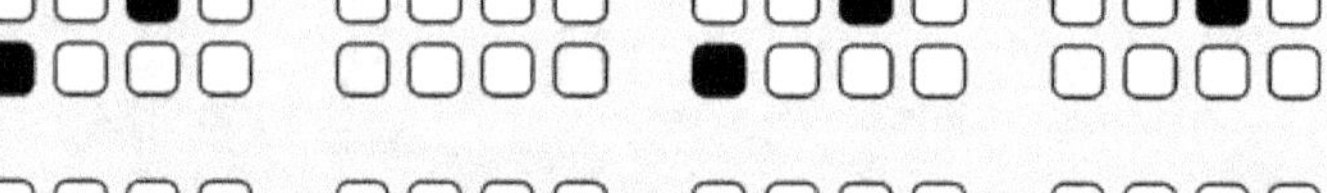

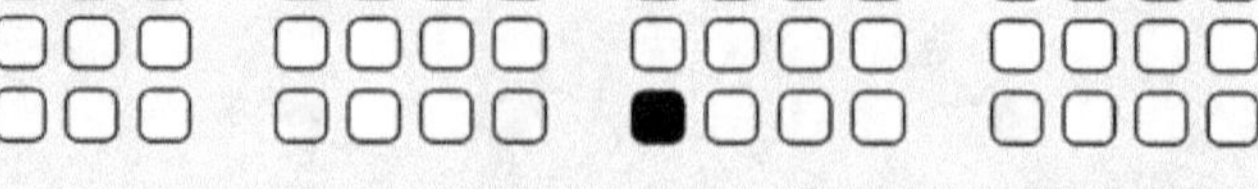
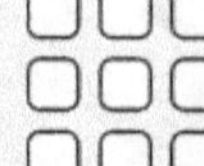

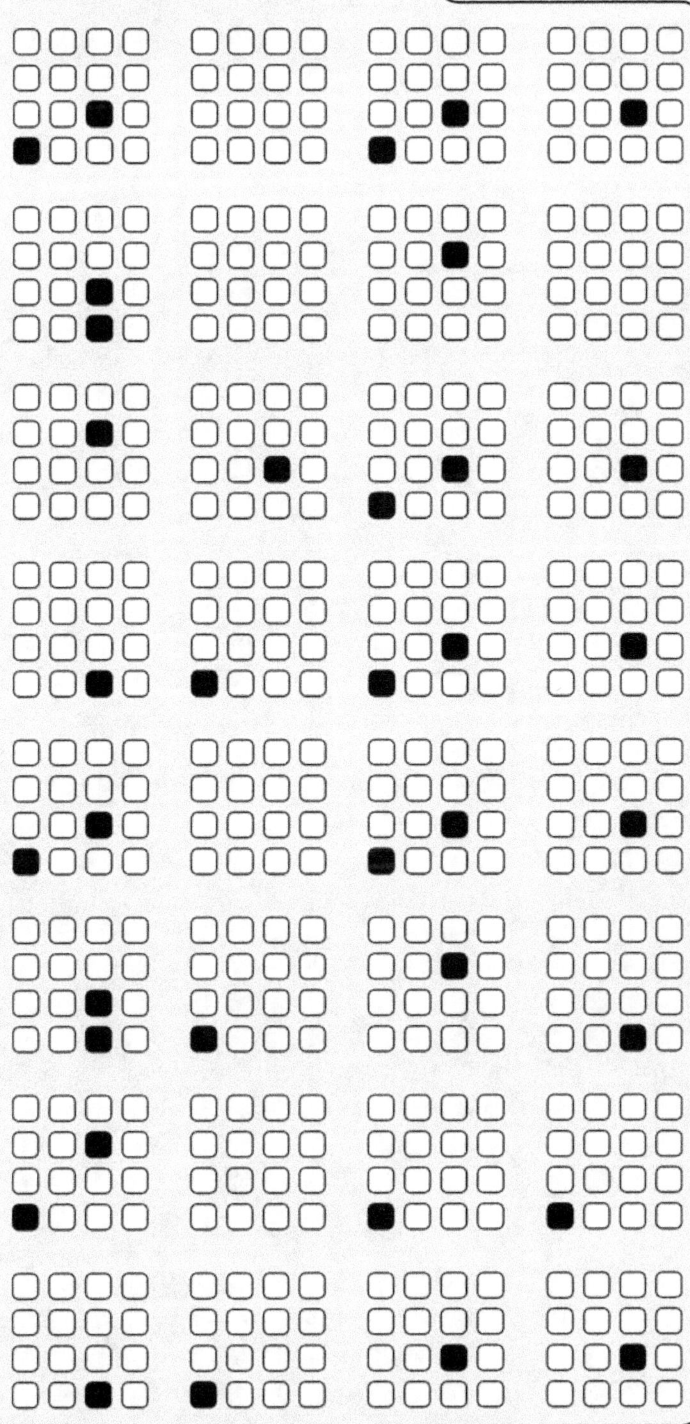

TIMESTREAM

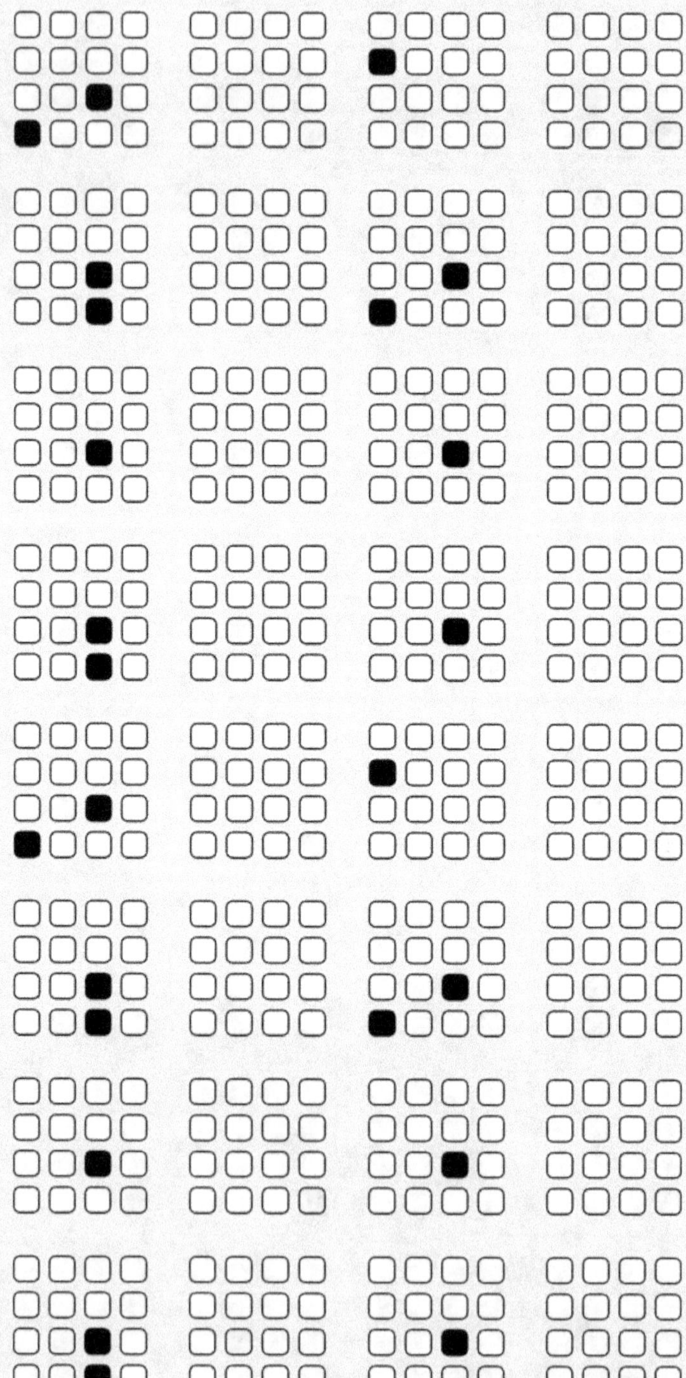

FAVORITES
110BPM
SPL
16
TITAN 1/2

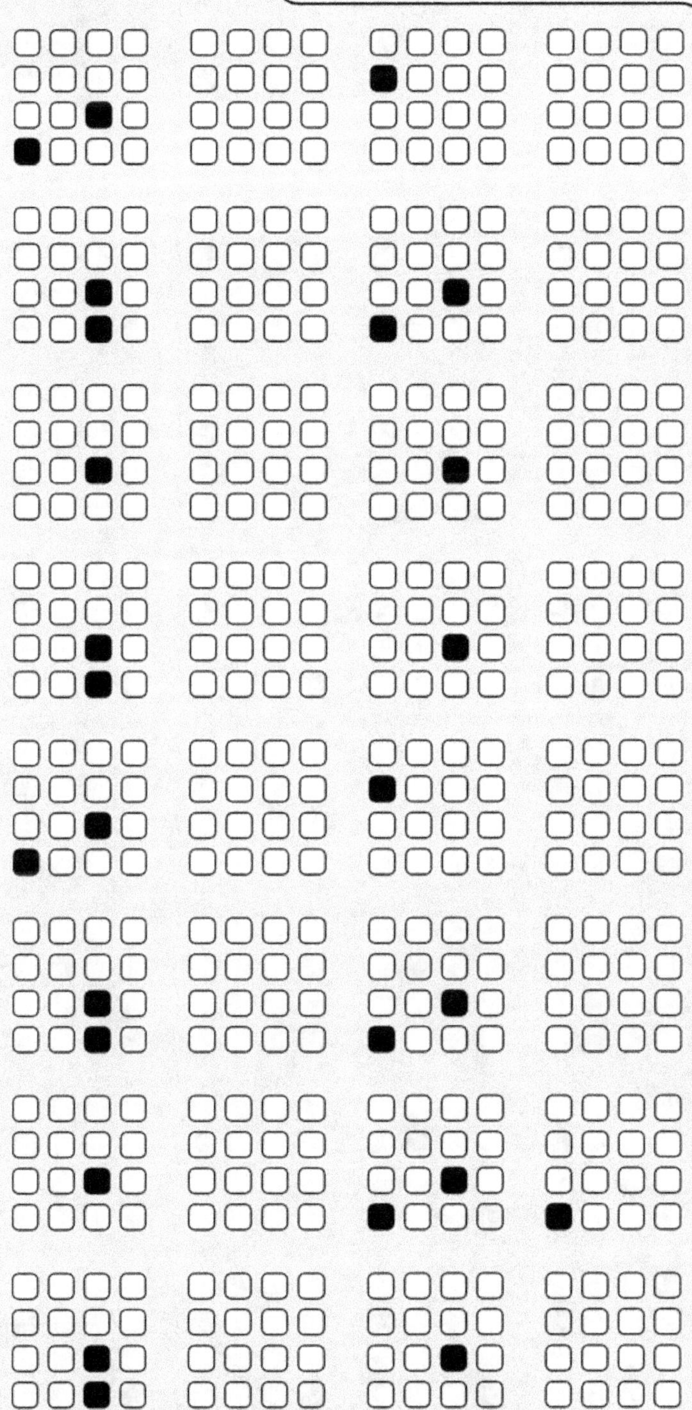

16

SPL

90BPM

FAVORITES

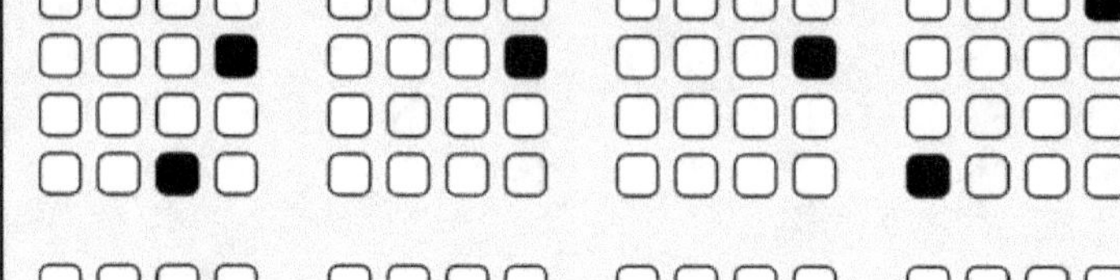
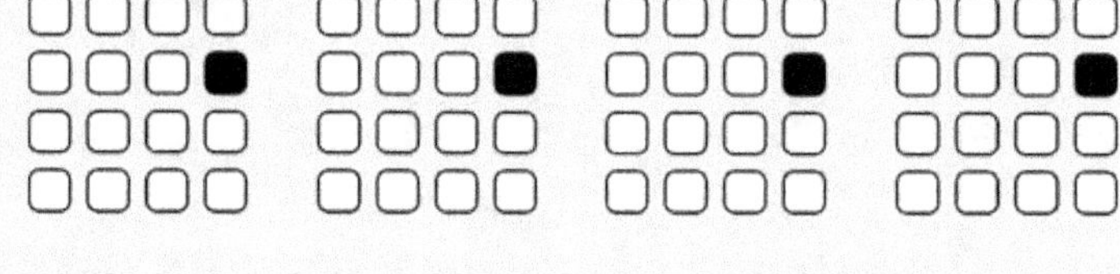
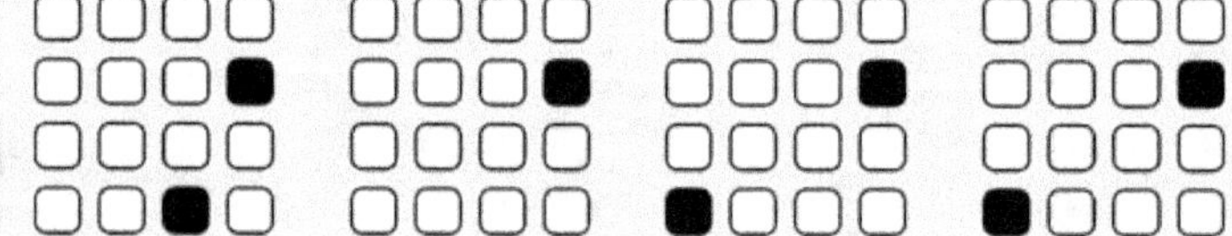

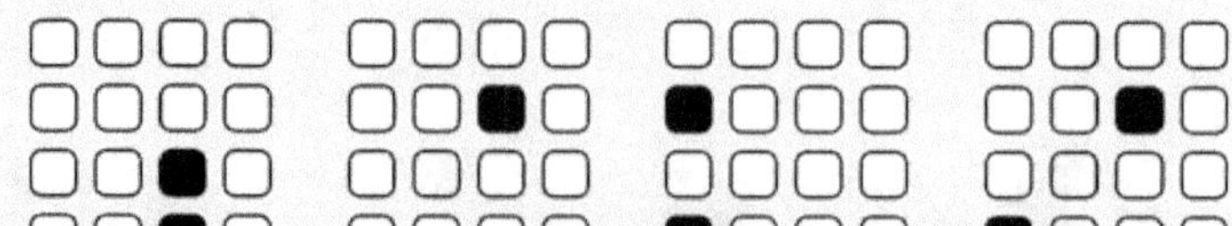
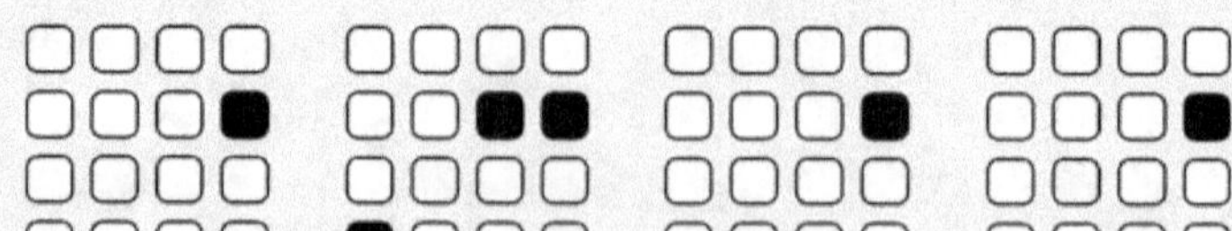

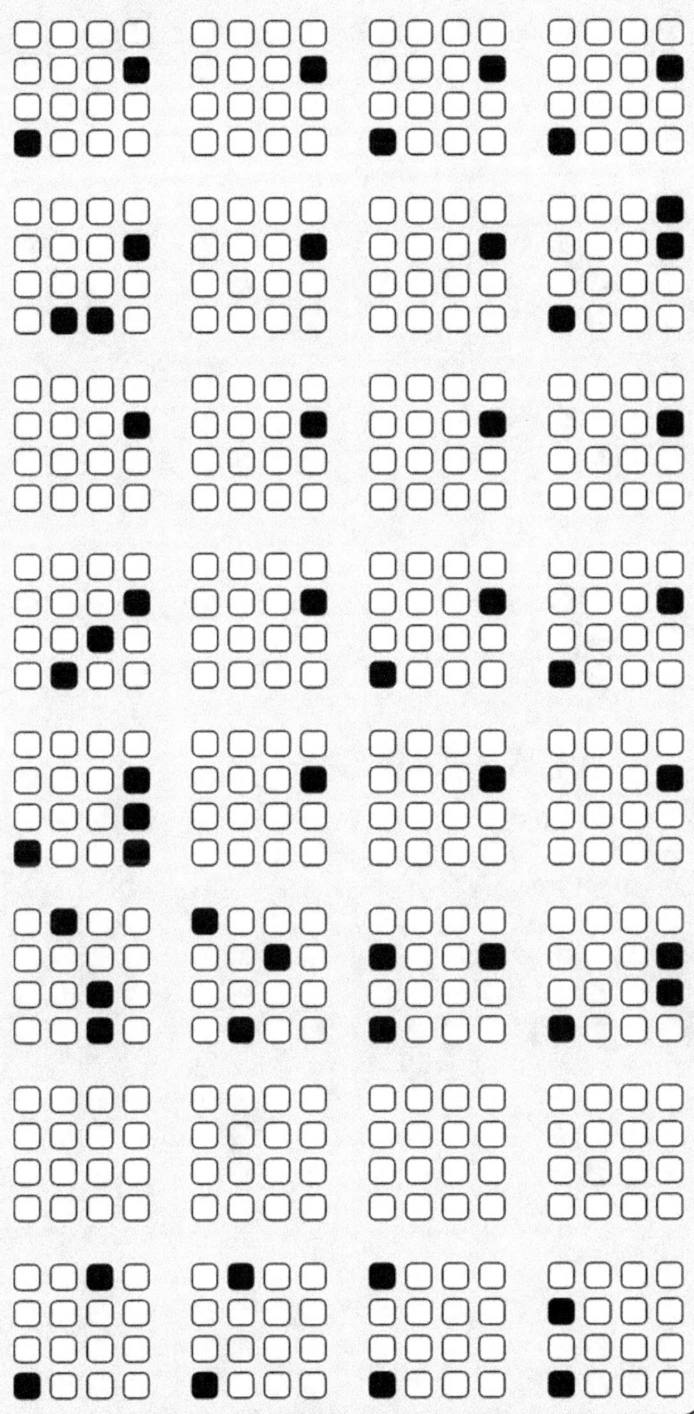

TRUDGE

FAVORITES
16
SPL
110BPM

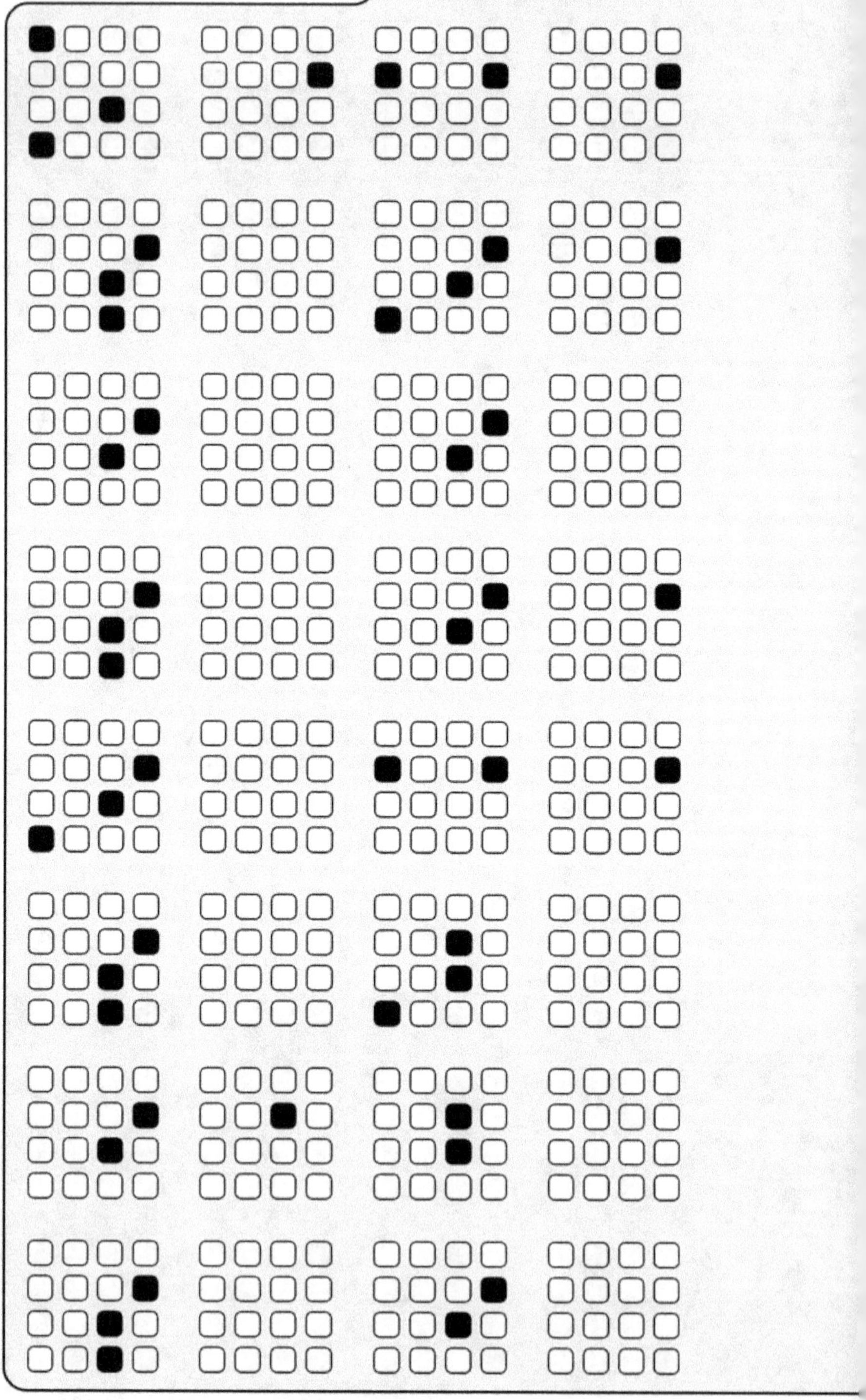

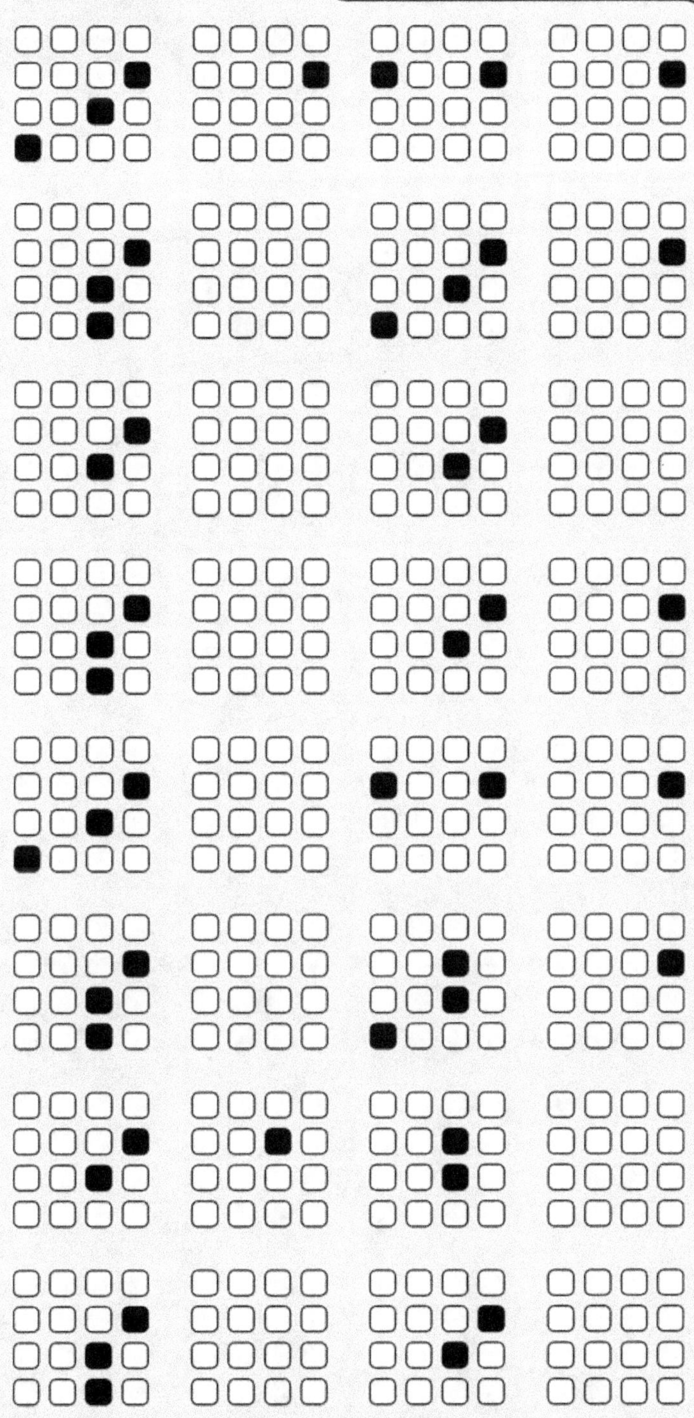

16

MIR

157BPM

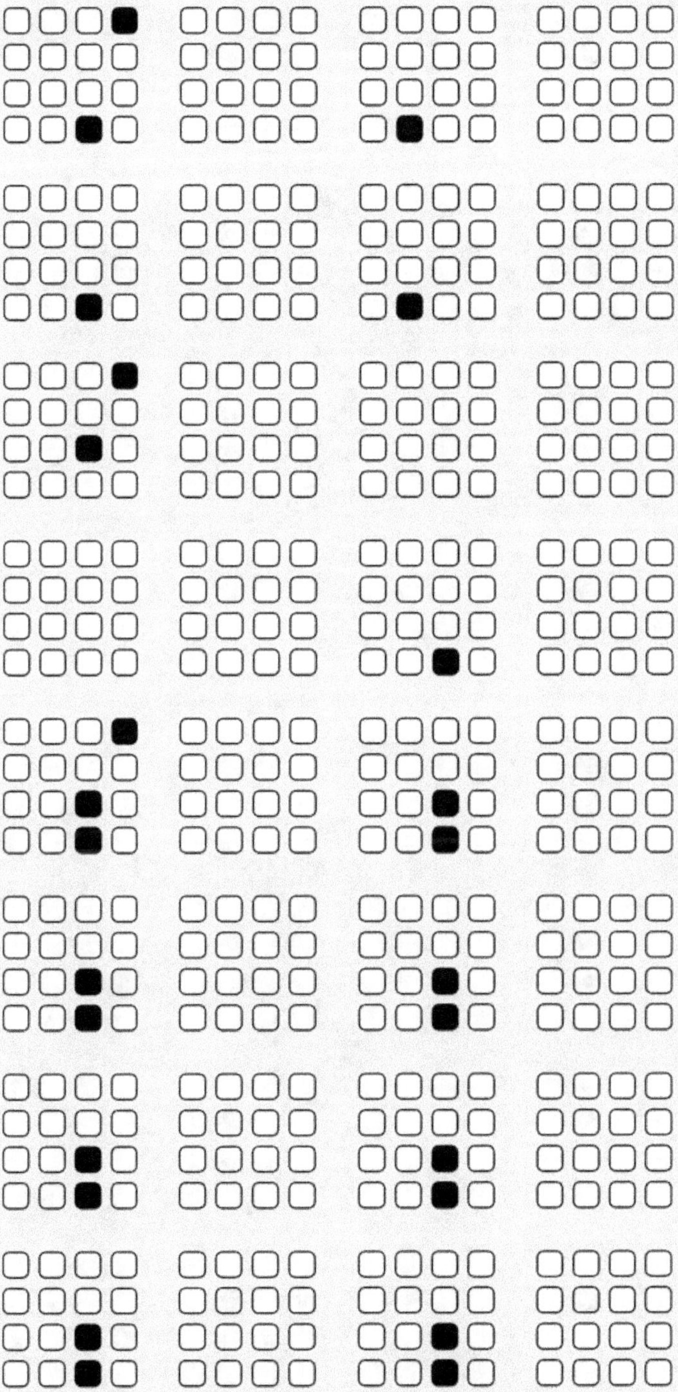

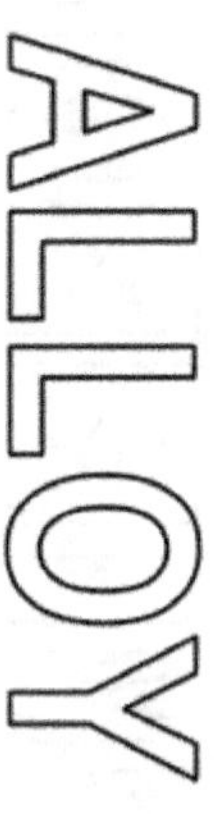

16

MIR

160BPM

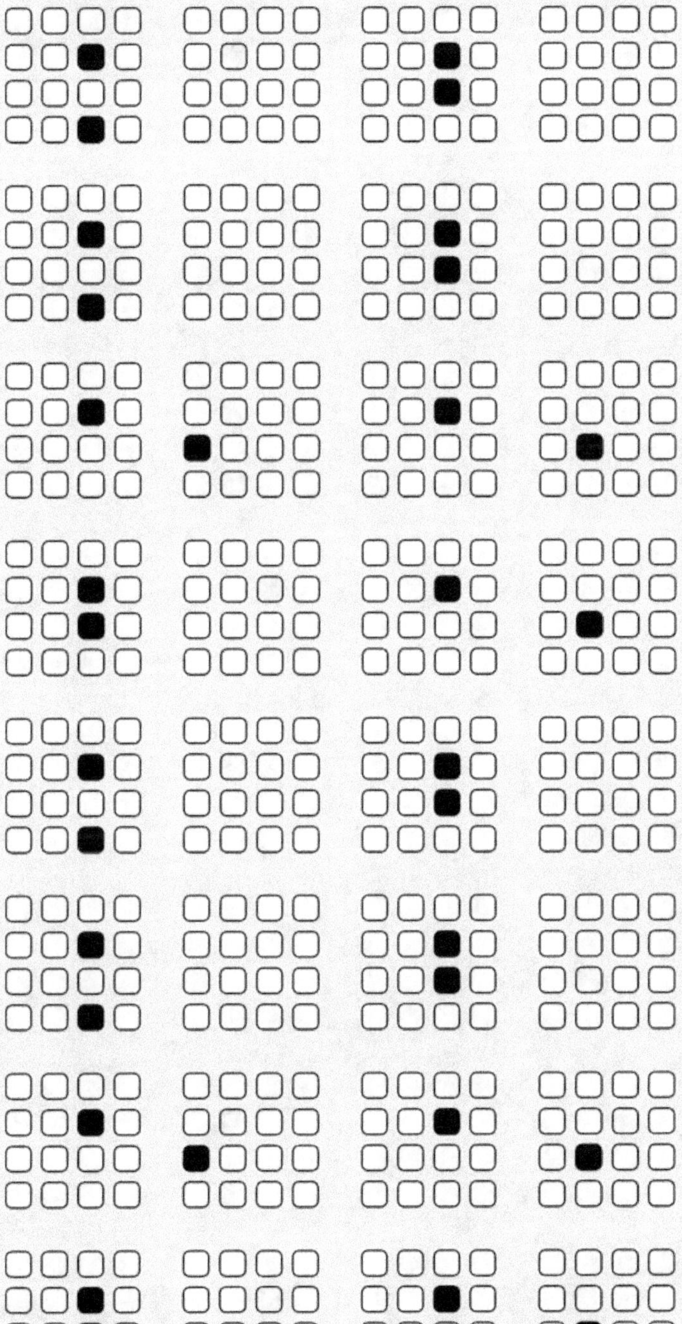

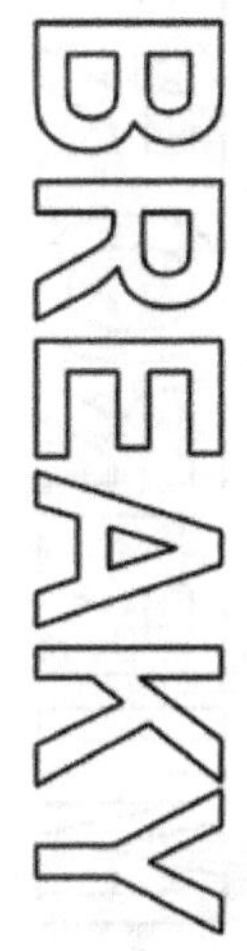
BREAKY

16

MIR

150BPM

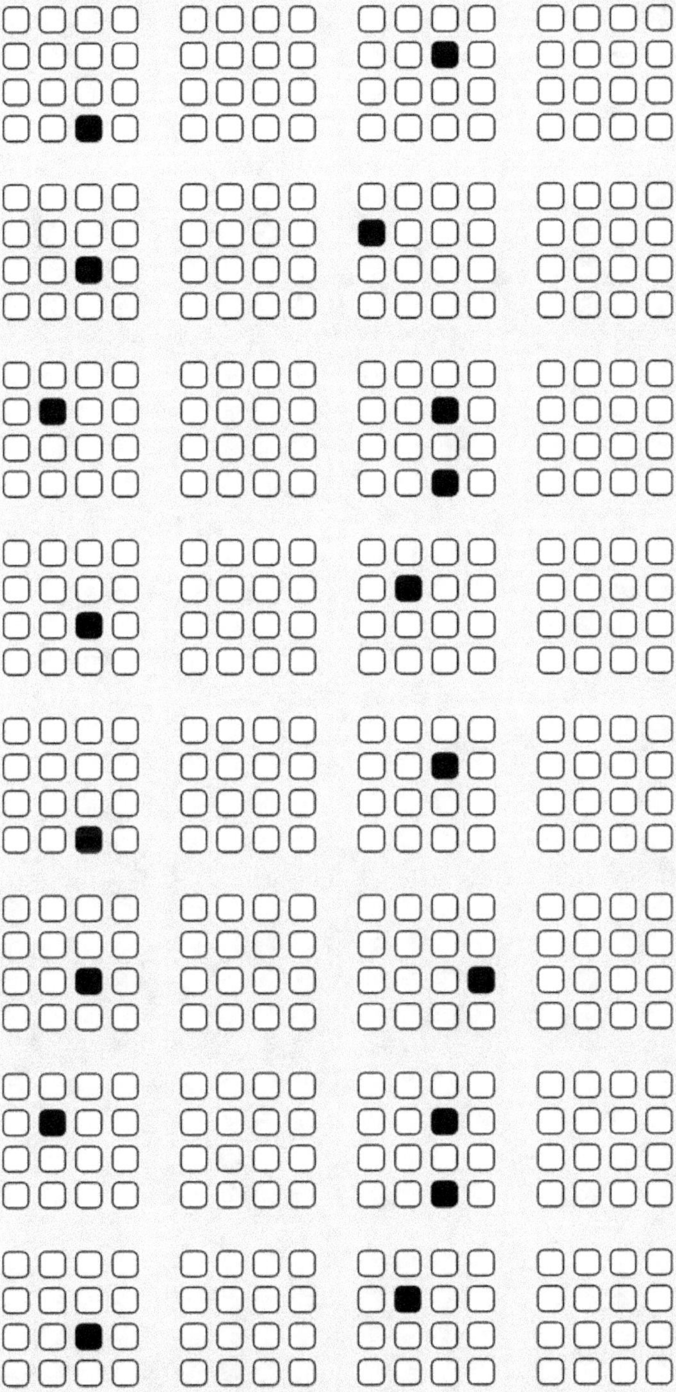

FUNGLE

MIRRORED

145BPM

MIR

16

GET DOWN 1/2

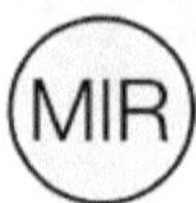

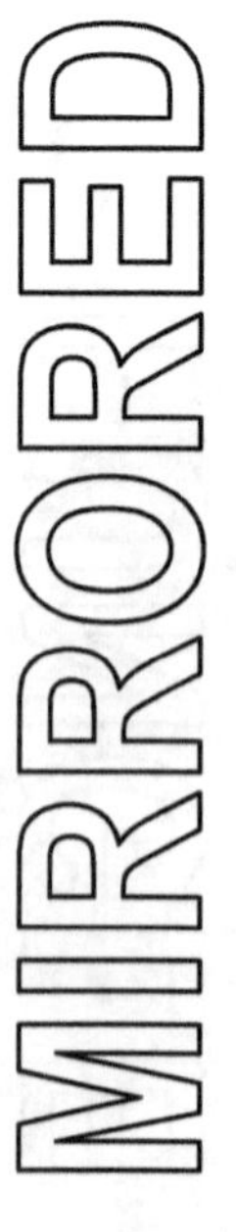

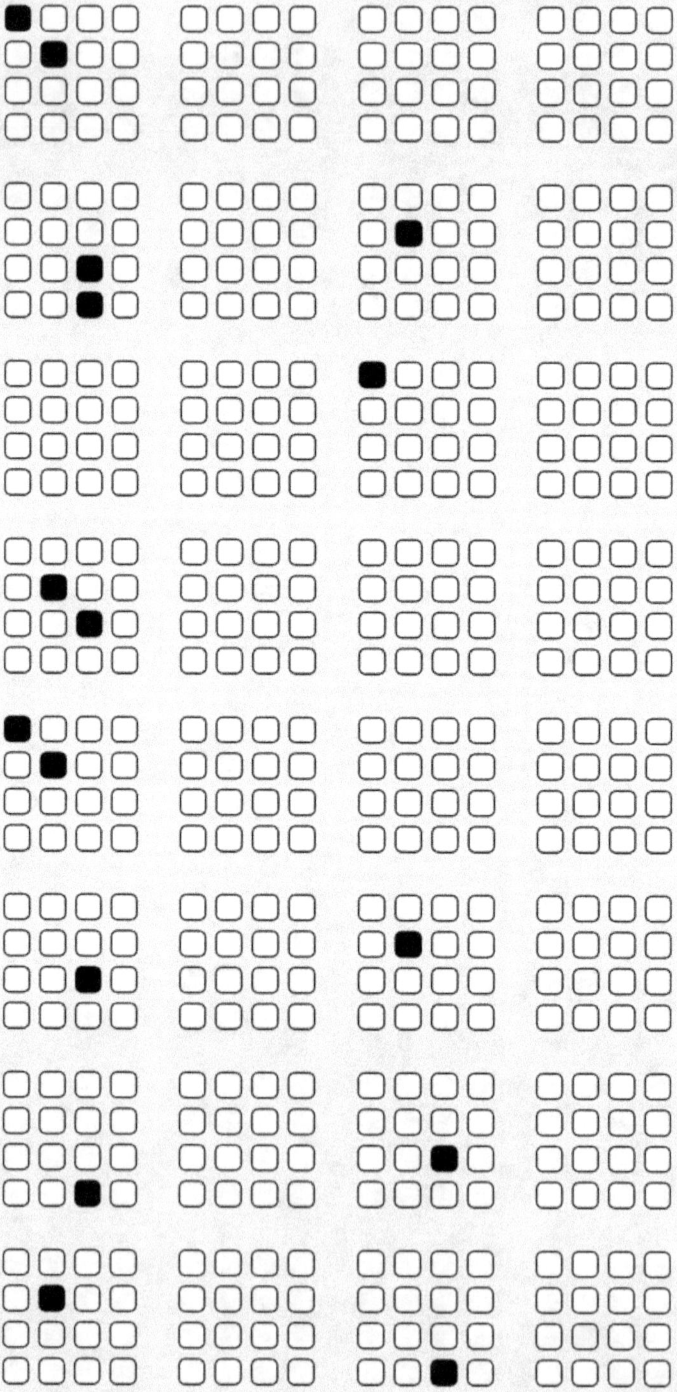

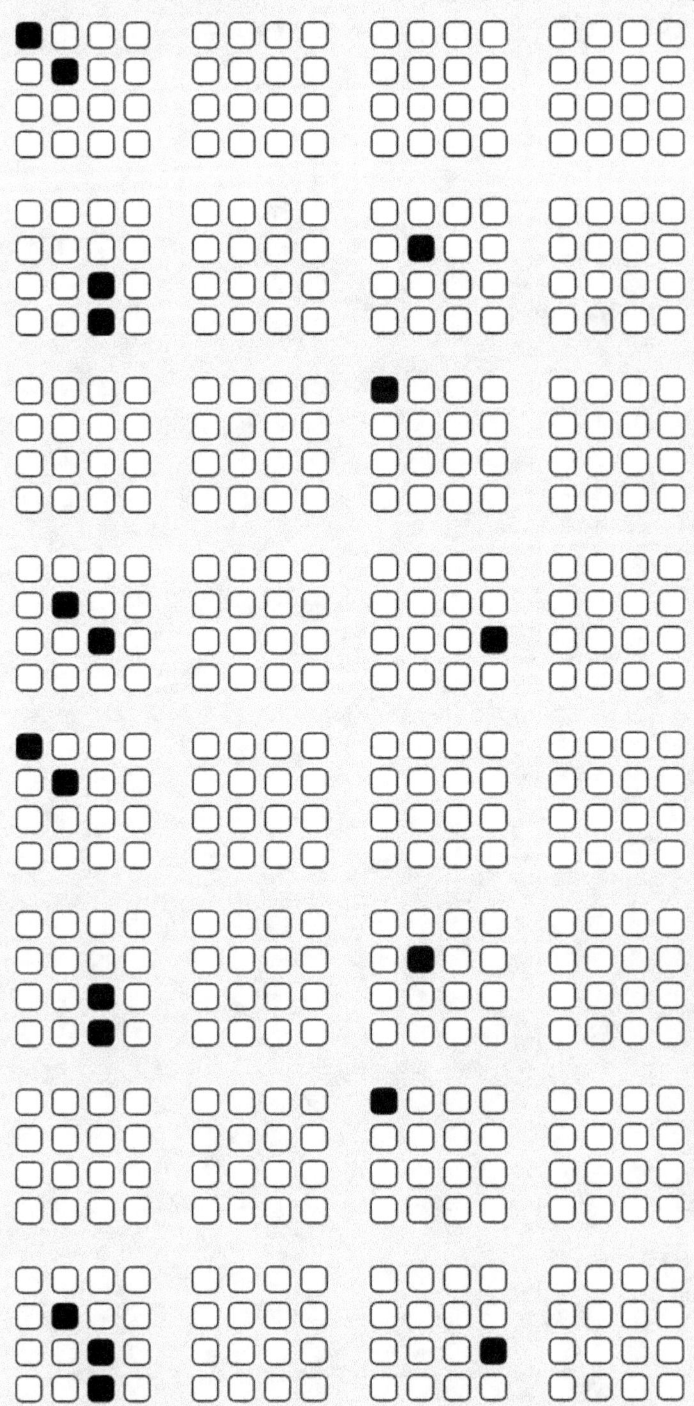

MATRIX 1/2
16
MIR
160BPM
MIRRORED

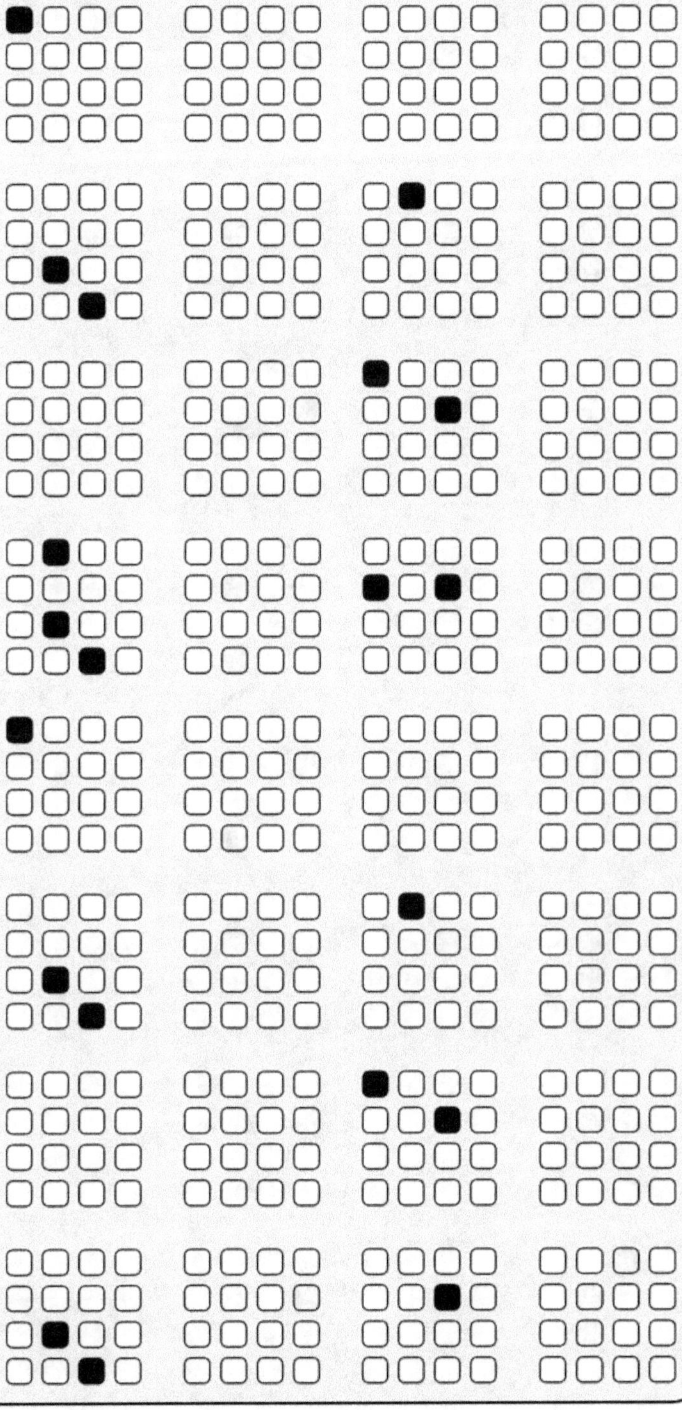

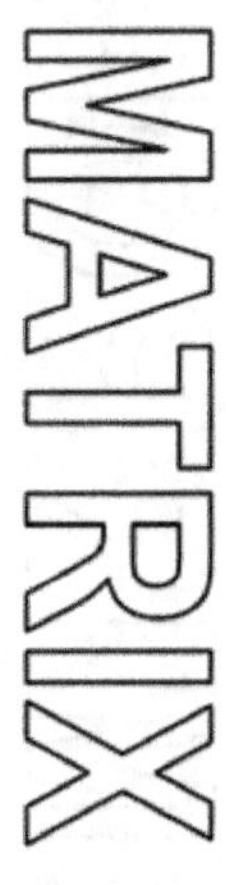

16

MIR

127BPM

MIRRORED

MICROVILLI 1/2

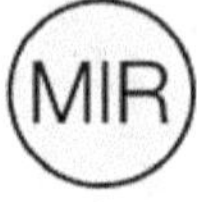

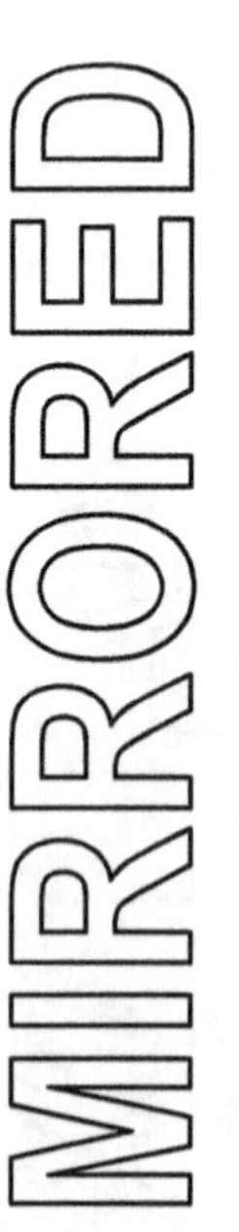

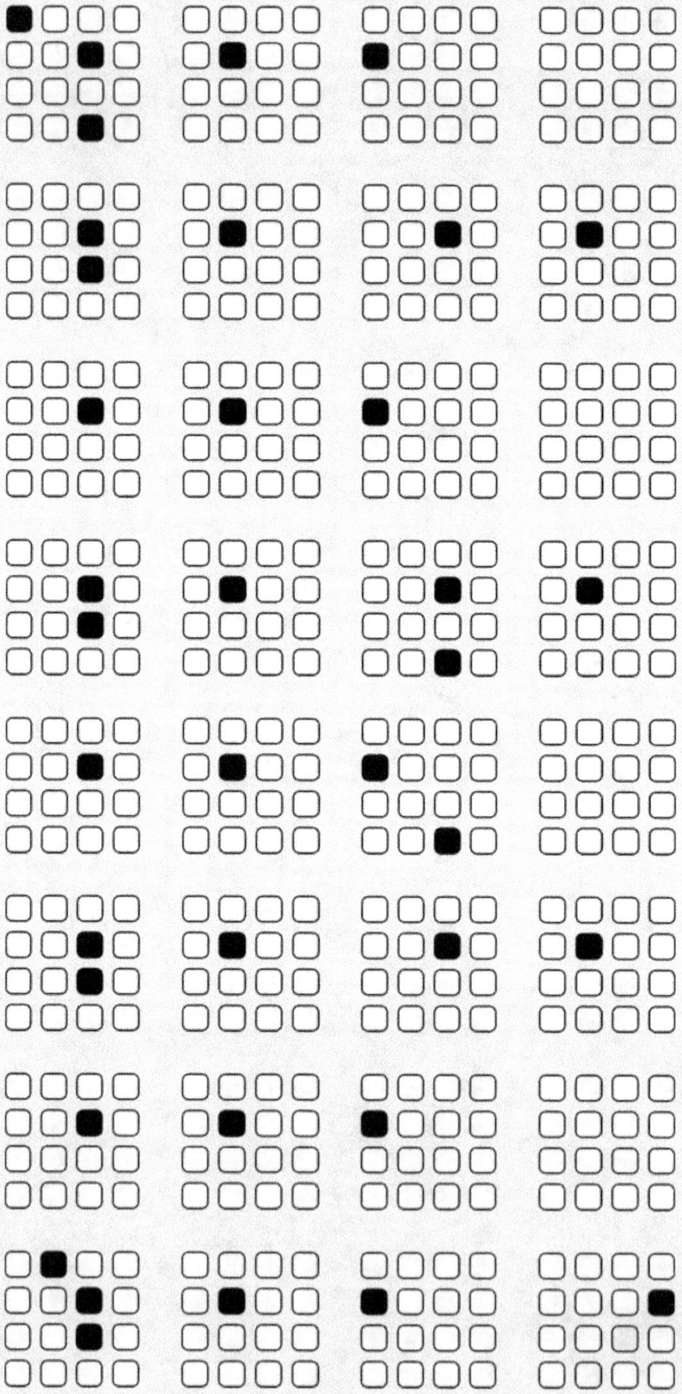

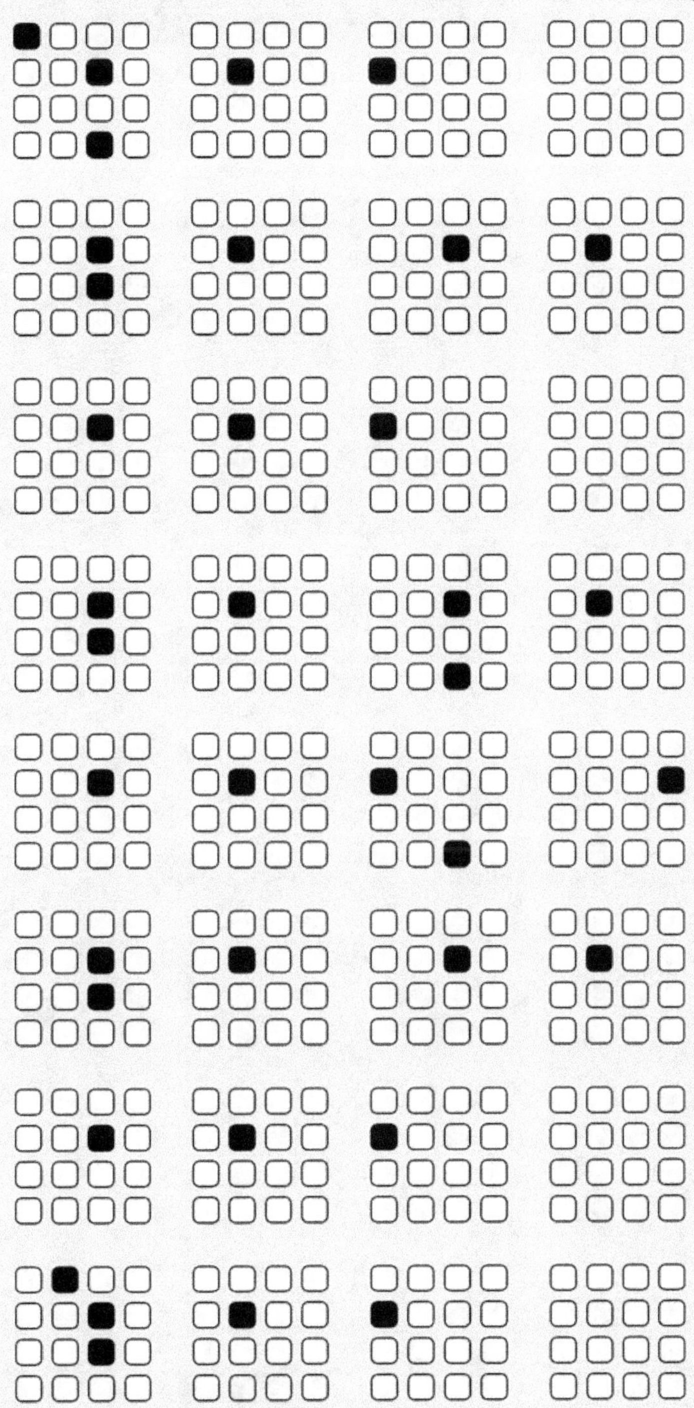

16

MIR

160BPM

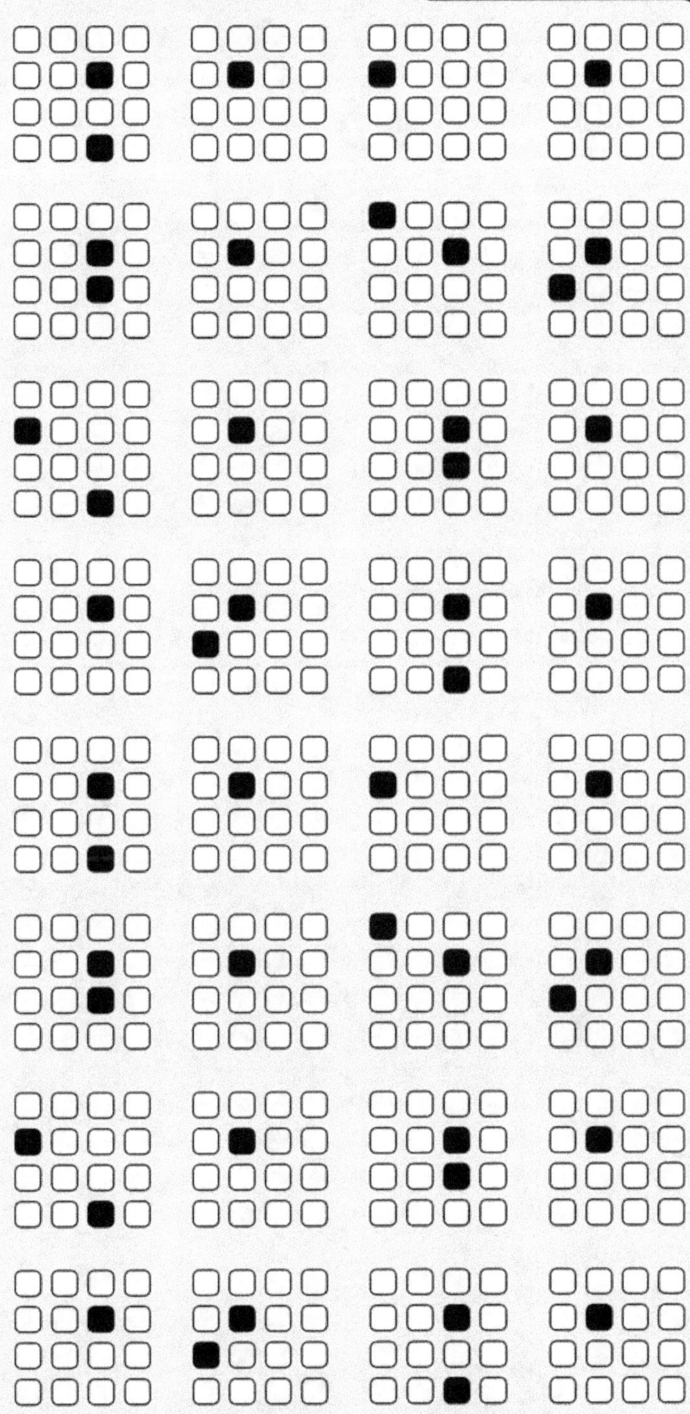

QUICKSTEP

16

MIR

150BPM

MIRRORED

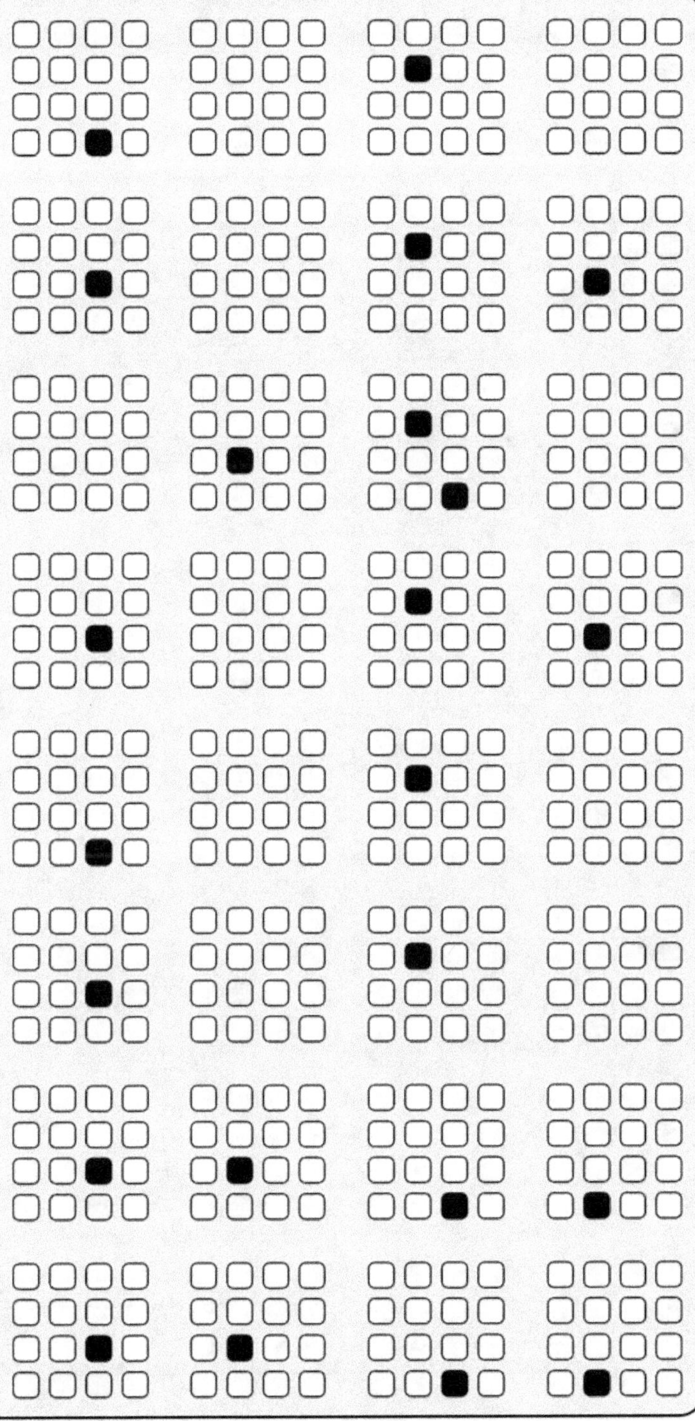

16

MIR

157BPM

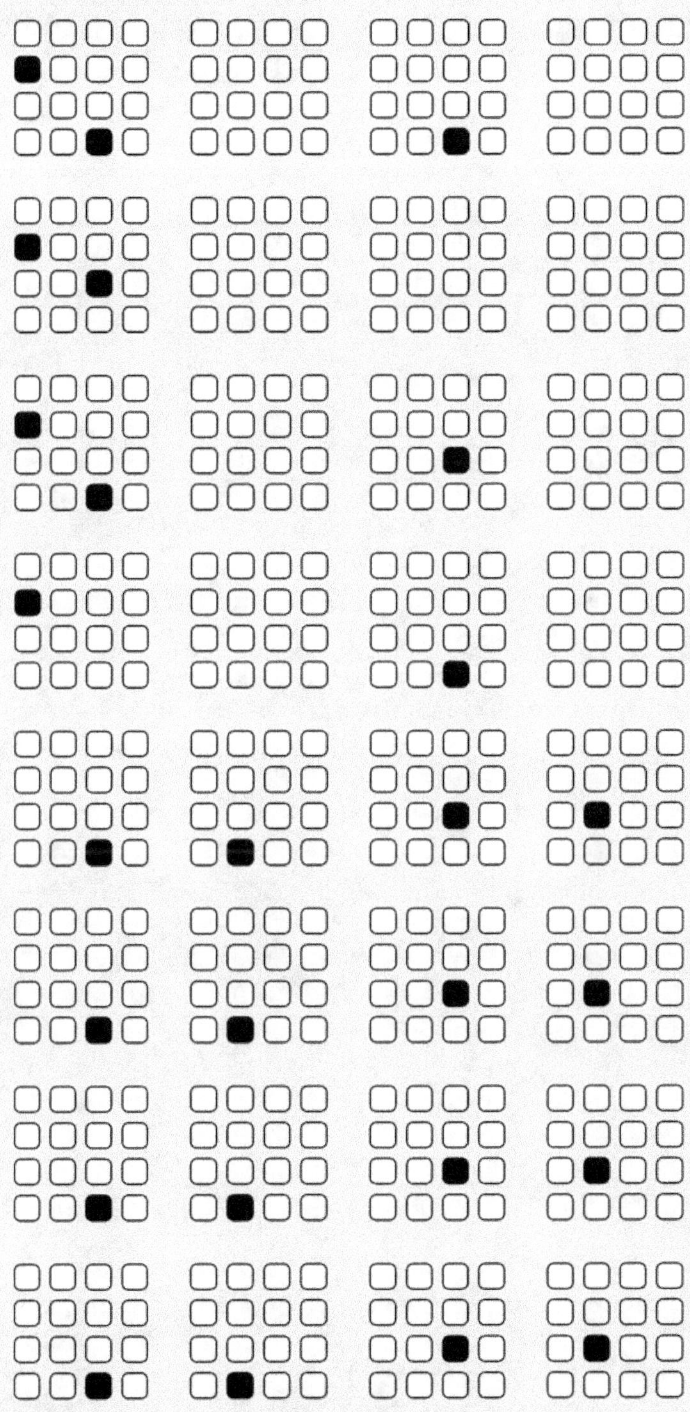

16

MIR

160BPM

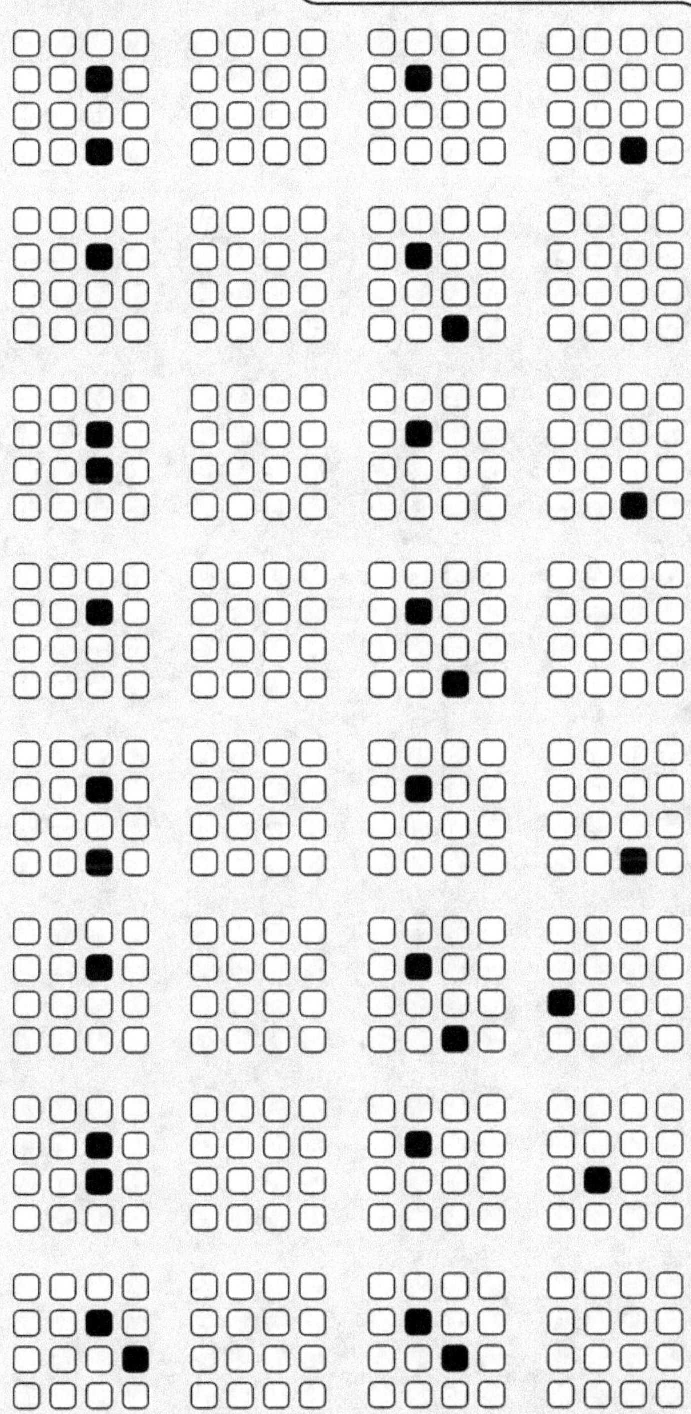

WHAT ARE DRUM FILLS?

Drum fills are rhythmic patterns or sequences that break away from the regular groove or beat in a song, usually occurring at the end of a musical phrase, section, or transition. These fills serve as a form of punctuation in the music, adding variety, excitement, and dynamics to a performance. They can range from simple, subtle embellishments to complex, high-energy passages, depending on the style of music and the drummer's intention.

WHY ARE DRUM FILLS USED?

Transition and Flow: Drum fills are essential for creating smooth transitions between different parts of a song, such as moving from a verse to a chorus or into a bridge. They help signal changes to the listener and maintain the flow of the music.

Dynamic Contrast: Fills add dynamic contrast, preventing the music from becoming monotonous. By varying the intensity and complexity of fills, drummers can build anticipation, create tension, or provide a release, enhancing the emotional impact of the music.

Highlighting Musical Phrases: Fills can be used to highlight important moments or phrases in a song, drawing attention to specific lyrics, melodies, or instrumental solos. This helps to create memorable moments within the performance.

Showcasing Skill and Creativity: For drummers, fills are an opportunity to showcase their technical abilities and creativity. Well-executed fills can demonstrate a drummer's sense of timing, coordination, and musicality, adding a personal touch to the performance.

DRUM FILLS

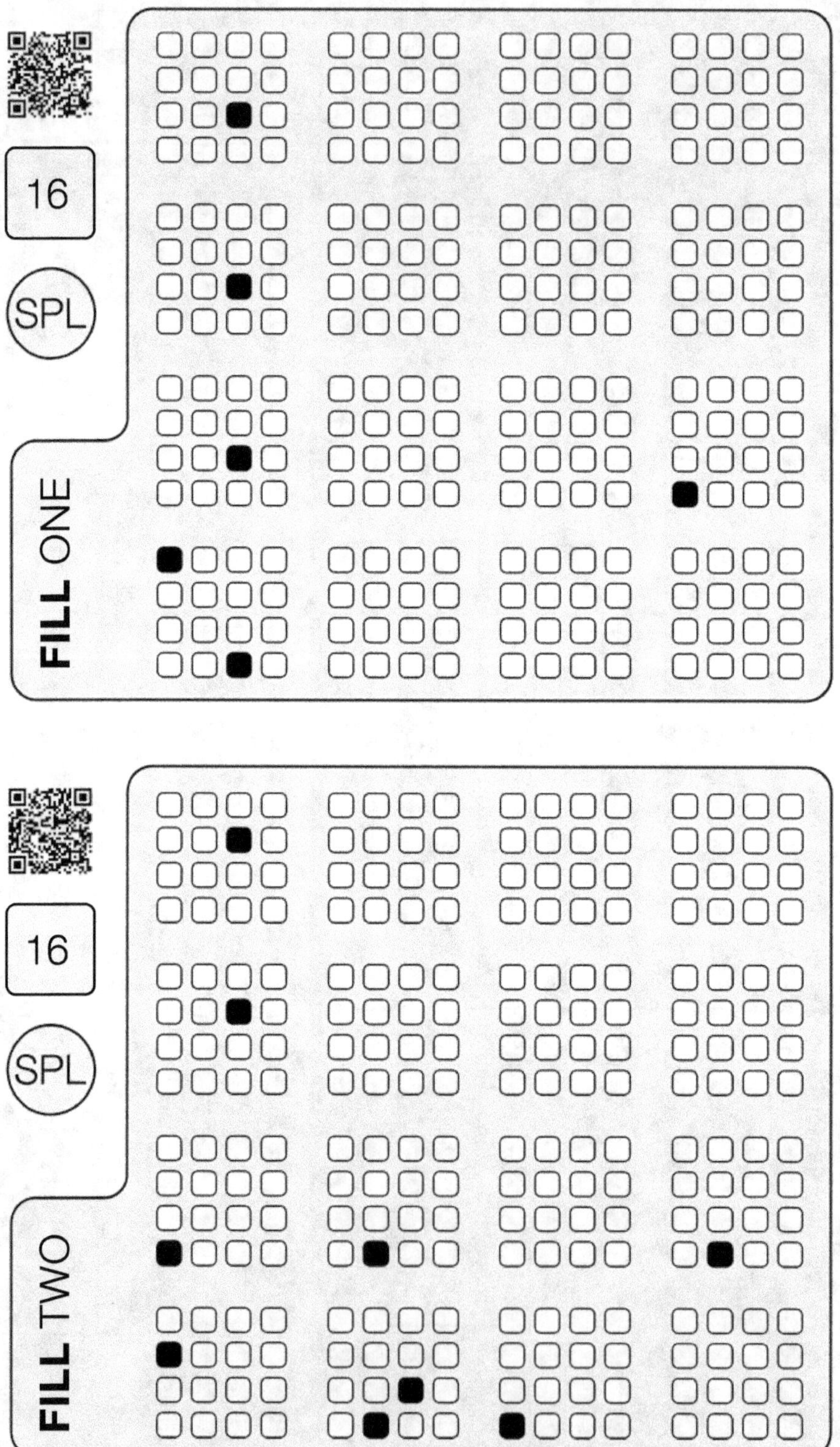
16
SPL
FILL ONE
16
SPL
FILL TWO

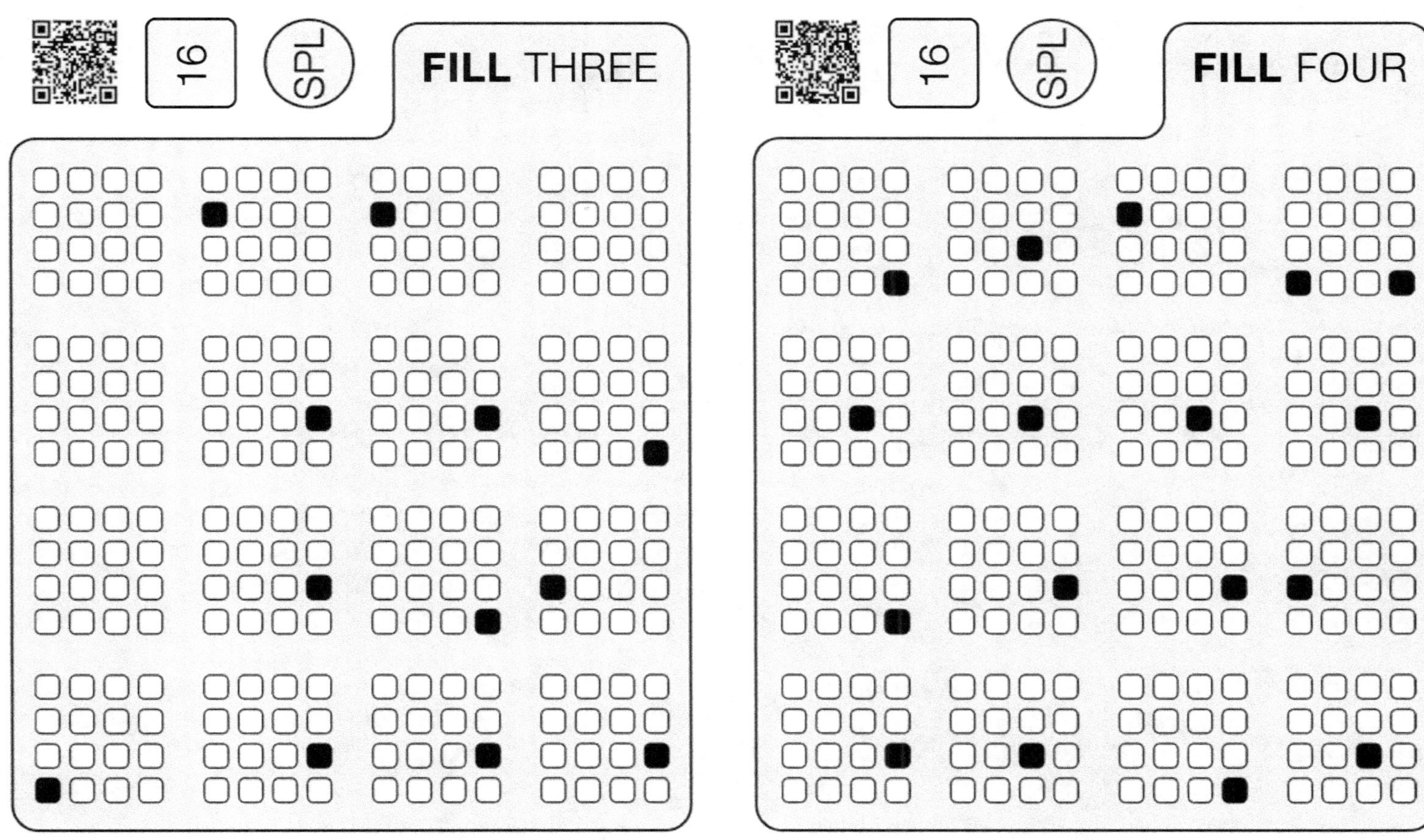
16
SPL
FILL THREE
16
SPL
FILL FOUR

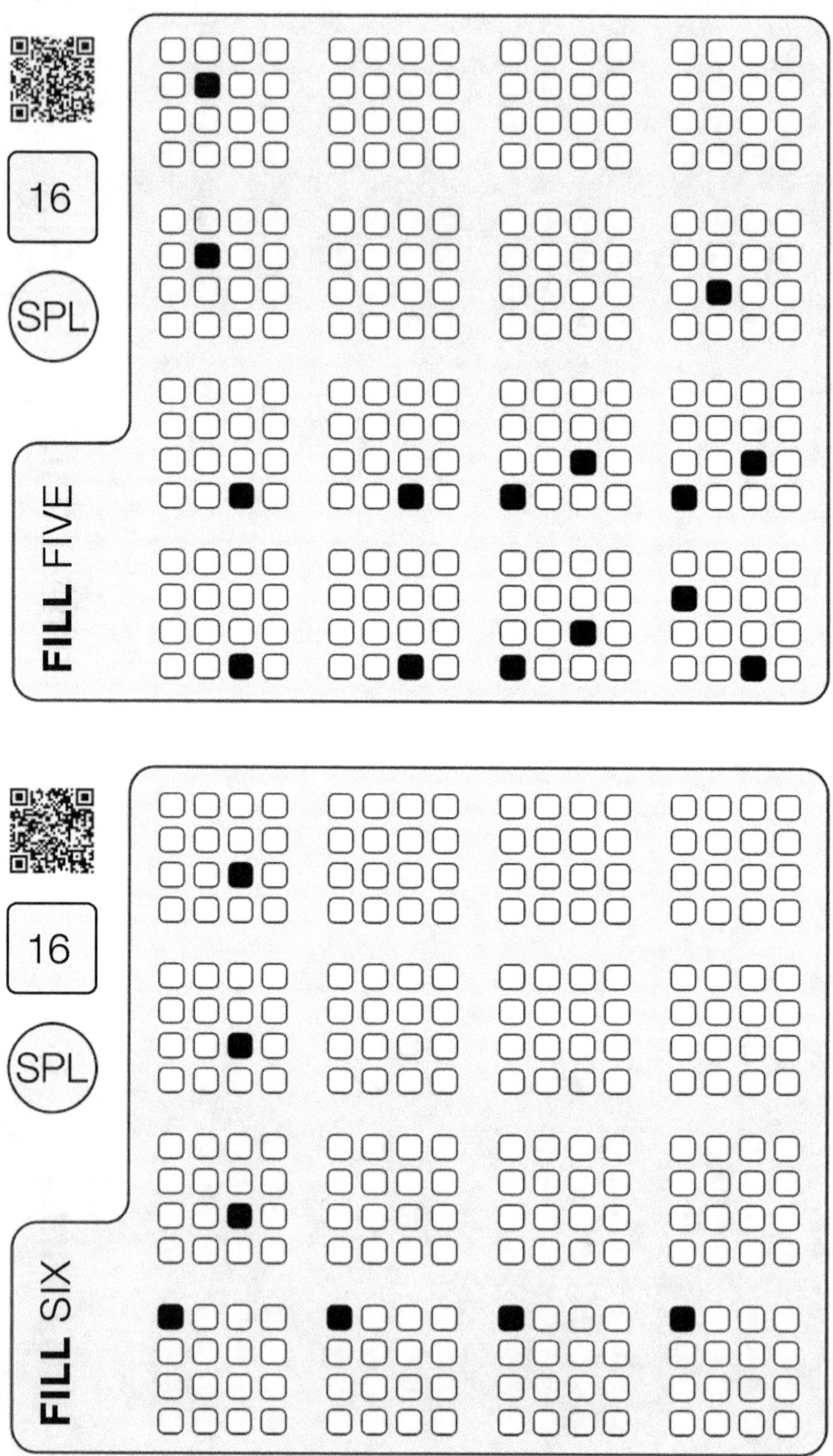

16
SPL
FILL FIVE
16
SPL
FILL SIX

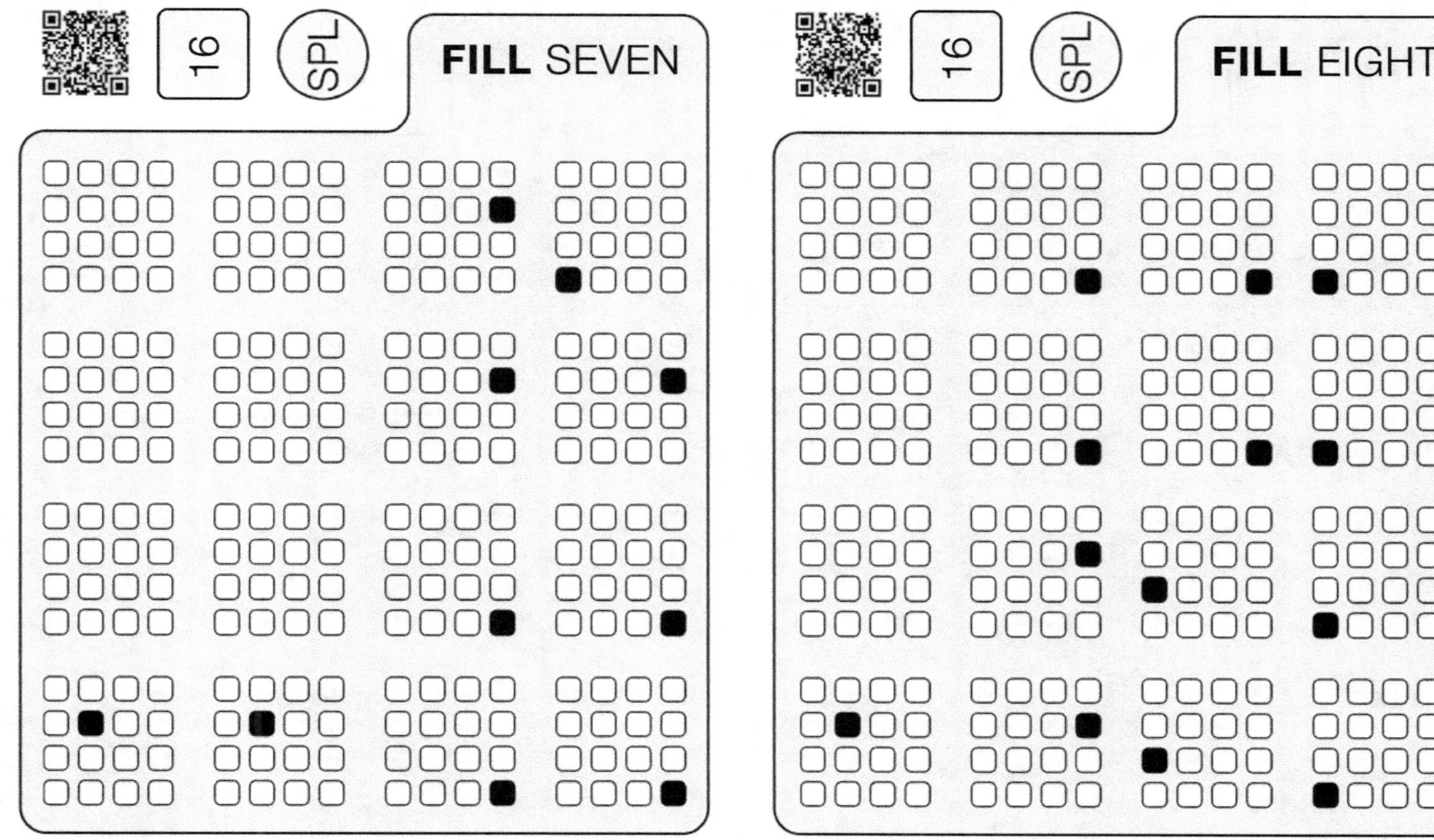
16
SPL
FILL SEVEN
16
SPL
FILL EIGHT

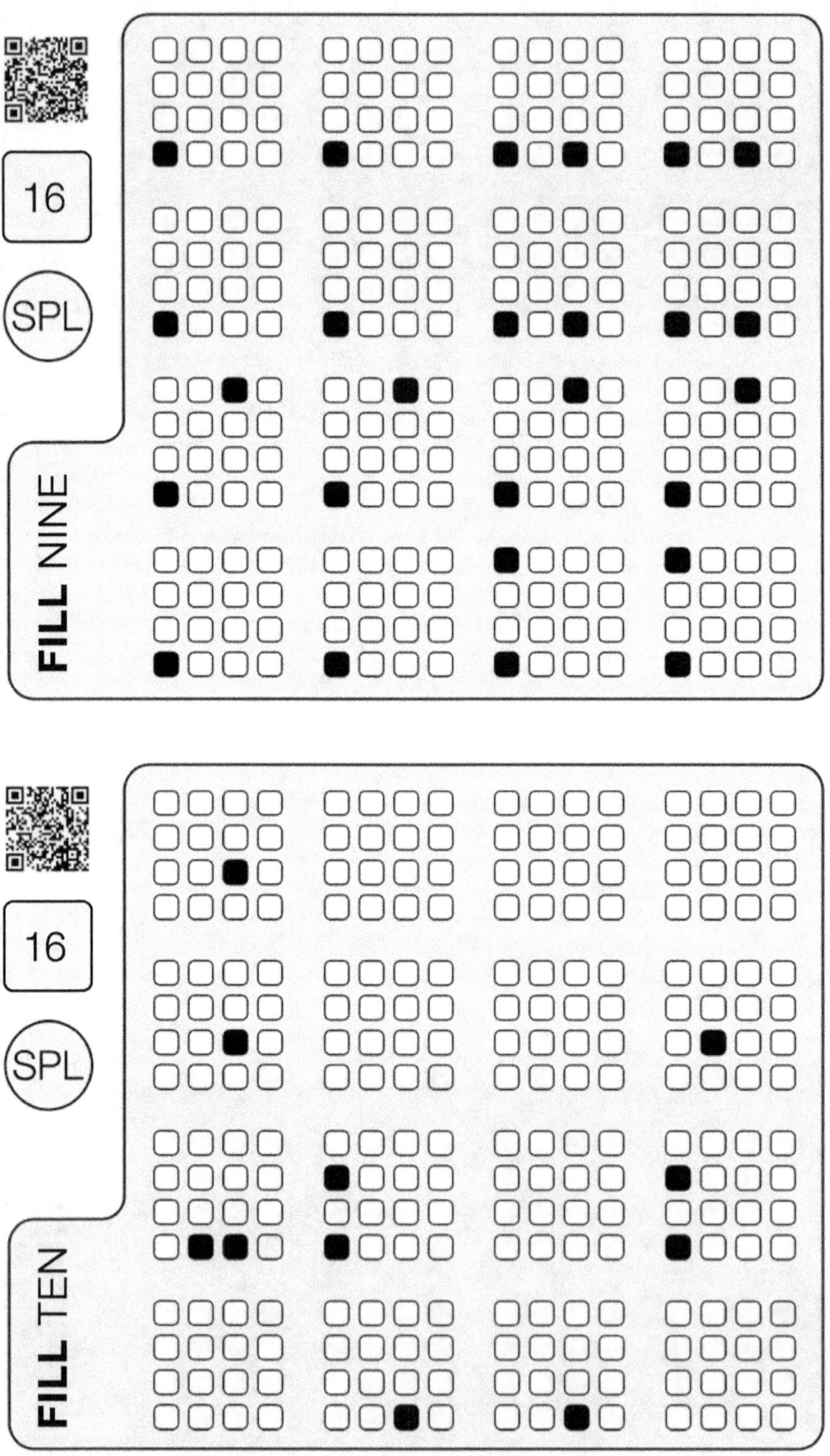
16
SPL
FILL NINE
16
SPL
FILL TEN

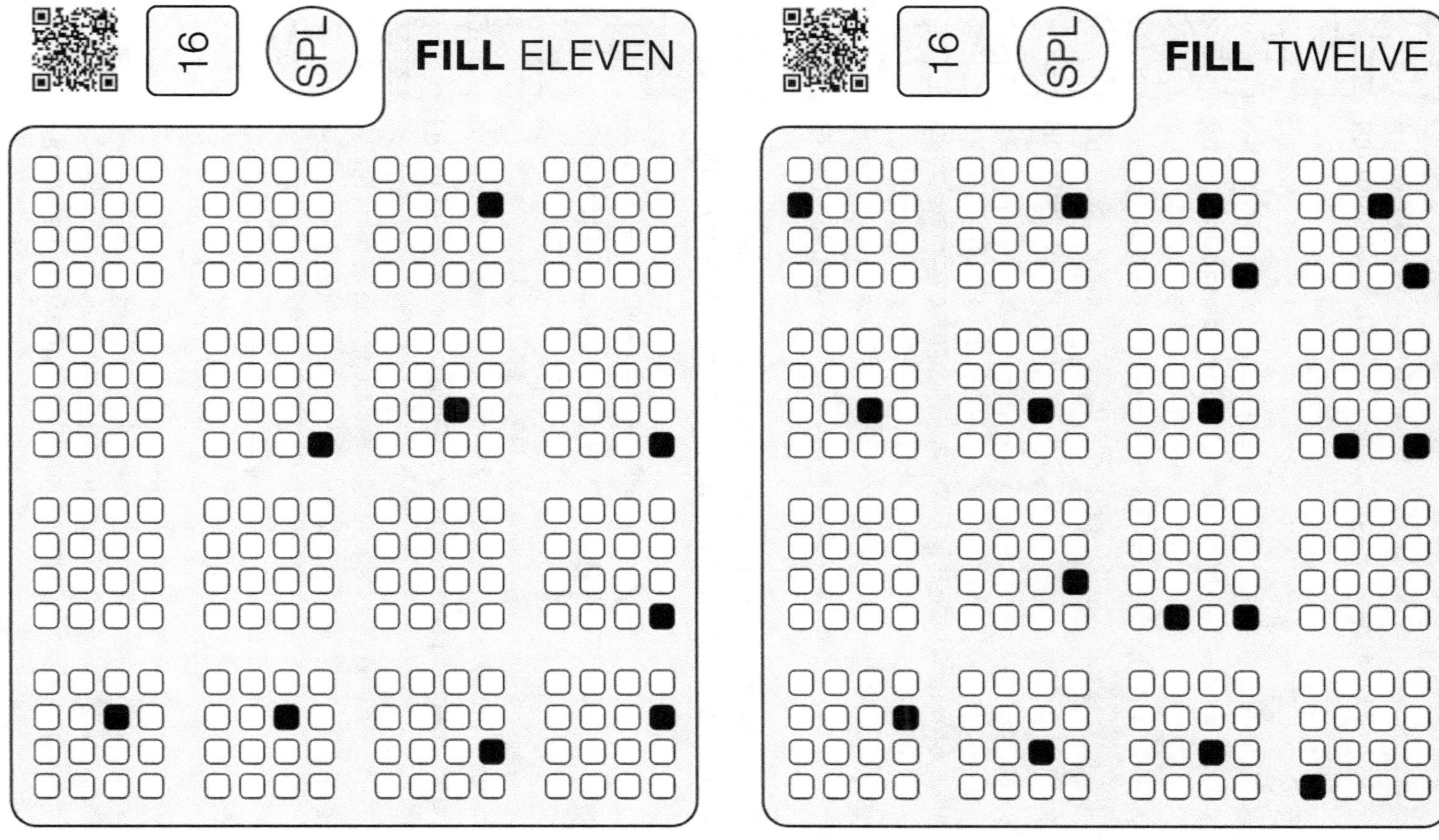

16
SPL
FILL ELEVEN
16
SPL
FILL TWELVE

Alternative Layouts: Different pad arrangements designed for specific drumming styles and techniques, such as Mirrored and Sample Chops layouts.

Beats Per Minute (BPM): A measure of the tempo of a piece, indicating the number of beats in one minute.

Crash Cymbal: A circular cymbal producing a bold, explosive sound used to punctuate significant musical moments.

Drum Fills: Rhythmic patterns or sequences that break away from the regular groove or beat in a song, usually occurring at the end of a musical phrase, section, or transition.

Eighth Notes: Rhythmic units worth half a beat in 4/4 time, making them twice as fast as quarter notes.

Finger Assignment: Specific fingers designated for triggering the pads, usually indicated by numbers assigned within each pad.

Grid Tablature: A unique notation system used in the Finger Drum Bible series to represent rhythms and exercises.

Hand Assignment: The method of assigning specific hands to trigger pads during finger drumming exercises.

Hi-Hats: Small cymbals mounted on a stand, producing a high-pitched sound when clamped together (closed hi-hat) or a longer, resonant sound when apart (open hi-hat).

Kick Drum/Bass Drum: A large, cylindrical drum producing a deep, low-frequency thud, serving as the fundamental pulse of a track.

Metronome: A tool for counting BPM and maintaining a steady tempo, used to strengthen the sense of timing.

One-Shots: Singular, isolated sounds triggered to play once each time they are activated, without looping.

Quarter Notes: Fundamental rhythmic notation representing a single beat in 4/4 time.

Ride Cymbal: A circular cymbal used to maintain a steady rhythm, often providing a constant background pulse.

Rudiments: Fundamental patterns and techniques forming the foundation of more complex rhythms and beats in finger drumming.

Sampling: The process of taking a portion of a sound recording and reusing it in a different song or piece of music.

Sixteenth Notes: Rhythmic units worth a quarter of a beat in 4/4 time, making them twice as fast as eighth notes.

Snare Drum: A cylindrical drum with metal wires stretched across the bottom head, producing a sharp, crisp sound.

Stabs: Quick, intense bursts of sound from various instruments, used to punctuate parts of a track.

Swing Feel: A rhythmic concept involving uneven eighth notes, often associated with jazz music.

Tambourine: A circular frame with metal discs producing a bright, jingling sound, used in various musical genres.

Tempo: The speed or pace of a piece of music, typically measured in BPM.

Toms: Cylindrical drums used for fills and rhythmic sequences, adding depth and dramatic flair to drumming patterns.

Voice Recorder: A device or app used to record practice sessions for self-evaluation of rhythm and accuracy.

Kick on '&': A drumming pattern involving a kick drum placed on the off-beat, enhancing rhythmic complexity and syncopation.

Nonadjacent Pair Lifts: Exercises involving lifting non-adjacent fingers simultaneously to build finger independence and strength.

Palms Down Exercise: A strengthening exercise involving lifting and holding each finger while keeping the palm flat against a surface, focusing on finger isolation and control.

Rolls: Drumming technique involving quick successive strikes on the pads, used for building speed and fluidity.

Speed Roll: A technique involving rapid successive strikes on the pads, used to build speed and fluidity in finger drumming.

Triples: A rolling technique that introduces speed and groove by alternating strikes between fingers in a triple pattern.

Voice Recorder: A tool used to record practice sessions, allowing for self-evaluation and improvement of rhythm and timing.

Wrist Alignment: Maintaining straight wrists to prevent strain and reduce the risk of repetitive motion injuries during finger drumming practice.

Controller Orientation: The positioning of the drum controller, which can be set in traditional horizontal orientation or diamond orientation (45-degree angle) for ergonomic play and ease of access to pads.

808 Kick: A sustained, tonal bass drum sound originating from the Roland TR-808 drum machine, widely used in hip-hop, trap, and electronic music for its distinctive low-frequency impact.

Four on the Floor: A dance rhythm pattern where the kick drum hits on every beat, common in house and electronic dance music, providing a steady and driving pulse.

Hand Assignment: The method of assigning specific hands to trigger pads during finger drumming exercises, indicated by outlined grids or pads in the tablature.

Finger Numbering: Assigning numbers to each finger and thumb (1-5) to indicate which finger should trigger specific pads, aiding in the learning of patterns and techniques.

Flams: A drumming technique involving two nearly simultaneous strokes, where the first stroke (grace note) is softer and slightly earlier than the second (main note), adding a dynamic feel to rhythms.

Sampling: The practice of using portions of pre-recorded sounds or music in new compositions, a common technique in electronic music production.

Round Robin Sequences: A technique used to trigger multiple samples in a rotating or cycling manner to create variation and a more natural sound.

Layering: The process of combining multiple sounds or samples to create a richer, more complex sound, often used in music production to enhance depth and texture.

DAW (Digital Audio Workstation): Software used for recording, editing, mixing, and producing audio files, such as Ableton Live, FL Studio, and Logic Pro.

Stem Splitting: The process of isolating different elements (stems) of a track, such as vocals, drums, and instruments, for separate processing or remixing.

Royalty-Free Samples: Pre-cleared samples that can be used without additional permissions or fees, commonly sourced from websites like Splice, Loopmasters, and FreeSound.org.

AI Music Generators: Tools that create original samples or compositions using artificial intelligence, providing unique sounds and sequences free of copyright restrictions.

Clearing Samples: The legal process of obtaining permission to use samples from other artists, necessary to avoid legal repercussions for unauthorized use.

Musique Concrète: A form of experimental music that uses recorded sounds as raw material, pioneered by Pierre Schaeffer in the 1940s and 1950s.

Turntablism: The art of manipulating sounds and creating music using turntables and a DJ mixer, often involving techniques like scratching and beat juggling.

EQ (Equalization): The process of adjusting the balance of different frequency components in an audio signal, used to enhance or modify the sound.

Side-Chaining: A dynamic range compression technique where the level of one audio signal is used to control the level of another, commonly used in dance music to create a pumping effect.

Volume Envelopes: Tools used to shape the amplitude of a sound over time, typically including parameters for attack, decay, sustain, and release (ADSR).

Frequency Range: The spectrum of frequencies that an audio signal encompasses, important for understanding the tonal characteristics of different sounds and instruments.

Harmonics: Overtones that accompany the fundamental frequency of a sound, contributing to its timbre and richness.

Dynamic Contrast: Variations in volume and intensity within a piece of music, used to create interest and emphasize certain parts of the composition.

Groove: The sense of rhythmic feel or swing in music, often created by the interaction of different rhythmic elements.

Clipping: Distortion that occurs when an audio signal exceeds the maximum level that can be accurately reproduced, resulting in a harsh, distorted sound.

Sample Chops: Small segments of a larger sample, often used in hip-hop and electronic music to create new patterns and sequences.

Stem Splitting: The process of separating a track into its individual components (e.g., vocals, drums, bass) for remixing or re-editing purposes.

Triggering: The act of initiating a sound or sample using a pad, key, or other controller, fundamental in finger drumming and electronic music production.

FOUNDATIONAL RHYTHMS

LINK GLOSSARY

THE BASICS

DOWNLOADS

MUSIC CHOPS

FAVORITES

MIRRORED

FILLS

ADDITIONAL LINKS

My friend, you've made it through the Finger Drum Genesis! Beyond just rhythms to practice, I hope this book sparks your creativity and ignites new ideas for your unique productions. Sometimes, all it takes to get a brilliant idea is practicing new concepts and blending them with your current knowledge and experience. I genuinely hope the information in this book has helped you move closer to your music goals, whatever they may be. The pursuit of anything meaningful can be challenging, so take it one day at a time and enjoy the journey!

Every sunny day you've enjoyed, every hardship you've faced, every powerful experience you've had, and every fear you've conquered contributes to the unique and wonderful person you are. With this in mind, be patient with yourself and trust your intuition. The world is vast, and with the internet as a tool, there's a huge audience out there eager to hear the music and creativity you have to offer.

When you inevitably feel frustrated while practicing, or envious when you see someone else shredding the pads, remember that these feelings are signs of how much music means to you. Turn that emotion into excitement and motivation to keep practicing. We're all just humans seeking purpose and fulfillment each day. Why not reach out to someone you admire and let them know how much their music and creativity inspire you?

I'm thrilled at the thought of you achieving your dreams, one day at a time! If you'd like to share your progress, I'd be honored to hear from you. You can reach me through my website (Spacefood.ca) using the chat bubble, and I'll respond as soon as I can. Oh, and I've done my best to ensure the book is accurate, with all downloads and resources in place, but I'm still human. If you notice anything that seems off, please let me know so I can fix it. Thanks a million!

Thank you again, and happy finger drumming!

Sincerely,
Aaron Spacefood

If you enjoyed this book, I invite you to join my modest Patreon community. There, you'll find a wealth of exciting projects and exclusive content that might interest you, including Ableton Live courses, finger drumming videos and tutorials, expansion and sample packs, unreleased music, music walkthroughs, and opportunities to participate in future editions of the *Finger Drum Bible* series.

Your patronage would greatly support my ongoing creative endeavors and enable me to produce even more in-depth educational content. I hope to see you there and continue our musical journey together!

ABOUT THE AUTHOR

Hello, I'm Aaron Spacefood! I am an avid student of finger drumming and a lifelong pursuer of musical expression. My journey through music has taken many forms, including ghost production, sound design, music education, film sound, and production—basically anything that keeps me immersed in music and sound. My passion for music began early in life with my dad, a drummer in various bands, and my older brother following suit. I started with piano but soon realized it couldn't fully express the multi-timbral arrangements I dreamed up. Discovering computers as a medium for music creation was a game-changer, and I was immediately hooked, diving deeply into the world of electronic music.

My formal training at Metalworks Institute in Toronto laid the foundation for my career in Audio Engineering and Sound Production. For over 15 years, I've worked professionally, producing and engineering various genres such as Trance, Techno, Dubstep, Downtempo, Psytrance, Rock, Country, Pop, and Jazz. Teaching has also been a significant part of my journey, with experiences at Long & McQuade (the largest music franchise in Canada), YouTube, Zoom sessions, and my website, Spacefood.ca.

In recent years, I've yearned to perform my electronic music in a more organic and traditional way. While DJing is fantastic, I wanted a method to perform in real time. This led me to finger drumming, which for me, is the perfect intersection of piano, drumming, and electronic production. Creating the Finger Drum Bible series has been a labor of love, with Finger Drum Genesis being the second book. My hope is that this book will ignite your passion and enhance your skills in finger drumming.

Aaron Spacefood

Photo credit: Geena M. Grim

Grim Photography, Nova Scotia

The Finger Drum Routine Planner is packed with hundreds of blank grid tabs, just like those found in the Finger Drum Bible series. This versatile journal is perfect for anyone looking to design their own rhythms and routines without worrying about forgetting the sequences they've created. The following pages offer a sneak peek into the Finger Drum Routine Planner.

Get your copy of the Finger Drum Routine Planner today, available on Amazon!

FINGER
DRUM
ROUTINE
PLANNER

13
14
15
16
9
10
11
12
5
6
7
8
1
2
3
4

BPM

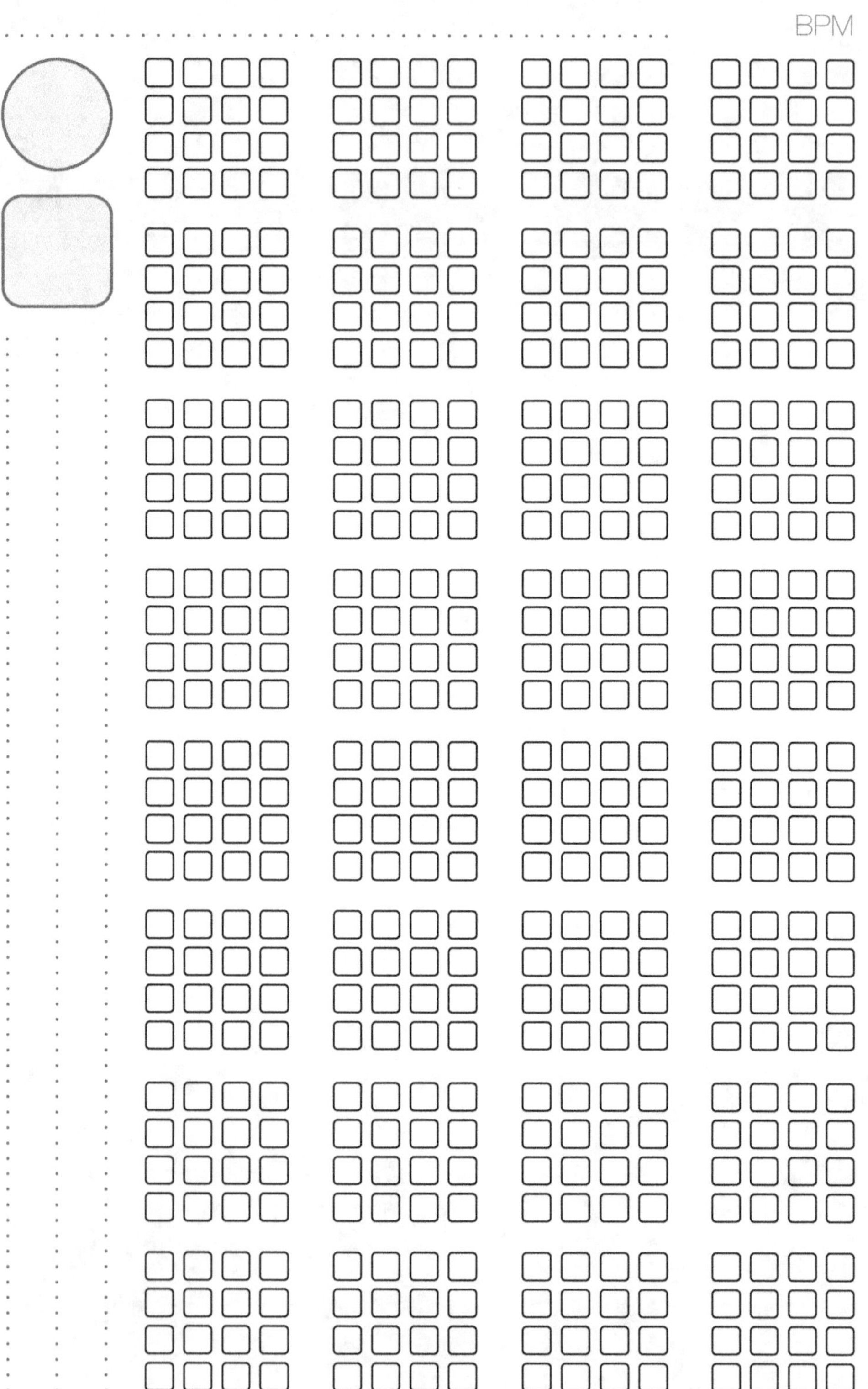